# Grand Strategies of the Left

Why are progressives often critical of US foreign policy and the national security state? What would a statecraft that pulls ideas from the American left look like? *Grand Strategies of the Left* brings the progressive worldview into conversation with security studies and foreign policy practice. It argues that American progressives think durable security will only come by prioritizing the interconnected conditions of peace, democracy, and equality. By conceiving of grand strategy as worldmaking, progressives see multiple ways of using foreign policy to make a more just and stable world. US statecraft – including defense policy – should be retooled not for primacy, endless power accumulation, or a political status quo that privileges elites, but rather to shape the context that gives rise to perpetual insecurity. Progressive worldmaking has its own risks and dilemmas but expands how we imagine what the world is and could be.

Van Jackson is a professor of international relations at Victoria University of Wellington and Senior Research Scholar at Security in Context, where he codirects the Multipolarity, Great-Power Competition, and the Global South project. A leading voice of progressive foreign policy thought, Jackson is also the author of *Pacific Power Paradox* (2023).

# Grand Strategies of the Left

*The Foreign Policy of Progressive Worldmaking*

**VAN JACKSON**

*Victoria University of Wellington*

**CAMBRIDGE**
UNIVERSITY PRESS

**CAMBRIDGE**
UNIVERSITY PRESS

Shaftesbury Road, Cambridge CB2 8EA, United Kingdom

One Liberty Plaza, 20th Floor, New York, NY 10006, USA

477 Williamstown Road, Port Melbourne, VIC 3207, Australia

314–321, 3rd Floor, Plot 3, Splendor Forum, Jasola District Centre,
New Delhi – 110025, India

103 Penang Road, #05–06/07, Visioncrest Commercial, Singapore 238467

Cambridge University Press is part of Cambridge University Press & Assessment,
a department of the University of Cambridge.

We share the University's mission to contribute to society through the pursuit of
education, learning and research at the highest international levels of excellence.

www.cambridge.org
Information on this title: www.cambridge.org/9781316518663

DOI: 10.1017/9781009002080

First published 2024

A catalogue record for this publication is available from the British Library

A Cataloging-in-Publication data record for this book is available from the
Library of Congress

ISBN 978-1-316-51866-3 Hardback
ISBN 978-1-009-00988-1 Paperback

# Contents

v

# Tables

# Preface and Acknowledgments

I started this book in 2018 – a time when I saw the world very differently than I do today.

As a one-time "defense intellectual" and a longtime creature of the national security state, I always had a hard time reconciling the unspoken politics of my vocation with what I gleaned from having one foot in the progressive movement. For a while, circumstances made it possible to avoid acknowledging internal contradictions. Obama's presidency encouraged people like me to get out of the streets and put down radical texts in favor of being consultants and policy insiders. Because of what the Democratic Party has been my entire life, I was "on the left" only in the thinnest, American-hegemony sense of what that meant – vague cosmopolitanism and an antiwar sensibility, yet reflexively in support of the going concerns of the Democratic Party, including (paradoxically) military primacy. And let's face it, I led the bourgie, luxury hotel, brunch-filled, NPR cloth-bag-at-Whole-Foods existence of a foreign policy mandarin. That lifestyle didn't confront me with hard truths and intellectual contradictions; it sublimated them.

But the Trump years were topsy turvy, sending me searching. Initially, I sought succor in the liberal internationalism I had propped up my entire career, which naturalized a brief fling as a China hawk. But I quickly started recognizing the reactionary potentialities within liberal foreign policy – particularly on China issues.

Eventually, I came to see liberal internationalism as a worldview that not only obscured who benefited from US policy but also offered no satisfying way of either asking or answering the kinds of questions plaguing me.

How was Trump possible, and if Washingtonians find him so repugnant, why are most of them untroubled by the tremendous continuities of

Trump's policies with both his predecessors and successor? Why are policymakers (I was once one) incapable of acknowledging how the domestic and the international spheres of policy affect each other? What good is American power if perpetuating it requires horizonless war, or horizonless preparation for it? How do we justify the numerous hypocrisies in liberal foreign policy (from killing in the name of security to keeping secrets and allying with dictators in the name of democracy to sustaining spheres of influence while repudiating others doing the same), especially when there are alternatives available? Above all, why is the plight of workers – average Americans – totally absent from the geopolitical machinations of the national security state?

There is much more I could say about that period of my life, but this book allowed me to work through things the only way I know how – by reading and writing. Following the "soak and poke" model laid down by Richard Fenno in *Homestyle* so many years ago, I immersed myself in the ecosystem of global thought to the left of liberal internationalism, spanning from left-liberal reformists to labor historians to anti-imperialists to radical communists, and everything in between.

*Grand Strategies of the Left* stands on its own merits as an analytical work that speaks to several audiences as once ... but it is also unmistakably personal. While I do not actually endorse all the prescriptions and wagers presented in these pages – even, paradoxically, when citing some of my own older work – any reader familiar with my background will see parts of me in both the overall claim (the solutions to global insecurity lay in the political and economic conditions at their root) and the numerous tensions within leftist thinking that the book tries to identify and navigate.

For help in seeing liberal internationalism more clearly and rethinking what security ought to mean, I owe an immense debt to a lot of people who are active in the public intellectual (and sometimes activist) scene. In no particular order, Jeannie Morefield, Patrick Iber, Michael Kazin, Matthew Specter, Brian Mueller, John Feffer, Mike Brenes, Kate Kizer, Christopher McKnight Nichols, Tim Barker, Tobita Chow, Jake Werner, Spencer Ackerman, Adom Getachew, Gabe Winant, Promise Li, Olufemi Taiwo, Sam Ratner, Lacie Heeley, Patrick Porter (whom nobody should mistake for a leftist), Ted Fertik, Stephen Wertheim, Malcolm Harris (who may have reservations about this book), John Carl Baker, Stephen Miles, Kelsey Atherton, Daniel Immerwahr, Loren Schulman, Adam Mount, and Ganesh Sitaraman were among the many folks who either shared their time with me or whose work guided my political evolution (often both). Reading them, I would frequently end up investigating/ rediscovering more canonical writers ranging from Harry Braverman and Paul Sweezy to W.E.B. Du Bois and Antonio Gramsci. Matt Duss, Bernie Sanders's former foreign policy adviser, started out as an object of my research before eventually becoming a friend and recurring collaborator. The work of Peter Dombrowski and Simon Reich helped me realize grand strategy was a tradition worth both critiquing and rescuing. My conversations with Charles Knight helped me better grasp the world of "non-offensive defense," which I hope to bring back en vogue. Danny Bessner, someone I once thought of quasi-adversarially, has become someone whose work I respect, and whose intellectual style I appreciate. His desire to heighten, rather than obscure, the differences between socialism and liberalism pushed me to sharpen how I characterized anti-hegemonism.

Dan Nexon has my biggest debt of gratitude. His work on empire and liberal internationalism was clarifying. His early-career work on relational IR theory shaped how I think about the world and primed my receptivity to historical materialism and world-systems analysis. The *Duck of Minerva* blog he started long ago became an outlet where I road-tested a lot of the ideas that made its way into this book. And his writing about progressive foreign policy – even just the idea that there are policy-relevant alternatives beyond the horizon of liberal internationalism – made me think this project was possible.

Beyond gratitude, I'm compelled to make three brief clarifying points about what follows in the coming chapters.

First, anarchism is barely mentioned in this book. To be sure, anarchists and progressives have different political sensibilities when it comes to non-state violence, but they also have radically different dispositions toward the idea of state power. The scope of this book – concerned with the demands we should make of the state as a vehicle for a more peaceful, democratic, and egalitarian world – rests on a premise that many anarchists might reject. And anarchism, for all its rich history and potential allure, is not much of a resource for foreign policy or statecraft (notwithstanding Proudhon).

Second, this book only indirectly invokes world-systems analysis – a research tradition offering a powerful repertoire for making sense of the world that has historically found an audience on the left but has gotten short shrift in the academy. The primary reason for not leaning on world-systems thinking more heavily is quite simply that progressives and leftists expressing views about foreign policy today show scant awareness of it. The grand strategies of progressive worldmaking presented in this book are constructed out of prevailing discourses, and precious little policy advocacy is grounded in an explicit world-systems perspective. Moreover, as of this writing, world-systems analysis has been far better used for describing the terrain of global politics (literally a system-level view) than it has been a guide for the foreign policymaking of individual states (the unit level view). Still, consistent with world-systems thinking, there is an implicit understanding of the planet running through this book that distinguishes core from periphery, differential developmental trajectories, and the material constraints of being positioned within not only a given historical conjuncture or a given economic order but also a given geography.

Third, the choice to make this book about "progressive" foreign policy may prove controversial to some friends on the left, particularly those who either look to Marx as a North Star or recognize the reactionary strands that were once bound up with the progressive movement. I'm occasionally discomfited by how capacious "progressive" is, and I'm sensitive to the stark differences between what passes for progressivism inside the Beltway and the straightforward democratic socialism that has a more rightful historical claim to "leftism."

In other words, I'm self-conscious about conflating leftism and progressivism but I sometimes do it anyway. Why? I give a lengthier rationale in Chapter 3, but some of it is because the historical moment that birthed this book was one in which alternative foreign policy proposals from "the left" consistently fell under the category of *progressive*. In both popular discourse and among the presidential campaigns of the Trump years (I was involved in several of them), everything to the left of liberal internationalism was called "progressive." But even if that weren't the case, I want liberals to look to the left of liberal internationalism. This is the book I wish we had while searching for viable alternatives to liberal hegemony in those presidential campaigns. There are ideas here that could be taken up in a pragmatic spirit, even by those who are dismissive of (or find threatening) socialism and more radical currents. The *progressive* signifier is useful in that sense.

Finally, this book is the culmination of a larger project, some of which has appeared in other places. Portions of Chapters 1 and 4–7 originally appeared in "Left of Liberal Internationalism: Grand Strategies within Progressive Foreign Policy Thought," *Security Studies* Vol. 31, no. 4 (2022), pp. 553–92. The editor of *Security Studies* at the time of publication, Ron Krebs, also deserves my thanks for helping me tighten how I think about the role of anti-militarism in social democracy. Chapter 8 is a revised and expanded version of an article I wrote for *International Journal*, set to appear under the title, "A Capital Critique: Progressive Alternatives to Neoliberal Economic Order." And Chapter 9 contains a paragraph that originally appeared in Security in Context's journal, *Insecurity Monitor*, under the title, "Security Is beyond the National Interest: Grand Strategy and Progressive Worldmaking," as well as several sentences from my author reply as part of a roundtable series of responses in *Security Studies* following my 2022 article (the series titled, "Progressivism and Grand Strategy: An Exchange").

Kristin Chambers has been patient and open-minded as I went on this life-altering research journey. But our young son, Anders, deserves far less credit for this book. If anything, I finished it in spite of him. He took every opportunity to disrupt my writing, albeit in sometimes cute ways. "Why do you spend so much time writing books that nobody needs?" he asked. I can only hope that future readers will be more charitable.

# Introduction

American progressives in the twenty-first century have vocally agreed that climate change and nuclear war are the truly existential threats about which politicians are all too complacent. That America's endless wars and the Global War on Terror have inflamed global conflict and poisoned US politics. That the United States spends too much on defense and invests too little in diplomacy and societal welfare. That selling weapons to dictators is folly. That neoliberal globalization has enriched oligarchs and kleptocrats at the expense of workers. And that inequality in its many forms (race, gender, and capital) has become dangerously extreme.

Yet progressive politics forms an eclectic tradition that does not emanate from any singular ideological commitment. The label "progressive" is often a floating signifier, and those who identify as such come to it from a variety of standpoints – liberal, pragmatist, democratic socialist, feminist, anti-colonialist, black internationalist, Marxian, environmentalist, and their numerous intersections. They sometimes stress different aspects of American, and global, history. Their expectations about and tolerances for the pace of policy change vary widely. And they harbor competing preferences about how – even whether – the state itself ought to be used and how much power ought to reside in it.

Within the American left, consequently, disagreements and differing priorities abound when it comes to foreign policy. What explains the left's myriad reactions to Chinese oppression at home and in its periphery, which includes insisting on everything from militarized resistance to tacit accommodation? Why do progressives broadly agree with scaling back the role of the military in US foreign policy yet only some seek to scale back US international military commitments? Why are there so many competing prescriptions for how best to reform – and the extent to which we must revolutionize – global political economy? Why do only some progressives lobby to create a US Department of Peace while others seek a Department of Economic Development, or neither? And how should we understand the occasionally vitriolic fights within the left about issues ranging from Syria and Palestine to Russia and the future of the North Atlantic Treaty Organization (NATO)?

## THE ARGUMENT

This book introduces the concept of progressive worldmaking – that is, grand strategies meant to generate alternative futures that are more egalitarian, democratic, and peaceful than today.[1] It argues that the progressive view of what America's place in the world ought to be foregrounds what progressives see as underlying causes of war and peace, violence and justice. As a root-cause "theory" of peace and security, progressive worldmaking locates the sources of conflict upstream of geopolitics, and finds solutions to the deadly games nations play in public policy more than in the military instrument.

In prioritizing what it sees as the foundational sources of global insecurity, the progressive perspective portrays itself as uniquely realistic compared to its prevailing liberal internationalist alternative. It diagnoses the problems that preoccupy militaries as the surface level of deeper political dysfunctions, making mainstream grand strategy and security studies appear solution-less insofar as they deal only with national defense policy or strategy. Progressive worldmaking, in other words, directs us to reshape the very context that gives rise to traditional security problems.

This view of things, which underwrites the progressive approach to grand strategy, follows from a commitment to shared principles of economic equality, solidarity, and anti-authoritarianism.[2] But these principles also help account for the numerous foreign policy cleavages within the American progressive movement. Those cleavages can be understood

---

[1] This book is the first to self-consciously conceive of grand strategy as projects of worldmaking, but its idea of worldmaking borrows directly from Adom Getachew, *Worldmaking after Empire: The Rise and Fall of Self-Determination* (Princeton: Princeton University Press, 2019), pp. 23–24. As subsequent chapters make clear, the anticolonial worldmaking of which Getachew wrote informs more than one logical configuration of progressive grand strategy.

[2] I think of these commitments as meta-principles – broad conceptual families that subsume or incorporate more specific principles like restorative justice, inclusion, anti-fascism, anti-imperialism, accountability, anti-capitalism, and anti-corruption.

TABLE I.I *Varieties of progressive grand strategy*

| | Progressive pragmatism | Anti-hegemonism | Peacemaking |
|---|---|---|---|
| Approach to security | -Political economy | -Restraint | -Peace |
| Goal sequencing | -Equality first | -US democracy first | -Peace first |
| Priority progressive principle | -Economic equality | -Anti-authoritarianism (US) | -Solidarity |
| Sources of insecurity | -Economic precarity <br> -Oligarchy and kleptocracy | -US military and economic power | -Structural and militarized violence <br> -Rivalries |
| Working assumptions | -Economic dislocation feeds neofascism and far right authoritarianism <br> -US power is necessary | -US is militarist/ imperialist <br> -Rivals have defensive intentions <br> -Force and coercion are ineffective | -Power balancing is counterproductive <br> -No national security w/out human security <br> -Revisionist actors can change |

as arising from appeals to distinct logics that differ in how they prioritize, make assumptions about, and interpret the meaning of progressive principles of statecraft. The result of such differences, summarized in Table I.I, is not a singular consensus progressive grand strategy but rather three – that of the progressive pragmatist, the anti-hegemonist, and the peacemaker. Each of these ideal-types has a basis for claiming fidelity to progressive principles, and from them it may be possible to construct a repertoire of progressive statecraft with some analytical transparency.

*Progressive pragmatism* is a grand strategy of political economy that re-orients foreign policy toward principles of economic equality and anti-authoritarianism. It treats oligarchic and kleptocratic authoritarianism as threats, sustains international commitments to democratic allies only, and prioritizes solutions that reduce economic inequality. An alternative mode of progressive thought, *anti-hegemonism*, is a grand strategy of robust restraint, privileging foremost an interpretation of anti-authoritarianism that focuses on what it sees as the imperialist conduct of the United States. As such, it expects the world to become more benign when the US military scales down and comes home. It treats the projection and threat of force as generally counterproductive, positing that US power per se makes the United States and others less secure, and seeking compromise with adversaries to stabilize relations. And a third logic, of *peacemaking*, is a prefigurative grand strategy of peace, building cooperative co-existence among nations and societies to unlock political and economic democracy. It pairs an ethic of anti-militarism with a praxis of solidarity across borders, and it aims to change the valence of world politics by combining nonviolent peacebuilding and support for democracy movements with a cooperative security regime that moves toward disarmament.

Progressive pragmatism, anti-hegemonism, and peacemaking represent different ways of making good on a more progressive vision of what foreign policy should be. They are grand strategies in the sense that each is a "theory of security"[3] – that is, they configure beliefs, wagers, assumptions, and implicit risk propositions that convey how the United States ought to make and orchestrate its choices in order to realize greater security. Although grand strategy is a term as contestable as security itself,[4] thinking this way encourages us to depict national role conceptions and the political imagination in a manner that "contains explanations for why threats enjoy a certain priority, and why and how the remedies proposed could work."[5]

Collectively and individually, these progressive grand strategies constitute an "intellectual architecture that gives form and structure to foreign policy."[6] They also stand on critiques of liberal internationalism, the intellectual tradition that, while capacious enough to accommodate everything from the Marshall Plan to the Iraq invasion, has suffused US statecraft since at least World War I. The myriad faults that progressives find in liberal internationalism are the openings to prescribe alternative ways of wielding (and bridling) US power and influence. This has

---

[3] Barry Posen originated this term to describe a particular way of conceptualizing grand strategy as the foreign policy practices and decisions of the state in aggregate. Barry R. Posen, *The Sources of Military Doctrine: France, Britain, and Germany between the World Wars* (Ithaca, NY: Cornell University Press, 1984), p. 13.

[4] Much ink has been spilled over what grand strategy ought to mean. For a summary of the summaries of the literature, see Daniel Nexon, "Strategies of Unusual Size," *Duck of Minerva Newsletter* (May 6, 2022), https://duckofminerva.substack.com/p/strategies-of-unusual-size?utm_source=%2Fprofile%2F87416445-duck-of-minerva&utm_medium=reader2&s=r.

[5] Posen, *Restraint*, p. 1.

[6] Hal Bands, *What Good Is Grand Strategy? Power and Purpose in American Statecraft from Harry S. Truman to George W. Bush* (Ithaca, NY: Cornell University Press, 2015), p. 3.

implications for everything from "great-power competition" to the future of alliances, overseas bases, economic redistribution, and the power relations between the core and periphery of the world system. And yet, the progressive grand-strategic imaginary in its multiple configurations is radical only in the sense that it gets at root causes – it is more pragmatic than revolutionary, though in some conjunctures, the former may call for the latter.

This book, then, is an analysis of contemporary American leftist thought about making a world beyond liberal internationalism – specifically to its left – expressed in a language that brings it into dialog with scholarship on grand strategy and international security. It is not a manifesto, it does not pretend to be and largely excludes from its analysis revolutionary thought, and it does not directly describe how progressives organize for power or produce political change (although I deal with this too in Chapter 9). Its focus is statecraft – what are progressive demands against the national security state and the foreign policy apparatus? On what analytical grounds do those demands rest? How are the demands different from one another, where do they converge, and what are their implications for the conduct of US foreign policy? Drawing out three progressive grand strategies is a way of answering these questions.

Progressive pragmatism, anti-hegemonism, and peacemaking are categories constructed out of progressive discourses in (primarily) the United States. Many political actors are hybrids of these categories depending on the issue, or shift over time. At particular moments, figures such as Bernie Sanders may adopt one mode of reasoning over another in advocating foreign policy.

On China, for example, Sanders has at times aggressively spoken out against mass human rights abuses in Xinjiang, labeled it a genocide, and supported economic sanctions. Sanders even went on *60 Minutes* and flatly confirmed that he would use military force to defend Taiwan if China attacked.[7] These statements vexed some on the left who thought the good-versus-evil subtext was an overwrought diagnosis that made for a dangerous prescription. At the same time, Sanders was the only major presidential candidate in the post–Cold War era to include an explicit commitment to anti-militarism in his platform. That sentiment came through loudly when Sanders wrote in *Foreign Affairs* – the premier

---

[7] "Bernie Sanders Says He Would Intervene if China Took Military Action against Taiwan," *60 Minutes* (February 3, 2020), www.cbsnews.com/news/bernie-sanders-democratic-presidential-candidate-military-intervention-60-minutes-2020-02-23/.

journal of the national security establishment – excoriating Washington for stoking a McCarthyist, redbaiting atmosphere around China, stressing instead the importance of cooperating with Beijing to both sidestep rivalry and address the greater shared threat of climate change.[8]

These positions – sanctioning human rights abuses, defending fellow democracies from attack, resisting the pull of geopolitical rivalry, and searching for common ground with potential adversaries – reflect competing ways of dealing with China that can all nevertheless claim a progressive genealogy. On this specific issue, Sanders embodied the tensions within leftist politics that make it hard to escape antagonizing one part of the base in taking up the preferences of another part. But in general, Sanders's celebrity speaks to his unique effectiveness at synthesis – in 2016 and in 2020, he managed to largely unify behind him the extremely diverse American left. He pulled this off by successfully integrating or appealing to different progressive orientations – including on foreign policy – without pitting one camp against another. Sanders displayed a rare ability to codeswitch across multiple modes of leftist thought, and I aim to reveal what those modes are.

### WHY IT MATTERS

Bernie Sanders's complex stance on China underscores the real-world relevance of this analytical project. Which progressive values and lineages people like Sanders tap into as they engage in contentious politics is not unconnected from the kinds of positions they take and the tradeoffs they deem worthwhile. As the China case brings into sharp relief, it is not always possible to optimize for all progressive principles simultaneously, and one progressive approach may suit a given set of circumstances better than another. And precisely because not everyone on the left sorts or interprets the same broadly held principles the same way, or with the same understanding, rendering ideal-type categories can help us see and evaluate more clearly.

The construction of ideal types through the "one-sided accentuation of one or more points of view ... occasionally absent concrete individual phenomena" can serve "heuristic as well as expository purposes."[9] As with

---

[8] Bernie Sanders, "Washington's Dangerous New Consensus on China," *Foreign Affairs* (June 17, 2021), www.foreignaffairs.com/articles/china/2021-06-17/washingtons-dangerous-new-consensus-china.

[9] Max Weber, as quoted in Edward Shills and Henry Finch (translated and edited) *Max Weber on the Methodology of the Social Sciences (1903–1917)* (Glencoe, IL: Free Press, 1949), p. 90.

ideal types generally, so too with the theories of security presented in this book. Grasping progressive pragmatist, anti-hegemonist, and peacemaking logics helps us surface how prioritizing progressive values in different ways may reflect different assumptions about the world and America's role in it, require accepting different kinds of risks, and exhibit different biases when taking positions on discrete foreign policy issues. Thus, the closer a politician or intellectual comes to a given school of thought, the easier it is to unpack what their positions assume, wager, and risk. This is important because advocates may be unaware of the causal beliefs or tradeoffs implied in their positions, and even if they are aware, it often serves the purpose of advocacy to mask debatable assumptions, dilute the specificity of causal claims, and demur about the potential price that might have to be paid.

The argument put forward here also builds on recent efforts to establish a beachhead for intellectual diversity in the study of grand strategy, which might appear as hostile terrain for leftist ideas. Indeed, leftists channeling a critical or radical perspective might altogether resist making leftist thought an object of analysis on the grounds that national security itself is a domain in opposition to their political cause.[10] Others may fear that strategy's bias toward methodological individualism and instrumental means-ends reasoning forecloses on the ecological and relational understandings of how world politics is produced.[11] But, as Stephen Walt once wrote, "The persistent belief that opponents of war should not study national security is like trying to find a cure for cancer by refusing to study medicine while allowing research on the disease to be conducted solely by tobacco companies."[12] To the extent the problem with grand strategy is its conservatism, its slavishness to power, its obsession with the military, or its topically limited scope, the solution lay not in shunning it but diversifying and contesting within it. Indeed, a recent turn in grand strategy research has begun to accommodate

---

[10] See, for example, John Carl Baker, "Our Revolution Must Dismantle the National Security State," *Jacobin Magazine* (February 19, 2020), https://jacobinmag.com/2020/02/our-revolution-must-dismantle-the-national-security-state.

[11] Derber, *Welcome to the Revolution*; Mark Neocleous, *Critique of Security* (Edinburgh: Edinburgh University Press, 2008); Steven Fuller, "Karl Popper and the Reconstitution of the Rationalist Left," *Science & Technology Studies* Vol. 16, no. 1 (2003), p. 191. Opposition to instrumentalist reasoning also suffuses the Frankfurt School. See especially, Max Horkheimer and Theodor Adorno, *Dialectic of Enlightenment: Philosophical Fragments* (Palo Alto: Stanford University Press, 2002 edition); Max Horkheimer, *Eclipse of Reason* (New York: Bloomsbury, 2013 edition), pp. 1–40.

[12] Walt, "The Renaissance of Security Studies," p. 216.

demilitarized – or at least instrumentally agnostic – approaches that this book consciously builds on.[13]

But not only is this the first attempt to render progressive ways of thinking about security into terms commensurate with how it is conceived in the theory and practice of "high" strategy. Mapping progressive worldmaking strategies exposes blind spots in both the dominant conversations about US grand strategy today and in left foreign policy discourses, making this book a bridge to an admittedly hard conversation. Grand strategy is filled with rationalists debating rationalists, as if the solutions to the world's problems lay entirely within the narrow range of what they think and assume. As their dialog has become impoverished, so too has the advice they have to give policymakers. The progressive value-add, accordingly, is not only in surfacing wager-risk propositions not captured elsewhere, but also consciously incorporating how non-military repertoires of statecraft make it possible – even preferable – to manage or preempt risks in the traditional sense of the ability to project or protect military power.

In turn, the progressive worldview involves a number of strategic risks that are never taken seriously or engaged with analytically precisely because no prior research has attempted to render progressive thinking into coherent theories of security. Irrespective of whether leftist politics is correct in its remedies to the enduring dilemmas and tragedies contained within narrowly rationalist conceptions of security, it too has risks and blind spots that deserve scrutiny on like-terms. Doing so here sharpens grand strategy debates, clarifies risks and opportunity costs, and expands the foreign policy imagination.

## THE WAY AHEAD

The rest of the book is organized in three sections. The first, consisting of the next four chapters, broadly establishes what American progressives are, what they believe, and why. Chapter 1 situates this project in relation to the larger grand strategy conversation, stressing above all how progressives think differently about security. Chapter 2 introduces liberal internationalism as a theory of security that has been the core

---

[13] Thierry Balzacq, Peter Dombrowski, and Simon Reich, eds., *Comparative Grand Strategy: A Framework and Cases* (New York: Oxford University Press, 2019); Elizabeth Borgwardt, Christopher McKnight Nichols, and Andrew Preston, eds., *Rethinking American Grand Strategy* (New York: Oxford University Press, 2021).

of US foreign policy since at least the early twentieth century. Because progressive visions of foreign policy are cast as alternatives to liberal internationalism, it is important to establish what liberal internationalism is, what its wagers are, and how progressives see and critique its evolution. These critiques include claims that liberal internationalism enables the unequal distribution of gains from economic globalization that fuels radical politics and corruption; it militarizes foreign policy, which has led to costly wars of choice and a high opportunity cost in domestic welfare; it ignores instances in which the size and scope of US military power encourage adversaries to pursue more belligerent policies that leave the United States less secure; it supports authoritarian regimes; and it habitually excludes voices outside an unaccountable Washington establishment. Chapter 3 unpacks the shifting meaning of progressivism over time, as well as the left's clashes and convergences with liberal politics in the Democratic Party. Chapter 4 then introduces each of the core principles of progressive foreign policy – economic equality, anti-authoritarianism, and solidarity – in a form that bridges evidence of these principles in contemporary progressive discourses with their historical antecedents.

The second section, Chapters 5–7, constructs each of the progressive grand strategies that make up the core of the book. It shows how sorting or interpreting the meaning of progressive principles differently yields distinct agendas grounded in contrasting forms of reasoning. Chapter 5 describes the assumptions, wagers, and risks of progressive pragmatism, which seeks to combat oligarchy, kleptocracy, and neofascism. Chapter 6 does the same for anti-hegemonism, which focuses on bridling US power, reducing it, and reaching strategic accommodations with adversaries. Chapter 7 then builds an alternative to both progressive pragmatism and anti-hegemonism grounded in the logic of "non-offensive defense" and peace activism, a two-pronged approach. At the interstate level, peacemaking seeks a cooperative security regime that penalizes military aggression but prioritizes defensive postures and signaling in the short term, gradually moving toward disarmament in the long term. At the civil society level, it involves "waging peace" by brokering, legitimating, and aiding oppressed peoples (including but not limited to democracy movements) against their oppressors in various ways.

The final section of the book, Chapters 8 and 9, presents a synthesis of progressive grand strategy. Chapter 8 surveys myriad progressive proposals for how to transform the global economic order, including neo-Keynesianism, justice for the Global South (which takes several forms), de-growth, and the global green new deal. That chapter makes its own self-contained argument that progressives aim to use the global economy to reduce inequality in the Global North, address the climate crisis, and improve living conditions in the Global South ... but competing models of economic order stress these priorities differently and consist of prescriptions that are not equally fungible across all three modes of progressive statecraft. Chapter 9 concludes the book with two tasks: identifying a consensus progressive foreign policy agenda compatible with all three variants of progressive grand strategy and considering how the contemporary political terrain affects the prospects of the United States relating to the world in a more consciously social democratic way. At stake is whether US statecraft ignores, worsens, or grapples with what progressives see as root causes of global insecurity.

Before proceeding though, a word is necessary to clarify how this book interacts with the landscape of leftist thought generally. First, as is already clear, I sometimes use the term "left" and "progressive" interchangeably. I do this partly for stylistic reasons, and the substantive reasons for it will be rationalized at length in Chapter 3, but suffice it to say now that (1) the scope of my argument here concerns the spectrum of ideas that lay to the left of liberal internationalism, which is necessarily wide and eclectic, and yet (2) some leftists are not progressive and would loathe to identify as such. At the same time, it would be redundant and exceedingly narrow to reduce American leftism to being only socialism (which itself takes a variety of forms), even though there is something socialistic in every meaningful claim to leftist politics.

Second, entire books can be, and in some cases have been, written elaborating on an implicitly "left" foreign policy from different epistemological standpoints. Black internationalism takes as its entry point the black experience, which is something different than that of democratic socialism or third-wave feminism or liberal progressivism in the mold of John Dewey, for example. The insights that come from various standpoints to the left of liberal internationalism are resources from which I construct progressive logics of worldmaking.

Third, some strategy-minded leftists see distinct categories of struggle as being connected through "chains of equivalence" – that is, a way of seeing the world that relativizes the importance of one kind of struggle versus another in the face of a hegemonic power structure.[14] To the

---

[14] Ernesto Laclau and Chantal Mouffe, *Hegemony and Socialist Strategy: Towards a Radical Democratic Politics* (New York: Verso, 1985), pp. 113–131.

extent this means that mobilizing for any just cause creates a lodgment for addressing others, it makes practical sense. But this book pushes back on the more caricatured sensibility that says there can be no prioritization, or that prioritization is a trap. As I discuss in Chapter 4, chain-of-equivalence reasoning is one way of making sense of the progressive commitment to a principle of solidarity. But strategy necessarily entails prioritization, and partly because the rich diversity of perspectives within the left can be overwhelming – particularly for scholars and policymakers who do not necessarily come from leftist politics – it is useful to grasp a few key logics of security at play both across and within different left-aligned global struggles. Competing priorities are part of the story of how these competing logics (progressive pragmatism, anti-hegemonism, and peacemaking) come into being. Diagnosing the problems of international security differently or sorting progressive principles in different ways can lead to agenda conflicts among advocates of a more progressive foreign policy. And on any given issue, there may be multiple ways of realizing a more progressive future.

Thus, the three approaches to progressive worldmaking described in this book are not meant to displace any left standpoint but rather to supplement them all with analytical transparency that makes clear both what is at stake and inner logics of a common progressive spirit. So doing offers a way of potentially bridging rather than isolating different ways of seeing.

# Thinking Differently about Security

The depictions of progressive statecraft in this book should be understood in relation to the ways that scholars and practitioners alike talk, think, and make claims in the idiom of security, which can obscure as much as it reveals. While "national security" and "national interest" dominate discourses of grand strategy, for instance, they leave much to be assumed and specified.

Scholars often represent the ends of grand strategy as vital or long-term "national interests," with "interests" being vague and highly fungible.[1] Where interests are defined clearly, they are typically reducible to narrow conceptions of security – national survival, battlefield victory, or power position.[2] Such language blurs the chasm of difference that often exists between that which serves the interests of an entire nation and that which serves (and works against) the interests of particular classes, races, genders, or institutions within that nation.

Security's referent object, meanwhile, rarely gets interrogated. "National security" is a misnomer referring to state or regime security,

---

[1] See, for example, Paul Kennedy, "Grand Strategy in War and Peace: Toward a Broader Definition," in *Grand Strategy in War and Peace*, edited by Paul Kennedy (New Haven: Yale University Press, 1991), p. 5; John Lewis Gaddis, *On Grand Strategy* (New York: Penguin Publishing Group, 2019), pp. 37, 55. This case is also made in Nina Silove, "Beyond the Buzzword: The Three Meanings of Grand Strategy," *Security Studies* Vol. 27, no. 1 (2018), p. 35.

[2] The comparative turn in grand strategy resists this trend, accommodating geostrategic objectives that include the fulfillment of identity attributes and the redress of historical injustices. Peter Dombrowski and Simon Reich, *Across Type, Space, and Time: American Grand Strategy in Comparative Perspective* (Cambridge: Cambridge University Press, 2021), pp. 11–12. See also Kevin Narizny, *The Political Economy of Grand Strategy* (Ithaca, NY: Cornell University Press, 2007), pp. 8–16.

theories of international politics exhibit a well-known state-centric bias, and the primary means of securing the state tends to be through the military. The assumption that "grand strategy is ultimately about fighting" is exceedingly common in grand strategy research.[3] The result is a fixation on "the threat or use of force for policy ends."[4] These tendencies are intrinsic in "classical" grand strategy scholarship, which places a premium on questions relating to the accumulation and deployment of military power as a way of securing states from foreign predation, annihilation, and/or battlefield defeat.[5] The traditional view of security studies as a discipline shares these classical priorities.[6]

## GRAND STRATEGY'S GRAND PROBLEMS

This obsession with military affairs invites a number of criticisms. Grand strategy's focus on war bleeds too easily into becoming a rationalizing instrument for war, lending to a reputation for being exceedingly reactionary and militarist.[7] It is guilty of a certain elite, "great-man" reading of history, making its connections to a notion of the common good threadbare. You could be forgiven for thinking that this form of analysis exists only to counsel those with power on how to retain or maximize it.[8] And to the extent grand-strategic studies have taken domestic political ideologies seriously, they have been confined only to conservative politics.[9]

---

[3] Barry Posen, *Restraint: A New Foundation for U.S. Grand Strategy* (Ithaca: Cornell University Press, 2014), p. 1.

[4] Colin Gray, *Strategy and History: Essays on Theory and Practice* (Abingdon: Routledge, 2007), p. 78.

[5] Dombrowski and Reich, *Across Type, Space, and Time*, p. 14; Thierry Balzacq, Peter Dombrowski, and Simon Reich, "Is Grand Strategy a Research Program? A Review Essay," *Security Studies* Vol. 28, no. 1 (2019), pp. 68–75.

[6] Stephen Walt, "The Renaissance of Security Studies," *International Studies Quarterly* Vol. 35, no. 2 (1991), pp. 211–39. "Traditional" security studies is a common way to describe the historical focus on militaries and hard power. See Barry Buzan and Lene Hansen, *The Evolution of International Security Studies* (Cambridge: Cambridge University Press, 2009), p. 156.

[7] Aaron Jakes, "A Yale Program Drew Fire over Donor Meddling. Its Real Problem Was Promoting War," *Washington Post* (October 11, 2021), www.washingtonpost.com/outlook/2021/10/11/yale-grand-strategy-beverly-gage-kissinger/.

[8] Thomas Meaney and Stephen Wertheim, "Grand Flattery: The Yale Grand Strategy Seminar," *The Nation* (May 9, 2012), www.thenation.com/article/archive/grand-flattery-yale-grand-strategy-seminar/.

[9] See, for instance, Paul Miller, *American Power and Liberal Order: A Conservative Internationalist Grand Strategy* (Washington, DC: Georgetown University Press, 2018);

But the biggest problem with classical grand strategic thinking is that it limits the possibilities for how America relates to the world, and in the grimmest way. Specifically, a rationalist bias pervades debates about US grand strategy. For instance, Barry Posen and Andrew Ross described four ideal-type categories of grand strategy at the dawn of the post–Cold War era that endure in most analyses today: primacy, cooperative security, selective engagement, and neo-isolationism.[10] A generation later, scholars still describe America's grand strategic choices in roughly these terms – restraint, deep engagement, liberal internationalism, and conservative primacy.[11]

But as Posen and Ross freely acknowledge, the theoretical traditions underpinning their typology are all rationalist – three variations of realism (primacy, selective engagement/offshore balancing, and neo-isolationism, respectively) and one variant of neoliberal institutionalism (cooperative security/deep engagement). This not only perpetually privileges questions of military force and the aggregation of hard power but also constrains how scholars diagnose and policymakers respond to security/insecurity in the world. Realism typically black-boxes the state, obscuring problems and solutions that come from within it.[12] And rationalism, the larger epistemic commitment that realism falls within, caricatures reality in ways that can be unhelpful.[13] International actors are not always and everywhere rational

Colin Dueck, *Hard Line: The Republican Party and U.S. Foreign Policy since World War II* (Princeton: Princeton University Press, 2010); Colin Dueck, *Age of Iron: On Conservative Nationalism* (New York: Oxford University Press, 2019). See also the discussion of "conservative primacy," elevated to an ideal-type category of grand strategy in Paul C. Avey, Jonathan N. Markowitz, and Robert J. Reardon, "Disentangling Grand Strategy: International Relations Theory and U.S. Grand Strategy," *Texas National Security Review* Vol. 2, no. 1 (2018), pp. 28–51.

[10]  Barry Posen and Andrew Ross, "Competing Visions for U.S. Grand Strategy," *International Security* Vol. 21, no. 3 (1996/97), pp. 5–53.

[11]  Paul C. Avey, Jonathan N. Markowitz, and Robert J. Reardon, "Disentangling Grand Strategy: International Relations Theory and U.S. Grand Strategy," *Texas National Security Review* Vol. 2, no. 1 (2018), pp. 28–51. In practice, debates about US grand strategy have been even narrower, primarily dwelling on deep engagement and offshore balancing. Balzacq, Dombrowski and Reich, "Is Grand Strategy a Research Program?," p. 62.

[12]  All versions of realism take a reduced view of matters internal to the state, but not all are equally guilty of black-boxing it. See Bernard Finel, "Black Box or Pandora's Box: State Level Variables and Progressivity in Realist Research Programs," *Security Studies* Vol. 11, no. 2 (2001), pp. 187–227; Brian Rathbun, "A Rose by Any Other Name: Neoclassical Realism as the Logical and Necessary Extension of Structural Realism," *Security Studies* Vol. 17, no. 2 (2008), pp. 294–321.

[13]  Alexander Wendt and James Fearon, "Rationalism v. Constructivism? A Skeptical View," in *Handbook of International Relations*, edited by Walter Carlsnaes, Thomas Risse, and Beth Simmons (New York: Sage, 2001), pp. 52–72; Brian Rathbun, *Reasoning*

utility maximizers, and the assumption that causality in the observable world must follow from microfoundations is at best questionable when we know that certain patterns of world politics reflect and are reflected in macro-level social structures and relational processes of interaction.[14]

Such biases may offer analytical advantages from time to time, but they are a shoddy foundation for an entire research program meant to inform real-world politics. They are the kinds of limitations that narrow the imagination regarding what America's international role and conduct ought to or could be. If this rationalist tilt in US grand strategy debates covered the full range of real-world political thinking, occluding alternatives might have analytical merit. But it does not. So we must illuminate what lay beyond it.

## THE PROGRESSIVE WORLDVIEW
## AND DURABLE SECURITY

The modes of reasoning discoverable in progressive thought stand as implicit critiques of the narrow band of choices available in grand strategy debates. They also share a number of attributes that distinguish them from prevailing discourses about grand strategy.

One is that while progressives can be said to hold security as the ultimate end of foreign policy, they define security as a necessarily political condition. "Security" does not refer to power position or national survival directly; it relates to greater peace, participatory democracy, and equality.[15] These visionary ends inform the progressive commitment to a set of core principles (economic equality, anti-authoritarianism, and solidarity), because there is no realizing the former without some fidelity to the latter. Security conceived in this way also presupposes national survival and the absence of war, but to seek such minimalist aims in a political and economic vacuum would not furnish security but rather precarity and outright militarism.

*of State: Realists, Romantics and Rationality in International Relations* (New York: Cambridge University Press, 2019), pp. 38–73.

[14] Patrick Thaddeus Jackson and Daniel Nexon, "Relations before States: Substance, Process, and the Study of World Politics," *European Journal of International Relations* Vol. 5, no. 3 (1999), pp. 291–332.

[15] Equality and democracy have been priorities of the left since the French Revolution. See Howard Brick and Christopher Phelps, *Radicals in America: The U.S. Left since the Second World War* (Cambridge: Cambridge University Press, 2015), pp. 5–11; Gary Dorrien, *American Democratic Socialism: History, Politics, Religion, and Theory* (New Haven: Yale University Press, 2021) pp. 1–2, 9; Michael Kazin, *American Dreamers: How the Left Changed a Nation* (New York: Vintage Books, 2011), pp. xiii–xiv.

Second, progressives view the conditions of security (peace, democracy, and equality) as interdependent, making the taproot of a progressive approach using and constraining the power of the state in a manner that, as much as possible, deals with underlying causes of insecurity. "The aim of security policy," argued fellows of the progressive Transnational Institute, "should be the establishing of the long-term social and ecological conditions for well-being and justice – the necessary bases for genuine peace – rather than a reactive approach to short-term security threats."[16] This shares something of Karl Marx's dictum that "To be radical is to grab things by the root. But for man the root is man himself."[17] Similarly, in his "Letter to the New Left" in 1960, C. Wright Mills intoned that leftist demands ought to be based on an understanding of foundational causes; "our work is necessarily structural," he insisted.[18] Accordingly, the answers to the problems of war and injustice – which are related – are presumed to be upstream of the decisions of "great men," the shape of militaries, and the outcomes of battles.[19]

This view – even more than a thick versus thin conception of security – is the most striking break between progressive grand strategy and the rest. Progressives see the geopolitical games nations play as symptoms of a security deficit whose solutions are found mostly in public policy, which vastly expands the *ways and means* available in progressive grand strategy while also rendering more realistic evaluations of the costs and risks of military tools. National "defense," by contrast, is a largely negative project – at least in the way it has been deployed since the early Cold War. Traditional national security is really a domain of proximate causes. Dwelling exclusively in it confines the world to perpetual *in*security.

Third, progressives find talk of "interests" obfuscatory. It is not that interests do not exist; they do. But if security is a political and ecological condition, then "interests" should not be something apart from it. The question that subsumes "Whose interests?" and even "What are interests?" is "Security for whom?"[20] Rare is the policy that benefits both the

---

[16] Ruth Blakeley, Ben Hayes, Nisha Kapoor, Arun Kundnani, Narzanin Massoumi, David Miller, Tom Mills, Rizwaan Sabir, Katy Sian and Waqas Tufail, *Leaving the War on Terror: A Progressive Alternative to Counter-Terrorism Policy* (Amsterdam: Transnational Institute, 2019), p. 58.

[17] Karl Marx, "Contribution to the Critique of Hegel's Philosophy of Right Introduction," in *The Marx-Engels Reader*, 2nd ed., edited by Mark Tucker (New York: W.W. Norton and Co., 1978), p. 162.

[18] C. Wright Mills, "Letter to the New Left," *New Left Review* (July 4, 1960), p. 21.

[19] On Mills's radicalism and its inspiration to the New Left, see Todd Gitlin, *The Intellectuals and the Flag* (New York: Columbia University Press, 2006), pp. 27–48.

[20] Security in the progressive sense *is* freedom, understood more precisely than its colloquial right-wing usage. Conservatives drape themselves in terms like "freedom" and

masses and their ruling classes, and oligarchs from different countries have far more in common with each other than they do the workers – of whatever national origin – whose surplus value they hoard. State/ national security is a public good only insofar as it functions as a tool servicing more peaceful, democratic, and egalitarian ends. As such, the progressive view of security is self-consciously internationalist, but in a manner that dissolves hard distinctions between domestic and international imperatives to begin with. This is true of democratic socialists,[21] neo-Keynesians,[22] and left-liberal progressives like Democratic Senator Chris Murphy, who argued that progressive "issues don't exist in a vacuum. If you care about democracy, or human rights or the environment here, then you have to care about these fights everywhere, and you need to be engaged in them everywhere."[23]

But as Daniel Bessner, a self-identified anti-hegemonist quipped, "Sad to be an internationalist in a world of nation-states."[24] "Internationalism" has a flattened, co-opted meaning in most debates; progressives' internationalism is not reducible to military operations or security commitments abroad. Progressives believe long-term security is indivisible. While they have competing theories for realizing it (and sequencing the goals that constitute it), the state or nation will only realize durable security for itself when humanity has greater security. But when should security come at the point of a gun?

## Anti-militarism

That question is why it is vital to understand the centrality of anti-militarism to the progressive worldview. Progressives' anti-militarist

"liberty" but often in a manner that obscures both who benefits from the policies implemented in their name and what hierarchical and exclusionary power arrangements lay underneath the rhetoric. Leftists and progressives see equality, democracy, and peace as antecedent conditions for realizing liberation. See Corey Robin, "Reclaiming the Politics of Freedom," *The Nation* (April 25, 2011), www.thenation.com/article/archive/ reclaiming-politics-freedom/.

21  Aziz Rana, "Renewing Working-Class Internationalism," *New Labor Forum* (2019), https://newlaborforum.cuny.edu/2019/01/25/working-class-internationalism/.
22  Zack Beauchamp, "What Should a Left Foreign Policy Look Like? An Elizabeth Warren Adviser Offers His Vision," *Vox* (May 7, 2019), www.vox.com/ world/2019/5/7/18525841/elizabeth-warren-foreign-policy-ganesh-sitaraman.
23  "Progressive Foreign Policy: A Conversation with Senator Chris Murphy," Remarks at the Council on Foreign Relations, New York (September 13, 2019), www.youtube.com/ watch?v=Kicd3npHSys&feature=emb_logo.
24  @dbessner (February 25, 2022), https://twitter.com/dbessner/status/149695294816055 7059.

commitment distinguishes them from liberal internationalists more than any other (and separates those who identify as progressives in domestic politics only from those with a progressive worldview). When militarism became a diagnosed problem in industrial societies during the nineteenth century, it was understood narrowly as circumstances where "the military aspect of politics became a state's overriding concern ... preparations for war gained the upper hand over considerations of 'the steady art of statecraft'."[25] Today, militarism is sometimes broader, taken to mean "the social and international relations of the preparation for and conduct of organized political violence."[26]

Because military-first politics are a blight on democracy, anti-militarism has always been a through-line for the American left that informs its anti-war sensibility.[27] The American Union Against Militarism, the institutional vanguard against not just America's participation in World War I but also the military buildup that would have been required to wage the war, gave birth to a spinoff organization called the Committee for Democratic Control. The latter's very name points to the conceit of anti-militarism – preserving democracy, which war and war preparation risks denuding of any real meaning.[28]

Opposition to militarism also persisted as a through-line for the American left from the global peace and nuclear disarmament movements of the early Cold War to the New Left's opposition to the Vietnam War, and later the Nuclear Freeze Movement of the 1980s.[29] C. Wright Mills condemned militarism as "The doctrine of violence, and the inept opportunism based upon it," because it "substitutes for political and economic programs. That doctrine has been and is the fundamental basis of U.S. policy. And that policy is bankrupt .... It has increased the insecurity of the United States and the world at large."[30] By the early twenty-first century, with *liberal* representing cultural and identity politics associated

---

[25] V.R. Berghahn, *Militarism: The History of an International Debate, 1861–1979* (Cambridge: Cambridge University Press, 1984), pp. 105–106.

[26] Chris Rossdale, *Resisting Militarism: Direct Action and the Politics of Subversion* (Edinburgh: Edinburgh University Press, 2019), p. 45.

[27] Petra Goedde, *The Politics of Peace: A Global Cold War History* (New York: Oxford University Press, 2019). See also Michael Kazin, *War against War: The American Fight for Peace, 1914–1918* (New York: Simon & Schuster, 2017).

[28] McKnight Nichols, *Promise and Peril*, p. 150.

[29] On this historical continuity, see especially Petra Goedde, *The Politics of Peace: A Global Cold War History* (New York: Oxford University Press, 2019).

[30] C. Wright Mills, *The Causes of World War Three* (New York: Ballantine Books, 1960), p. 20.

with the left, the thing that defined *progressive* more than anything was opposition to war – especially the Iraq War.[31]

Despite a century-long tradition of anti-militarist activism and a vibrant feminist and critical literature naming the problem of militarism in societies (depicting it as bound up with patriarchy, imperialism, and white supremacy),[32] militarism as a concept is alien to the discourses of Washington policymakers, "defense intellectuals," and mainstream security studies. The threat, deployment, and use of military force is so central to America's modern national security state that to critically invoke the idea of militarism at all risks indicting the very edifice of US foreign policy.

But anti-militarism does not inherently rule out the use of force, which means it is not reducible to pacifism.[33] It proscribes wielding the use or threat of force *when* such actions are understood as tragically self-perpetuating or self-undermining. As Matt Duss, Bernie Sanders's foreign policy adviser, explained, "because military violence leads to so many unintended consequences, to outcomes that we can neither foresee nor control, American foreign policy needs to dramatically de-emphasize military power" in its engagement with the world.[34] Anti-militarism thus does not denote an absolute commitment to nonviolence; it indicates an earned skepticism of military responses to foreign policy problems that requires diagnosing and resisting dynamics of self-entrapping violence. This guards against the liberal "imperial temptation" and distinguishes

---

[31] In keeping with *progressive* as a floating signifier though, even anti-war beliefs were a contested basis for being progressive because centrist Democrats had occasionally appropriated *progressive* – and specifically *progressive internationalism* – as a way to refer to a globally hegemonic military project. See, for example, *Progressive Internationalism: A Democratic National Security Strategy* (Washington, DC: Progressive Policy Institute, 2003).

[32] On militarism's intersectional nature, see Davis, *Freedom is a Constant Struggle*; Derber, *Welcome to the Revolution*; Cynthia Cockburn, *Anti-militarism: Political and Gender Dynamics of Peace Movements* (New York: Palgrave Macmillan, 2012); Cynthia Cockburn and Cynthia Enloe, "Militarism, Patriarchy, and Peace Movements," *International Feminist Journal of Politics* Vol. 14, no. 4 (2012), pp. 550–57; Carol Cohn, "Sex and Death in the Rational World of Defense Intellectuals," *Signs: Journal of Women in Culture and Society* Vol. 12, no. 4 (1987), pp. 687–718.

[33] On the anti-militarism of pacifism, see Judith Butler, *The Force of Nonviolence: An Ethico-Political Bind* (New York: Verso, 2021).

[34] Matt Duss as quoted in "The Bernie Sanders Doctrine on Foreign Policy: An Interview with Matt Duss," *Jacobin Magazine* (August 20, 2020), https://jacobinmag.com/2020/08/bernie-sanders-foreign-policy-matt-duss?fbclid=IwAR0GZfbgCxAzDGgJ38q-qE7fqsTJi6xF2N9clYiH5JHwYfVh6LPsLFkGOKE.

progressive security thinking from the liberal primacist or neoconservative logic of simply promoting global democracy at the point of a gun.[35]

The problem, as foreign-policy progressives see it, is that the military as a security tool presents a fundamental mismatch between problem and solution in most instances. As a matter of budget, attention, and imagination, US foreign policy is heavily invested in warriors and weapons systems "despite not offering a credible solution to modern problems like cyber attacks, pandemics, and climate change."[36] Bertrand Russell's truth is instructive about the progressives' sense that militarism is bad strategy – "To advocate democracy by war is only to repeat, on a vaster scale and with far more tragic results, the error of those who have sought it hitherto by the assassin's knife and the bomb of the anarchist."[37] US participation in World War I, for example, unleashed antidemocratic forces, needlessly securitizing politics and stigmatizing egalitarian values for a century to come.[38]

The war exposed violence as a crude, risky means of achieving political ends – one that tends to work for reactionary aims better than progressive ones. Similarly, when the progressive Institute for Policy Studies formed in 1963, it did so on the basis of many specific critiques of Cold War foreign policy, but above all it resisted what it saw as attitudes of militarism substituting for rigorous policy arguments. The justifications for arms racing and threat-making had been too shallow – even nonsensical – to justify risking democracy and the planet itself.[39] Even in the Biden era, sitting Senators opposed national infrastructure investment and spending on a green climate fund on the grounds that the Pentagon needed those resources to compete with China.[40]

Such myopic statecraft is militarism in action – the same myopia that has kept America continuously in conflict overseas for a century while

[35] Daniel Nexon and Paul Musgrave, "American Liberalism and Imperial Temptation," in *Empire and International Order*, edited by Noel Parker (London: Ashgate, 2013), pp. 131–48.

[36] Yasmeen Silva, "When All You Have Is a Hammer …," *Outrider Post* (November 24, 2021), https://outrider.org/nuclear-weapons/articles/when-all-you-have-hammer/.

[37] Bertrand Russell, "The Ethics of War," *International Journal of Ethics* Vol. 25, no. 2 (1915), p. 138.

[38] Kazin, *War against War*; Nichols, *Promise and Peril*; Adam Hochschild, *American Midnight: The Great War, a Violent Peace, and Democracy's Forgotten Crisis* (New York: Mariner Books, 2022).

[39] Exposing the irrationality of rational arguments for deterrence was one of the tactics of IPS and peace intellectuals in the early Cold War. See Mueller, *Democracy's Think Tank*.

[40] Julia Conley, "Manchin Only Dem to Join GOP to Reroute Billions in Climate Funds to Pentagon," *Common Dreams* (May 6, 2022), www.commondreams.org/news/2022/05/06/manchin-only-dem-join-gop-reroute-billions-climate-funds-pentagon.

only taking notice of it in spurts and starts.[41] So while there are people who vote Democrat and can think of themselves as "progressives except for U.S. primacy,"[42] they are liberal internationalists (not progressives) on matters of foreign policy. Anti-militarism insulates the progressive worldview from the reactionary potential within progressivism.

## AVOIDING FALSE FRAMES

What makes progressive grand strategies projects of worldmaking, then, is that even the most restrained versions counsel how to build toward something. To think of grand strategy as worldmaking is to center "how state power ought to be wielded, on behalf of whom, and at whose expense."[43] Contrary to how mainstream grand strategic ideas tend to function, progressive worldmaking is expressly *not* about entrenching the interests of a ruling class, accruing power for its own sake, or preserving an unbalanced political status quo. In an academic sense, that makes this book part of a wave of recent grand strategy research that surfaces social logics of power,[44] seeks comparative-empirical (rather than just theoretical) grounding,[45] and takes

[41] This is the bedrock claim underwriting Marilyn Young's entire career of anti-war historiography. For an overview, see Mark Philip Bradley and Mary Dudziak, eds., *Making the Forever War: Marilyn B. Young on the Culture and Politics of American Militarism* (Amherst: University of Massachusetts Press, 2021).

[42] Theodore Roosevelt represented a kind of reactionary progressivism. World War I fractured the progressive movement because some progressives saw war as a means of realizing global democracy (though most later regretted it). Some progressives working for Obama and Biden – notably Kurt M. Campbell – treated military superiority as an explicit aim and promoted a pro-corporate economic agenda. See Kurt M. Campbell, *The Pivot: The Future of American Statecraft in Asia* (New York: Twelve Books, 2016). See also Dominic Tierney, "The Rise of the Liberal Hawks," *Atlantic*, 4 September 2022, www.theatlantic.com/ideas/archive/2022/09/liberal-democrat-military-support-ukraine-trump/671328/. At least one longtime progressive proponent of Elizabeth Warren also aligned himself with reactionary militarism. See Van Jackson, "Why the Elizabeth Warren Pipeline Goes Left and Far Right," *Un-Diplomatic Newsletter*, October 19, 2022, www.un-diplomatic.com/why-the-elizabeth-warren-pipeline-goes-left-and-far-right/.

[43] Van Jackson, "Grand Strategy Is Worldmaking," *Duck of Minerva* (October 25, 2022), www.duckofminerva.com/2022/10/grand-strategy-is-worldmaking.html.

[44] Stacey Goddard and Ronald Krebs, "Rhetoric, Legitimation, and Grand Strategy," *Security Studies* Vol. 24, no. 1 (2015), pp. 5–36; Ronald Krebs, *Narrative and the Making of U.S. National Security* (Cambridge: Cambridge University Press, 2015); Simon Reich, *Global Norms, American Sponsorship and the Emerging Patterns of World Politics* (Basingstoke: Palgrave MacMillan, 2010); Peter Dombrowski and Simon Reich, "The Strategy of Sponsorship," *Survival* Vol. 57, no. 5 (2015), pp. 121–48.

[45] Thierry Balzacq, Peter Dombrowski, and Simon Reich, eds., *Comparative Grand Strategy: A Framework and Cases* (New York: Oxford University Press, 2019); Lukas Milevski, *The Evolution of Modern Grand Strategic Thought* (London: Oxford University Press, 2016).

domestic history and ideology seriously.[46] In a practical sense, that makes this book uniquely transparent in its willingness to not just acknowledge but foreground how superficially apolitical security analysis does political work. Grand strategy is worldmaking because grand strategy always has grand political implications – any strategy with the ambition of directing the national security state presupposes allocating resources and exercising (state) power, often at scale. But progressive grand strategy is worldmaking for the many, rather than the few.

As subsequent chapters make clear, progressive grand strategy has much to say about even defense policy. But contra classical grand strategy and traditional security studies, it also finds affinity with the more expansive "nontraditional" security concerns that have marked the evolution of security studies since the 1980s.[47] The human security agenda, for example, which stresses anthropogenic threats (climate change) and naturogenic threats (pandemics), has historically gotten short shrift in grand strategy literature but is instrumental in how progressives think about security.[48] But the reason that progressives take these issues seriously is that they believe foreign policy ought to attend to the root causes of geopolitical problems, which are necessarily located disproportionately in the "non-traditional" policy spaces rather than in debates about the threat and use of military force.

There is a tendency among traditional national security analysts to think of nonmilitary security issues as "values-based" ones, and then to contrast that with some kind of supposedly hard-nosed analysis that boresights on guns and bombs and the like. The implication being that tools and techniques of war ought to have primacy over "values." But this is a false contrast. To prioritize guns and bombs at the expense of other issues is often to claim a particular set of values – specifically militarist, hierarchical, exclusionary, and functionally antidemocratic values – over others. It also mischaracterizes what progressives are doing. Unlike guns-and-bombs enthusiasts, progressives' values do not bracket off but rather are based on claims about the roots of insecurity.

---

[46] Elizabeth Borgwardt, Christopher McKnight Nichols, and Andrew Preston, eds., *Rethinking American Grand Strategy* (New York: Oxford University Press, 2021).

[47] On the rise of "non-traditional" security, see Buzan and Hansen, *The Evolution of International Security Studies*, pp. 118–52, 200–11.

[48] A rare exception is Bruce Jentleson, "Refocusing US Grand Strategy on Pandemic and Environmental Mass Destruction," *Washington Quarterly* Vol. 43, no. 3 (2020), pp. 7–29.

# 2

# Liberal Internationalism and Its Critics

The challenge of presenting liberal internationalism as a foil for leftists and progressives is that it has a "thin and shape-shifting character."[1] This leaves room for advocates and critics to talk past each other by appealing to not only different aspects of the same phenomenon today, but also to different historical versions of it. And as I discuss the Biden presidency in Chapter 9, liberal internationalism sometimes fuels itself by siphoning ideas from its left flank.

For advocates, this is a virtue that makes liberal internationalism a vehicle for progress. For opponents, however, appropriating tokens from the left without transforming the liberal foreign policy project is at the heart of the problem. In either case, the contours of liberal internationalism are reasonably well understood, especially the elements that make it function as a theory of security.

## WASHINGTON AND THE "LIBERAL INTERNATIONAL ORDER"

As practiced in the United States, liberal internationalism consists in a mix of realist and liberal/neoliberal wagers, premised on American exceptionalism – military superiority, alliances, economic interdependence through capital markets, and multilateral institutions. These

---

[1] G. John Ikenberry, *A World Safe for Democracy: Liberal Internationalism and the Crises of Global Order* (New Haven: Yale University Press, 2020), p. 8. Some critics, incidentally, also view liberal internationalism this way. See Beate Jahn, *Liberal Internationalism: Theory, History, Practice* (New York: Palgrave MacMillan, 2013), p. 39.

combined wagers follow from principles cherished in liberal political theory – individual rights, institutions that govern by consent, and private property and commerce.[2] It also represents a paradox.

On the one hand, liberal internationalism has proven prone to triumphalism and is shot through with an optimistic view of history; that today is better than yesterday and tomorrow promises to be better still.[3] On the other, there is a "liberalism of fear," to borrow Judith Shklar; a hypervigilance against threats in the form of cruelty, disorder, or intolerance.[4]

The notionally realist elements in the liberal internationalist theory of security respond to the latter sensibility – military superiority, understood as the ability to overmatch all plausible opponents in war, and alliances, which make it possible for the United States to project power into distant regions. US officials, who have been the historical torchbearers of liberal internationalism, believe a position of military dominance buys deterrence on behalf of allies. As the thinking goes, threats to repel aggression around the world will lack credibility (and therefore fail to deter) unless the United States has the capacity to defeat would-be aggressors in worst-case scenario struggles.[5] The forward military positioning necessary to sustain such an overmatch posture is also thought to restrain allies from aggression, forestall nuclear proliferation, and enforce open sea lanes for trade in energy and commodities.[6]

---

[2] On the philosophical principles that bolster liberal internationalism, see especially Jahn, *Liberal Internationalism*; Michael Doyle, "Three Pillars of the Liberal Peace," *American Political Science Review* Vol. 99, no. 3 (2005), pp. 463–66; Michael Doyle, "Kant, Liberal Legacies, and Foreign Affairs," *Philosophy and Public Affairs* Vol. 12, no. 3 (1983), pp. 205–35.

[3] Jahn, *Liberal Internationalism*, p. 172; G. John Ikenberry, "Liberal Internationalism 3.0: America and the Dilemmas of Liberal World Order," *Perspectives on Politics* Vol. 7, no. 1 (2009), p. 72.

[4] Judith Shklar, "The Liberalism of Fear," in *Liberalism and the Moral Life*, edited by Nancy Rosenblum (Cambridge: Harvard University Press, 1989), pp. 21–37. See also Robert Meister, "The Liberalism of Fear and the Counterrevolutionary Project," *Ethics and International Affairs* Vol. 16, no. 2 (2002), pp. 118–23. For the claim that liberalism's fear of fear could lead to security complacency, see Michael Williams, "Securitization and the Liberalism of Fear," *Security Dialogue* Vol. 42, no. 4–5 (2011), pp. 453–63.

[5] Van Jackson, "American Military Superiority and the Pacific Primacy Myth," *Survival* Vol. 60, no. 2 (2018), pp. 107–32.

[6] Mira Rapp-Hooper, *Shields of the Republic: The Triumph and Peril of America's Alliances* (Cambridge, MA: Harvard University Press, 2020); Terence Roehrig, *Japan, South Korea, and the United States Nuclear Umbrella: Deterrence after the Cold War* (New York: Columbia University Press, 2017); Peter Dombrowski, *The End of Grand Strategy: U.S. Maritime Operations in the Twenty-First Century* (Ithaca, NY: Cornell University Press, 2018).

This commitment to unrivaled military power, while central today, only arose with the onset of the Cold War.[7] Earlier versions of American liberal internationalism, in the Wilsonian and inter-war periods, did not conceptualize military might as being so vital to American security,[8] even though military conquest has featured in American statecraft from its earliest days.[9]

The more "liberal" wagers of liberal internationalism include multilateral intergovernmentalism and economic interdependence through capital markets, each of which are thought to reinforce the other. In the classic Washington formulation that G. John Ikenberry popularized, international institutions are important not simply because they coordinate peaceable relations and serve as instruments of global governance, but because the United States uses them as mechanisms of "strategic restraint."[10] If, in theory, the world's greatest power allows itself to be checked by the rules of international institutions of which it is part, then it lends credibility and legitimacy to those institutions, thereby instantiating a stable hegemonic order.[11] But there is also a supplemental view that multilateral institutions promote democracy – both in the sense of socializing members to become democratic and in the sense that they coordinate cooperative activities that literally promote democracy (like election monitoring and development assistance).[12] Less abstractly too, multilateral institutions directly function as protectors of the stock and flow of global capital from national level politics. The "ordoliberals," neoliberal thinkers concerned with building a financial architecture that made the world safe for capital, were advocates for and engineers of

---

[7] Stephen Wertheim, *Tomorrow, The World: The Birth of U.S. Global Supremacy* (Cambridge: Harvard University Press, 2020).

[8] Ikenberry, "Liberal Internationalism 3.0."

[9] William Appleman Williams, *The Contours of American History* (New York: Verso, 2011); Daniel Immerwahr, *How to Hide an Empire: A History of the Greater United States* (New York: Picador, 2020).

[10] G. John Ikenberry, *After Victory: Institutions, Strategic Restraint, and the Rebuilding of Order after Major Wars* (Princeton: Princeton University Press, 2001); G. John Ikenberry, *Liberal Leviathan: The Origins, Crisis, and Transformation of the American World Order* (Princeton: Princeton University Press, 2011).

[11] This is not the only way hegemonic orders can be produced or sustained. See G. John Ikenberry and Daniel Nexon, "Hegemony Studies 3.0: The Dynamics of Hegemonic Orders," *Security Studies* Vol. 28, no. 3 (2019), pp. 395–421.

[12] Robert Keohane, Stephen Macedo, and Andrew Moravcsik, "Democracy-Enhancing Multilateralism," *International Organization* Vol. 63, no. 1 (2009), pp. 1–31; Tony Smith, *Why Wilson Matters: The Origin of American Liberal Internationalism and Its Crisis Today* (Princeton: Princeton University Press, 2017), pp. 95–129.

the World Bank, International Monetary Fund (IMF), and World Trade Organization (WTO) for precisely this reason.[13]

The other wager of liberal internationalism, economic interdependence through capital markets, is not just a means of statecraft but also a primary end. A liberal foreign policy seeking an "open world" cannot but have among its aims the freedom to transact and move capital around. Woodrow Wilson sought a League of Nations partly because he was spooked by the takeover of communism in Russia, which threatened the regime of global capital. Even in mainstream histories of liberal internationalism, "a world safe for democracy" was always a world safe for the fusion "democratic capitalism."[14] And yet, liberal internationalism's advocates also see economic interdependence as a way to produce a "capitalist peace." Economic interdependence causes stability, in this view, through multiple mechanisms, the foremost being a "shadow of the future." High levels of trade and economic integration through shared supply chains and transnational production networks are supposed to foster expectations of future cooperation and increase the costs of war so as to be unthinkable.[15]

American exceptionalism, meanwhile, refers to a preternatural self-regard. An admixture of narcissism and global obligation makes the United States uniquely responsible for the world, which is why it must bear the burden of military superiority, alliances, multilateral institutions, and economic interdependence. Sometimes rephrased as "leadership," exceptionalism means that "American nationalism is ... transmuted from being parochially self-interested into being universal in its concerns."[16] For liberal internationalists, the goals of a more open and peaceable world "can be accomplished only through Washington's leadership, failing which crisis upon crisis is sure to occur."[17]

---

[13] For the argument that international financial institutions exist to ensure freedom for capital, see Quinn Slobodian, *The Globalists: The End of Empire and the Birth of Neoliberalism* (Cambridge: Harvard University Press, 2018).

[14] Cyrus Veeser, *A World Safe for Capitalism: Dollar Diplomacy and America's Rise to Global Power* (New York: Columbia University Press, 2002); Melvyn Leffler, *Safeguarding Democratic Capitalism: U.S. Foreign Policy and National Security, 1920–2015* (Princeton: Princeton University Press, 2017).

[15] The logic of the capitalist peace (which may or may not be real) has multiple mechanisms, of which the "shadow of the future" is one. Dale Copeland, "Economic Interdependence and War: A Theory of Trade Expectations," *International Security* Vol. 20, no. 4 (1996), pp. 5–41; Erik Gartzke, "The Capitalist Peace," *American Journal of Political Science* Vol. 51, no. 1 (2007), pp. 166–91.

[16] Tony Smith, *Why Wilson Matters: The Origin of American Liberal Internationalism and Its Crisis Today* (Princeton: Princeton University Press, 2017), p. 15.

[17] Smith, *Why Wilson Matters*, p. 16.

Because a liberal internationalist foreign policy is so broadly drawn, there is a lot of room for variation within the elements described above. And indeed, US foreign policy since Wilson has changed dramatically from presidency to presidency. Nobody can doubt that President Obama's foreign policy was different from that of President George W. Bush, just as Trump's was of a vastly different color than Obama's. But such differences occurred within a bipartisan consensus or settled "national security narrative" about America's role in the world that made the thrust of liberal internationalism overwhelmingly stable and little contested by policy elites.[18]

## BLIND SPOTS AND BAD WAGERS: CRITIQUES FROM THE LEFT

If you judge the wagers of liberal internationalism narrowly and on their own terms – without observing their full historical context, opportunity costs, or unintended effects – you might think them not half bad. Although the post–Cold War unipolar world gradually evaporated as the twenty-first century marched forward, it has been one without great-power wars or arms races, and with scant nuclear proliferation – all outcomes that liberal internationalists attribute to the order that springs from their foreign policy designs.[19]

Yet, even liberal internationalism's most stalwart proponents believe that much of US foreign policy taken in its name – especially since the 1990s – has failed to live up to its promise.[20] In fact, Ikenberry, the international-relations scholar who has probably done more to conceptualize and justify this tradition than any other, has, since the end of the Trump era, tried to de-center Wilson's legacy in liberal internationalism in favor of Franklin Delano Roosevelt – a decidedly more progressive anchor than Wilson and one with less of a checkered history on racism and authoritarianism at home.[21] Once Wilson entered World War I in

---

[18] Patrick Porter, "Why America's Grand Strategy Has Not Changed: Power, Habit, and the U.S. Foreign Policy Establishment," *International Security* Vol. 42, no. 4 (2018), pp. 9–46; Ronald Krebs, *Narrative and the Making of U.S. National Security* (New York: Cambridge University Press, 2015).

[19] G. John Ikenberry, "The Future of the Liberal World Order: Internationalism after America," *Foreign Affairs* (May/June 2011), www.foreignaffairs.com/articles/2011-05-01/future-liberal-world-order.

[20] Smith, *Why Wilson Matters*, p. 28.

[21] Ikenberry, *A World Safe for Democracy*, pp. xiv, 141–76. It bears acknowledging that Roosevelt is not free from charges of racism or authoritarianism, only less so than Wilson.

1917, he became an enemy to many on the left and broke liberal solidarity with socialists and progressive liberals, not entirely because of the war so much as his brutal suppression of dissent and civil liberties – targeting socialists in particular – in the United States as part of the war.[22] Roosevelt, by contrast – and despite his New Deal reforms being racially compromised and failing to go as far toward equality as leftists hoped – was the most progressive president of the twentieth century.[23]

Advocates like Ikenberry see liberal internationalism's historical association with racism, militarism, and imperialism as unfortunate misappropriations.[24] Critics like Jeanne Morefield see those convergences as a feature rather than a bug of liberal foreign policy.[25] At issue is whether liberal internationalism should be understood as a high-minded justification for manifestly illiberal conduct, or whether the illiberal (and outright imperial) aspects of US foreign policy are negative externalities that owe not to liberalism per se but rather its intersections with other factors. Regardless who is more correct about the nature of liberal internationalism, many of the specific charges against it are based on lived experience – that is, how critics see liberal internationalist foreign policy as having functioned in the real world. These grievances are eclectic, but can be organized into roughly three types – inequality, militarism, and un-democracy or elite unaccountability.

### Globalized Inequality and Its Consequences

The expanding global reach of trade and finance since the 1970s has dramatically increased global growth. World economic productivity has never been higher. There have never been so many millionaires and billionaires in the world. Globalization is the word we give to the process of capital efficiently crossing borders to produce this bounty, and liberal internationalism has sought to nurture it.

---

[22] On Wilson's authoritarianism at home, see Michael Kazin, *War against War: The American Fight for Peace, 1914–1918* (New York: Simon & Schuster, 2017), pp. 204–12, 231–4. On how Wilson broke left-liberal solidarity, see Doug Rossinow, *Visions of Progress: The Left-Liberal Tradition in America* (Philadelphia: University of Pennsylvania Press, 2008), pp. 63–81.

[23] For a favorable portrayal of FDR's progressivism given the constraints of the historical moment, see Ira Katznelson, *Fear Itself: The New Deal and the Origins of Our Time* (New York: Liveright, 2014).

[24] Ikenberry, *A World Safe for Democracy*, pp. 212–54.

[25] Jeanne Morefield, *Empires without Imperialism: Anglo-American Decline and the Politics of Deflection* (Cambridge: Oxford University Press, 2014).

Yet, the bounty is hoarded, not shared. Globalization has wrought world-historic levels of inequality and fiscal volatility. As I discuss in Chapter 4, progressives see this as allowing transnational corruption to thrive, fueling right-wing extremism, committing structural violence against workers the world over, and abetting dictators with market-friendly economies. Contrary to once-commonplace representations of globalization as some inexorable and agent-less force that the US economy must adapt to,[26] it has been an output of US policy design. For all practical purposes, economic interdependence – a key wager of liberal internationalism – *is* globalization.[27]

Notwithstanding the productivity growth that globalization has unlocked, progressive critics cast doubt on whether the game has been worth the candle. Globalization, they charge, has become less efficient and more exploitative over time, and has not actually alleviated global poverty, which is globalization's most cherished talking point.[28] In places like India, absolute poverty actually *increased* in tandem with growing inequality, rendering the proposition of globalization as a rising tide that lifts all boats questionable at best.[29] Globalization has also begun shifting around distributions of highly concentrated wealth without diluting it or creating new wealth. Payoffs from rents and speculation have become more valuable and less individually risky than payoffs from the production of goods and services. The globalized economy incentivizes monopoly strategies as the preferred path to firm-level growth, which stunts competition and corrupts democracy.[30] Over time, these conditions are bringing "not only slower growth and lower GDP but even

---

[26] Paul Musgrave, "The Beautiful, Dumb Dream of McDonald's Peace Theory," *Foreign Policy* (November 26, 2020), https://foreignpolicy.com/2020/11/26/mcdonalds-peace-nagornokarabakh-friedman/.

[27] By the late 1990s, "globalization" had become a common substitute for "economic interdependence," even in academic research. See Katherine Barbieri and Gerald Schneider, "Globalization and Peace: Assessing New Directions in the Study of Trade and Conflict," *Journal of Peace Research* Vol. 36, no. 4 (1999), p. 387.

[28] On the failure of globalization to reduce poverty as claimed, see Jason Hickel, *The Divide: Global Inequality from Conquest to Free Markets* (New York: W.W. Norton & Co., 2018), pp. 47–53.

[29] Prabhat Patnaik, "Why Neoliberalism Needs Neofascists," *Boston Review* (July 19, 2021), https://bostonreview.net/class-inequality-politics/prabhat-patnaik-why-neoliberalism-needs-neofascists.

[30] Leftists disagree about whether within-sector competition is actually desirable or a trap. See, for example, Doug Henwood, "Why Socialists Should Distrust Antitrust," *Jacobin Magazine* (July 17, 2021), https://jacobinmag.com/2021/07/antitrust-law-monopolies-small-business-competition-large-corporations-bigness; Matt Bruenig, "No, Small

more instability … a weakened democracy, a diminished sense of fairness and justice …" all of which unleashes graver and more immediate threats to both democracy and human life.[31]

Worse, these trends have obliterated the power of organized labor around the world and forced workers into a *Hunger Games*-like race to the bottom in terms of wage competition while governments engage in large-scale labor repression.[32] This has negatively affected the Global North and South but in different ways – it has taken jobs away from the Global North (especially in manufacturing) and relocated them to the Global South, where they exist as lower paying, more environmentally damaging, and tax avoiding gigs that rely on repressive working conditions. It has also given rise to a global "precariat" – billions of workers who are not only underemployed but whose jobs are chronically casual and insecure (think homeless Uber and Lyft drivers in the North, seasonal migrant workers in the South).[33]

The Marxist critique of liberal internationalism also stresses these concerns with inequality and poverty creation, but even more stridently. In so many words, "liberal ideals – popular sovereignty, individual rights – are what enable the capitalist state to act in the interests of the dominant classes."[34] Since liberalism is the ideology that defends capitalism, liberal internationalism is the foreign policy that works for the same and must therefore be opposed.[35] This is a complete rejection of liberal internationalism,

---

Isn't Beautiful," *Jacobin Magazine* (June 5, 2021), https://jacobinmag.com/2021/06/small-business-monopoly-socialism-collective-ownership.

[31] Joseph Stiglitz, *The Price of Inequality: How Today's Divided Society Endangers Our Future* (New York: W.W. Norton & Co., 2013), p. liii.

[32] Adam Dean, *Opening Up by Cracking Down: Labor Repression and Trade Liberalization in Democratic Developing Countries* (New York: Cambridge University Press, 2022); Paul Adler, *No Globalization without Representation: U.S. Activists and World Inequality* (Philadelphia, PA: University of Pennsylvania Press, 2021).

[33] As one survey of the global economy noted, "If you live in an expensive metropolitan area, it's likely you have received an Uber ride, package delivery, or takeout order from someone who spent the previous night in a shelter, car, or tent." Ned Resnikoff, "From the Labor Question to the Housing Question," *The Nation* (March 28, 2022), www.thenation.com/article/economy/housing-class-homelessness/. On the distinct color of precarity in the North, see Barbara Ehrenreich, *Nickel and Dimed: On (Not) Getting By in America* (New York: Picador, 2001). On precarity as a new post-neoliberal capitalism, see Albena Azmanova, *Capitalism on Edge: How Fighting Precarity Can Achieve Radical Change without Crisis* (New York: Columbia University Press, 2019).

[34] David Sessions, "Nicos Poulantzas: Philosopher of Democratic Socialism," *Dissent* (2019), p. 85.

[35] Leo Panitch and Sam Gindin, *The Making of Global Capitalism: The Political Economy of American Empire* (New York: Verso, 2011). For a Marxian critique that the classist

a view that is not universally shared within the progressive movement but that nevertheless appears in the form of calls for a post-capitalist economic order, or in an unyielding incredulity when a liberal internationalist foreign policy burnishes its most positive claims about defending human rights, political sovereignty, and the like. If liberal internationalism is simply class politics by other means, the working classes everywhere should understand themselves as the victims of liberal internationalism.

A liberal-internationalist avatar might argue that the inequities of globalization can be corrected within liberal internationalism. That the solution is policies that more equitably redistribute wealth. That there is nothing inherent in liberal internationalism that says worker disempowerment, economic precarity, and the proliferation of oligarchy are essential to liberal foreign policy. Indeed, at least one proudly Clintonite liberal has argued that "plutocracy is not liberalism's fulfillment. It is liberalism's antithesis."[36]

But those are abstract rejoinders to concrete criticisms. If liberal internationalism can "do better" than it has – an assertion that would not refute critics' premises – then when will it? Why has it not historically? And how will it without resorting to more progressive ideas, initiatives to the left of liberal internationalism? Liberal internationalist foreign policy as practiced in the twentieth and early twenty-first centuries has aligned itself with global economic integration via the liberalization and deregulation policies of the neoliberal "Washington Consensus." The creation of extreme inequality was not a goal of these policies, and indeed, the "New Democrats" who championed neoliberal globalization believed it would actually reduce inequality.[37] But that bet has failed, and as evidence of the failure accrued, advocates of neoliberal globalization continued to accept (or overlook) its inequality-widening consequences. Whether liberal internationalism can be saved from itself is beside the point. Maladies need redress. And it is far from obvious that economic interdependence can thrive except by privileging capital over labor, which is what begot extreme concentrations of wealth and precarity in the first place – conditions that liberal internationalism has implicitly defended and promoted.

nature of liberal internationalism makes it an ideology that must be removed root and branch, see Perry Anderson, *American Foreign Policy and Its Thinkers* (New York: Verso, 2015).

[36] Sean Wilentz, "Fighting Words," *Democracy* (Spring 2018), https://democracyjournal.org/magazine/48/fighting-words/.

[37] Lily Geismer, *Left Behind: The Democrats' Failed Attempt to Solve Inequality* (New York: PublicAffairs, 2022).

## Militarism as Foreign Policy

The critique that liberal internationalism has effectively become a military-first foreign policy – and that such militarism is a problem – comes in multiple forms. One is the cost of human lives, whatever the purported benefits. The Brown University Costs of War project calculates 929,000 casualties resulting from US wars in the two decades since September 11, 2001.[38] That figure is hard to stomach under any circumstances, but all the more so considering that a large portion of those deaths owe to the 2003 Iraq invasion – the Vietnam war of the twenty-first century – and considering that the number of Salafi-Jihadist extremists globally increased some 400 percent over that same period, implying America's remedy made the problem much worse.[39]

Another charge against the military superiority on which liberal internationalism depends is the classic argument about guns displacing butter. Military spending comes at the opportunity cost of federal investments in societal welfare. The unbalanced distribution of government spending – defense makes up as much as 55 percent of discretionary funding in the federal budget – is a measure of the problem.[40] So is the absolute cost of defense, which totaled $14 trillion dollars in the two decades since September 11, 2001.[41] Such large sums amount to de facto military Keynesianism, which plays an underappreciated role in producing the regional and global financial crises that have occurred since the Cold War.[42]

And there is a deeper rot that military Keynesianism risks. Martin Luther King, Jr. presented the problem poignantly in his 1967 speech against the Vietnam War: "A nation that continues year after year to invest more money on military defense than on programs of social uplift is approaching spiritual death."[43] King bemoaned the dramatic cuts to

---

[38] Costs of War, Watson Institute for International and Public Affairs, Brown University, https://watson.brown.edu/costsofwar/figures/2021/WarDeathToll.

[39] Seth Jones, Danika Newlee, and Nicholas Harrington, *The Evolution of the Salafi-Jihadist Threat: Current and Future Challenges from the Islamic State, Al-Qaeda, and Other Groups* (Washington, DC: Center for Strategic & International Studies, 2018).

[40] Committee for a Responsible Federal Budget, "Charting a Responsible Path for Discretionary Spending" (February 20, 2019), www.crfb.org/papers/charting-responsible-path-discretionary-spending.

[41] William Hartung, *Profits of War: Corporate Beneficiaries of the Post-9/11 Pentagon Spending Surge* (Washington, DC: Center for International Policy, 2021).

[42] Thomas Oatley, *A Political Economy of American Hegemony: Buildups, Booms, and Busts* (New York: Cambridge University Press, 2015).

[43] Martin Luther King, Jr., as quoted in Liz Theoharis, "MLK Was Right about America's 'Spiritual Death'," *The Nation* (April 5, 2021), www.thenation.com/article/society/mlk-anniversary-america/.

antipoverty programs that Cold War liberals made in order to finance the growing costs of America's military campaign in Vietnam.

And prioritizing Vietnam over poverty alleviation was not an anomaly but rather part of a pattern. The Cold War not only gave the military primacy in American politics, it created a bipartisan coalition that sought to use defense spending as a substitute for programs of domestic improvement after 1964.[44] Put differently, the military superiority of liberal internationalism eventually became a major reason to *not* invest in a "great society," especially once neoliberal orthodoxies around austerity became ascendant in the 1970s. When liberal internationalists today argue that great-power competition with China will be a boon to American domestic recovery,[45] it is the left that points out how America's previous great-power competition (with the Soviets) portends the opposite.[46]

Military superiority's coupling with liberal internationalism also arguably both reflects and abets liberalism's "imperial temptation."[47] From the colonization of the Philippines and Guam in 1898 to the occupation of Iraq in 2003, a desire to defend and spread political liberalism – militantly if necessary – pockmarks the history of American foreign policy.[48] Some imperial relations still linger in US foreign policy.[49] And the Iraq war is particularly difficult to imagine occurring except in the context of neoconservative beliefs that overtook official Washington during the George W. Bush presidency. Neoconservatism – a hawkish variant of liberal internationalism – pairs a belief in military dominance and unilateralism as the ultimate arbiter of world politics with a belief that

---

[44] Michael Brenes, *For Might and Right: Cold War Defense Spending and the Remaking of American Democracy* (Amherst: University of Massachusetts Press, 2020).

[45] Kurt Campbell and Rush Doshi, "The China Challenge Can Help America Avert Decline," *Foreign Affairs* (December 3, 2020), www.foreignaffairs.com/articles/china/2020-12-03/china-challenge-can-help-america-avert-decline.

[46] Michael Brenes and Van Jackson, "Great-Power Competition Is Bad for Democracy," *Foreign Affairs* (July 14, 2022), www.foreignaffairs.com/articles/united-states/2022-07-14/great-power-competition-bad-democracy; Michael Brenes and Daniel Steinmetz-Jenkins, "Legacies of Cold War Liberalism," *Dissent* (Winter 2021), www.dissentmagazine.org/article/legacies-of-cold-war-liberalism.

[47] Daniel Nexon and Paul Musgrave, "American Liberalism and Imperial Temptation," in *Empire and International Order*, edited by Noel Parker (London: Ashgate, 2013), pp. 131–48.

[48] Immerwahr, *How to Hide an Empire*; Christopher McKnight Nichols and David Milne, eds., *Ideology in U.S. Foreign Relations: New Histories* (New York: Columbia University Press, 2022).

[49] Van Jackson, "Trapped by Empire," *Dissent* (February 8, 2023), www.dissentmagazine.org/online_articles/trapped-by-empire.

liberal democracy and individual freedom are values worth defending and spreading. The fusion of an unsurpassed war machinery with the guiding impulse of neo-Wilsonian crusades makes empire-like conquest an interminable risk in liberal internationalism.

An overmilitarized foreign policy also crowds out alternative ways of thinking and biases policy action in favor of the military instrument. As Madeleine Albright famously quipped to Colin Powell, "What's the point of having this superb military that you're always talking about if we can't use it?"[50] Similarly, former CIA Director and Secretary of Defense Leon Panetta justified relying so heavily on drone strikes to prosecute the Global War on Terror with a supply-side explanation – they were "the only game in town."[51]

The underwriting role of military superiority in American liberal internationalism has quite simply distorted US foreign policy in the direction of war. C. Wright Mills groaned of militarism overtaking the policy mind, "The accumulation of military power has become an ascendent end in itself; economic and political maneuvers and hesitations ... are subordinated to and judged in terms of military forces and potentials."[52] Violence becomes more likely simply because the tools of violence occupy such a prominent place in American statecraft. It also leaves little room to address problems for which violence has not even the pretense of solution, such as climate change.

## Washington's Unaccountable Monoculture

Nothing in the content of liberal internationalism says it must be unaccountable, antidemocratic, and elite-centered, but critics believe it has proven to be precisely that since at least the dawn of the Cold War. In contrasting socialist preferences with liberal internationalism, Thomas Meaney wrote,

It is imperative that state power not be delegated to a cloistered elite, whether a Leninist vanguard or, as in the U.S. case, a liberal technocratic elite that has long conflated the interests of the nation with those of global capital. The U.S. foreign

[50] As quoted in Emma Ashford, "Even Colin Powell Ignored the Powell Doctrine. Now, America Is Starting to Listen," *Politico* (October 23, 2021), www.politico.com/news/magazine/2021/10/23/colin-powell-foreign-policy-expansionist-advice-516795.
[51] Noah Schachtman, "CIA Chief: Drones 'Only Game in Town' for Stopping Al Qaeda," *Wired* (May 19, 2009), www.wired.com/2009/05/cia-chief-drones-only-game-in-town-for-stopping-al-qaeda/.
[52] C. Wright Mills, *The Causes of World War Three* (New York: Ballantine Books, 1960), p. 61.

policy elite has barely questioned its commitment to free trade pacts and permanent military missions abroad.[53]

Critics apply the epithet "Blob" to describe an elite policymaking community that they see as trafficking in liberal-internationalist groupthink, and rewarding intellectual conformity.[54] If there were greater accountability and intellectual diversity, there would be fewer cases of egregiously poor and antidemocratic judgment.

While liberal internationalists too understand the Iraq war as regrettably poor judgment and eventually acknowledged that the Global War on Terror had perhaps gone too far,[55] critics on the left see these things as the latest in a longer history of unapologetic, antidemocratic, elite bloodletting in the name of questionable goals. In 1965–1966, the Johnson administration facilitated mass killings in Indonesia in the name of anticommunism – the "Jakarta method" – that it then applied throughout Latin America.[56] The Vietnam War, on the thinnest of analytical rationalizations,[57] saw not just aerial bombing campaigns against North Vietnam that included the use of napalm and Agent Orange (a poisonous chemical defoliant), large-scale bombings were secretly expanded to include neighboring Laos and Cambodia – countries with which the United States was not at war.[58] Throughout the Cold War, the United States supported overthrows of foreign governments more than 60 times, 44 of which involved taking the side of autocracy.[59] While the United States had allied itself with right-wing dictators from the start of the Cold War, in the 1980s, the "Reagan Doctrine" elevated arm-the-autocrats to a guiding principle of statecraft.[60] After the Cold War, the Global

---

[53] Thomas Meaney, "What U.S. Foreign Policy Will Look Like under Socialism," *Foreign Policy* (January 17, 2020), https://foreignpolicy.com/2020/01/17/socialist-us-foreign-policy-democratic-socialism/.

[54] Peter Henne, "Deconstructing the Blob," *Duck of Minerva* (March 16, 2020), www.duckofminerva.com/2020/03/deconstructing-teh-blob.html.

[55] Maria Ryan, "Bush's 'Useful Idiots': 9/11, the Liberal Hawks, and the Cooption of the 'War on Terror'," *Journal of American Studies* Vol. 45, no. 4 (2011), pp. 667–93.

[56] Vincent Bevins, *The Jakarta Method: Washington's Anticommunist Crusade and the Mass Murder Program That Shaped Our World* (New York: PublicAffairs, 2020).

[57] Yuen Foong Khong, *Analogies at War: Korea, Munich, Dien Bien Phu, and the Vietnam Decisions of 1965* (Princeton: Princeton University Press, 1992).

[58] Jennifer Milliken and David Sylvan, "Soft Bodies, Hard Targets, and Chic Theories: US Bombing Policy in Indochina," *Millennium* Vol. 25, no. 2 (1996), pp. 321–59.

[59] Lindsey O'Rourke, *Covert Regime Change: America's Secret Cold War* (Ithaca, NY: Cornell University Press, 2018).

[60] Richard Johnson, "Misguided Morality: Ethics and the Reagan Doctrine," *Political Science Quarterly* Vol. 103, no. 3 (1988), pp. 509–29.

War on Terror followed in this tradition, swapping out the threat of communism with the threat of terrorism but applying the same prescription – arming and allying with dictators around the world. In the name of counter-terrorism, America was even complicit in China's persecution of Muslim Uighurs in Xinjiang, despite making so much noise about Uighur genocide since the Trump years.[61]

Should these damning appraisals of US foreign policy be attributed to liberal internationalism per se? Defenders of the ideology might point out that elite unaccountability should not be conflated with poor judgment. They might highlight the fact that the "Blob" epithet overstates how monolithic Washington elite culture is, that claims of elite failure do not even attempt counterfactual reasoning, and that obsessing on US domestic determinants of foreign policy overlooks logical comparisons with national security elites in other states.[62] They might also note that what looks like unaccountability among foreign policy elites follows from a Walter Lippman-esque turn in liberal democracy generally, toward elite stewardship and governance by technocracy.

In this view, liberal foreign policy, like liberalism itself, could in principle accommodate a more Deweyan conception of democratically accountable foreign policy.[63] More decisions could be put to the public. Bad judgment could come with a professional price. The stock of policy practitioners could be more representative of and directly connected to society itself.

But "A system that does not punish poor foreign-policymaking is a system doomed to repeat its mistakes."[64] The elitist and secretive nature of national security is thus bound up with it being a force *against* democracy at home and abroad – unaccountability makes it possible to run a foreign policy disconnected from the judgments and preferences of the public, the substance of which frequently supports authoritarianism

---

[61] Richard Bernstein, "When China Convinced the U.S. That Uighurs Were Waging Jihad," *The Atlantic* (March 19, 2019), www.theatlantic.com/international/archive/2019/03/us-uighurs-guantanamo-china-terror/584107/.

[62] Robert Jervis, "Liberalism, The Blob, and American Foreign Policy: Evidence and Methodology," *Security Studies* Vol. 29, no. 3 (2020), pp. 434–56.

[63] Some left-aligned critics of liberal internationalism have also acknowledged this point. See Daniel Bessner and Stephen Wertheim, "Democratizing U.S. Foreign Policy," *Foreign Affairs* (April 5, 2017), www.foreignaffairs.com/articles/united-states/2017-04-05/democratizing-us-foreign-policy.

[64] Daniel Bessner, "What Does Alexandria Ocasio-Cortez Think about the South China Sea?" *New York Times* (September 17, 2018), www.nytimes.com/2018/09/17/opinion/democratic-party-cortez-foreign-policy.html.

abroad. As long as Washington's monoculture exists – which, again, is not necessarily a product of liberal internationalism though liberal internationalism is clearly its object of consensus – there is a promise of still more Vietnams and Iraqs and Jakarta Methods in the future. Or worse.

These various charges against liberal internationalism – that it fuels inequality and precaritizes workers, that it is overmilitarized, and that it is in many ways functionally undemocratic and prone to bad judgment – are not unique to the left. Libertarians, conservatives, and a disenfranchised working class have also railed against neoliberal globalization and the military excesses of US foreign policy.[65] And various "post-liberal" thinkers in particular – which range from economic nationalists to paleoconservatives to MAGA-aligned right wing groups – harbor tremendous distrust of technocratic expertise.[66] The complaints are cross-class and cross-partisan in nature, which somewhat insulates them from counter-criticism; at a minimum it suggests these charges ought not be dismissed as merely pathologies of the left.

Because they highlight deficiencies in the way things are and have been historically, these critiques are also a useful entry point for exploring the progressive worldview. Going back to World War I, American progressives have often sought and built transpartisan coalitions to challenge some US foreign policy decision or another. Where they differ from other political and ideological opponents of liberal internationalism is not only in their epistemology of world politics, but what to do about international security as a consequence.

---

[65] See, for example, Christopher Preble, "The Right Way to Cut Wasteful Defense Spending," *Politico Magazine* (January 18, 2017), www.politico.com/agenda/story/2017/01/the-right-way-to-cut-wasteful-defense-spending-000282/; David Hendrickson, *Republic in Peril: American Empire and the Liberal Tradition* (New York: Oxford University Press, 2017); Stephen Walt, *The Hell of Good Intentions*; Sustainable Defense Task Force, *Sustainable Defense: More Security Less Spending* (Washington, DC: Center for International Policy, 2019), https://static.wixstatic.com/ugd/fb6c59_59a295c780634ce88d077c391066db9a.pdf.

[66] Michael Lind, *The New Class War: Saving Democracy from the Managerial Elite* (New York: Penguin Random House, 2020); Michael Mazarr, "Abstract Systems, Social Trust, and Institutional Legitimacy," *American Affairs* Vol. 6, no. 1 (2022), https://americanaffairsjournal.org/2022/02/abstract-systems-social-trust-and-institutional-legitimacy/. Sohrab Ahmari, "The Political Economy of Dystopia," *The American Conservative* (October 5, 2021), www.theamericanconservative.com/articles/the-political-economy-of-dystopia/; James Pogue, "Inside the New Right, Where Peter Thiel Is Placing His Biggest Bets," *Vanity Fair* (May 2022), www.vanityfair.com/news/2022/04/inside-the-new-right-where-peter-thiel-is-placing-his-biggest-bets.

# 3

# The Politics of Progressivism

Even though this book focuses on progressive foreign policy rather than progressive politics, the former comes from the latter. It derives meaning from the latter. So to ultimately understand where progressive world-making principles come from, we must situate ourselves in an understanding of American leftism generally.

The politics of the left is an Enlightenment-rooted politics of emancipation, of human liberation.[1] Peace, equality, and democracy are the ultimate ends of progressive worldmaking because they represent fulfillment of that promise.[2] What form this content should take – constitutional republicanism, a cooperative commonwealth, a society with class harmony, a truly classless society, or a working class-led society – depends on one's standpoint, and for philosophical pragmatists, need not be determined with any granularity in advance.

And for all its eclecticism, there are thematic consistencies in what it means to be of or on "the left." As practiced in the United States, it is ideologically pluralist, including among its non-revolutionary ranks "socialists, democratic socialists, and left-liberals."[3] It stands with oppressed

---

[1] Mills, "Letter to the New Left," p. 21; Philip Abbott, "The Enlightenment Legacy of the New Left," *Polity* Vol. 15, no. 4 (1983), pp. 630–41. On the left's commitment to not just realizing the Enlightenment but pushing liberals to live up to their own ideals, see Immanuel Wallerstein, *The Global Left: Yesterday, Today, Tomorrow* (Abingdon: Routledge, 2022), pp. 1–8, 35–39.

[2] Brick and Phelps, *Radicals in America*, pp. 5–11; Dorrien, *American Democratic Socialism*, pp. 1–2, 9; Kazin, *American Dreamers*, pp. xiii–xiv.

[3] Michael Walzer, *A Foreign Policy for the Left* (New Haven, CT: Yale University Press, 2018), p. 9; Brian Mueller, *Democracy's Think Tank: The Institute for Policy Studies and Progressive Foreign Policy* (Philadelphia: University of Pennsylvania Press, 2020).

populations and against entrenched privilege and unfair distributions of power. Leftist politics are "built on claims to equal representation in political life, and have always claimed to speak for disempowered and nonprivileged groups."[4] Its politics are supposed to be worker-centered. In the United States, leftism came into existence with "the mass party, grounded in socialism and linked with organized labor,"[5] but it did not have an institutionalized home in the Democratic Party until the New Deal reforms of the 1930s.

There is also a sometimes-healthy tension within the left, between its commitment to critiquing power and its view that only the government is in a position to deal with capitalism, whether to tame it or defeat it. On the leftism of critique, C. Wright Mills's guidance to the then-nascent "New Left" generation of the 1960s is instructive. He noted that whereas being on the political right means "celebrating society as it is, a going concern," to be on the left ought to mean "structural criticism and reportage and theories of society … focused politically as demands and programmes."[6] Mills's analysis had a Marxian flair, but he presented it as explicitly anti-Stalinist *and* anti–Cold War liberal.

But leftist politics also presumes that government has primary responsibility for the economy. Soon after labor aligned with the Democratic Party, the meaning of leftism as a policy agenda shifted from centering labor to centering Keynesian economics – an evolution that stayed faithful to the notion that government ought to steward the economy, but on a different theory for how it would do so, prioritizing development and employment over redistribution and wages.[7] By the 1970s, Democrats had mostly abandoned Keynesianism in favor of neoliberalism – a view of the economy that subordinated public policy to the interests of capital – leaving leftists and the Democratic Party alien to one another on economic concerns. Subsequently, not all Democrats have belonged to the left, and not all leftists have belonged in the Democratic Party.

## WHAT IS A PROGRESSIVE?

Progressivism embodies the qualities found in descriptions of leftist politics above – reformist, critical of capital and power, and aligned with

---

[4] Mudge, *Leftism Reinvented*, p. 4.
[5] Stephanie Mudge, *Leftism Reinvented: Western Parties from Socialism to Neoliberalism* (Cambridge, MA: Harvard University Press 2018), p. 2.
[6] C. Wright Mills, "Letter to the New Left," *New Left Review* (July 4, 1960), p. 20.
[7] Mudge, *Leftism Reinvented*, pp. 1–2.

the interests of what Henry Wallace dubbed "the common man." But *progressive* is best understood as a nonrevolutionary subset of *left*. *Progressive* has proven useful (including here) for obscuring ideological differences in the name of unity-building.[8] And yet the label "progressive" must also be understood as a floating signifier, which it has been since the dawning of the Progressive Era in the 1890s. In the extreme, "Clintonite centrists, anti-imperialist peace agitators, and labor-union activists alike call themselves progressives, and no one can say definitely that any of them is wrong."[9]

Describing progressivism, *New Republic* editor Edmund Wilson once wrote that it is "the gradual and natural approximation to socialism."[10] Yet any number of progressives see themselves as having "a perspective that agrees with many liberal precepts but takes their critique of conservatives further and adds important considerations to the solutions liberals propose."[11] Others claim that if history matters at all, progressives are "emphatically anti-liberal."[12] But some emphatically disagree, claiming instead that "*progressive* and *liberal* are precisely synonyms in American life," and that *civic republicanism* is what progressives are really all about.[13] Still others identify as progressive while practicing outright democratic socialist or social-democratic politics.[14] And one of the most prominent writers offering progressive critiques of capitalism in the Progressive Era, Richard Ely, sought a "golden mean" between plutocrats and socialists, private and public property, and individuals and the state.[15]

---

[8] Although out of fashion now, for a time some on the left saw the important distinction as not being between socialist/progressive/liberal but rather between radical and not radical. See especially Christopher Lasch, *The New Radicalism in America, 1889–1963: The Intellectual as a Social Type* (New York: Norton, 1965).

[9] Doug Rossinow, *Visions of Progress: The Left-Liberal Tradition in America* (Philadelphia, PA: University of Pennsylvania Press, 2008), p. 1.

[10] Edmund Wilson, "An Appeal to Progressives," *The New Republic* (January 14, 1931), https://newrepublic.com/article/104618/appeal-progressives.

[11] Steven Klees, *The Conscience of a Progressive* (Winchester: Zero Books, 2019), p. 7.

[12] Sean Wilentz, "Fighting Words," *Democracy* (Spring 2018, no. 48), https://democracyjournal.org/magazine/48/fighting-words/.

[13] Win McCormack, "Are You Progressive?" *New Republic* (April 20, 2018), https://newrepublic.com/article/147825/progressive-vital-term-us-political-life-lost-significance.

[14] Sheri Berman, "Unheralded Battle: Capitalism, the Left, Social Democracy, and Democratic Socialism," *Dissent* (2009), www.dissentmagazine.org/article/unheralded-battle-capitalism-the-left-social-democracy-and-democratic-socialism.

[15] Richard Ely, *Studies in the Evolution of Industrial Society* (New York: MacMillan, 1913); Benjamin Rader, *The Academic Mind and Reform: The Influence of Richard T. Ely in American Life* (Louisville: University Press of Kentucky, 1966), pp. 82–89.

These varied assertions are evidence of *progressive* as a floating signifier. Nevertheless, the term, like ideas generally, does not float freely.[16] And its capaciousness reflects the varied reasons for its use.

When Henry Wallace, a progressive if ever there was one (having run for president as the nominee of the Progressive Party), gave a speech in 1943 describing a progressive politics, he called it "new liberalism," not progressivism. The historical timing of his speech was such that *progressive* had a connotation of Popular-Front politics aligning liberals with socialists and communists against fascism, though many progressives of the time *were* liberal. But the Popular Front, as I explain below, had become polarizing by 1943 because of deliberate campaigns by red-baiting conservatives and anti-communist liberals to stigmatize it.

Wallace's moment was thus one in which progressive policies were far more attractive than the label itself. Speaking to that moment, Wallace positioned a liberal as "a person who in all his actions is continually asking 'What is best for all the people – not merely what is best for me personally?'"[17] His speech then went on to promote a thoroughly progressive agenda as part of continuing New Deal reforms – the New Deal itself commonly described interchangeably as liberal or progressive in character.[18] The following year, at the Democratic national convention, Wallace defined liberalism again, this time pointedly as "both political democracy and economic democracy regardless of race, color or religion."[19] By force of rhetorical will, Wallace rendered what some considered an individualist ethos into a communitarian one. Neither was he the first to do so. In the earlier Progressive Era, it was entirely normal for liberals to charge with bayonets at the ills of capitalism, seeking progressive, egalitarian (albeit white) change in society and government while holding to a liberal creed.

And whereas Wallace found it politically convenient to refer to progressive reforms as liberal ones, the opposite was equally true in different eras. When *liberal* takes on a toxic meaning, as Reagan tried to cast it in the 1980s, *progressive* becomes a synonym for *liberal* with less political

---

[16] Thomas Risse-Kappen, "Ideas Do Not Float Freely: Transnational Coalitions, Domestic Structures, and the End of the Cold War," *International Organization* Vol. 48, no. 2 (1994), pp. 185–214.

[17] Henry Wallace as quoted in John Nichols, *The Fight for the Soul of the Democratic Party* (New York: Verso, 2020), p. 4.

[18] Whether the New Deal was labeled liberal or progressive did not change its substance, but denoted something different in each case.

[19] Henry Wallace as quoted in Rossinow, *Visions of Progress*, p. 188.

baggage.[20] In the 1990s, Clinton-era Democrats practiced a centrist neo-liberal politics but sometimes found the "progressive" label useful for its imprecision; they meant little by it intellectually but it evoked a sentimental working-man continuity in Democratic Party politics.[21]

During the Trump presidency and since, progressives have typically been those who identify with the Bernie Sanders and Elizabeth Warren wings of the Democratic Party in contrast with the party's centrist-liberal wing. For the former, the progressive signifier gestures toward the muck-raking, trust-busting, and anti-fascist left-progressive politics of the early twentieth century. Not the progressives who backed military "prepared-ness" and rationalized Woodrow Wilson's entry into World War I, but the ones who opposed it, and who opposed America's colonization of the Philippines, Guam, and Puerto Rico too.[22] In this contemporary usage, *progressive* connotes assiduous opposition to neoliberalism, and in foreign policy to aspects of liberal internationalism or liberal primacy. *Progressive* as used today tends to be a sliding scale between democratic socialism and radical (non-neoliberal) liberalism.

But it is worth parsing the terms adjacent to and overlapping with *progressive* too – democratic socialist, social democrat, and left-liberal. Sheri Berman pithily explains that socialists became social democrats "When they accepted the possibility of a peaceful parliamentary road to socialism" rather than revolution – a difference of means rather than ends.[23] Social democrats broadly work within capitalism and are primarily concerned with the unfair distribution of economic gains (rather than class distinctions per se),[24] and implicitly subscribe to a Polanyian view that market forces must be embedded within or subordinated to society for democracy to

---

[20] McCormack, "Are You Progressive?"

[21] Geismer, *Left Behind*, pp. 112–13.

[22] Theodore Roosevelt was a progressive in his time, but also a racist, militarist, and imperialist. Although that strain of progressivism is not the genealogy that today's progressives identify with, any liberal progressivism that does not guard against militarism may succumb to what Nexon and Musgrave describe as the "imperial tempt-ation." See Van Jackson, "Why the Elizabeth Warren Pipeline Goes Left and Far Right," *Un-Diplomatic Newsletter* (October 19, 2022), www.un-diplomatic.com/why-the-elizabeth-warren-pipeline-goes-left-and-far-right/.

[23] Berman, *The Social Democratic Moment*, p. 4.

[24] Adam Przeworski, "Social Democracy as a Historical Phenomenon," *New Left Review* no. 122 (1980), pp. 27–58. Labor progressive Henry George also argued that labor and capital were properly viewed as being in a fight with land owners who extracted rents without work. See Edward T. O'Donnell, *Henry George and the Crisis of Inequality: Progress and Poverty in the Gilded Age* (New York: Columbia University Press, 2015), pp. 33–68.

function.[25] Contra socialism, social democracy does not make the worker the only agent of political change and instead tries to "rely on multi- and even supra-class support."[26] Thomas Meaney has said of the distinction between social democracy and democratic socialism: "The first ... aims to blunt the harder edges of capitalism and make it sustainable. The second ... aims to replace the capitalist system with a socialist order."[27] Democratic socialists have a socialist/anti-capitalist agenda, but pursue it via what Erik Olin-Wright called a "symbiotic strategy," of working with and through state power.[28] There is significant slippage across these terms, however, as evidenced by Senator Bernie Sanders, who identifies as a democratic socialist yet defines democratic socialism as "completing the vision that Franklin Delano Roosevelt started some 85 years ago."[29]

The notion of "left-liberal," meanwhile, is even more permeable because of different interpretations of what economic liberalism should mean. Left-liberals embrace social programs and the forms of noneconomic equality that make up cultural or identity politics. But to the extent that left-liberals adhere to some version of the "third way" liberalism that dominated the Democratic Party from the Clinton presidency onwards, they have made their peace with economic neoliberalism – a pro-globalization, pro-corporate, anti-regulatory view of the economy that gradually crept into the Democratic Party starting in the 1960s.[30]

Thus, neoliberalism complicates how we understand the left-liberals today. Neoliberalism is precisely the ideology of the primacy of capitalism in all its excesses.[31] The "left-liberal tradition" in America, by

---

[25] Karl Polanyi, *The Great Transformation: The Political and Economic Origins of Our Time* (Boston: Beacon Press, 1944), pp. 57, 61.

[26] Przeworski, "Social Democracy as a Historical Phenomenon," p. 27.

[27] Thomas Meaney, "What US Foreign Policy Will Look Like under Socialism," *Foreign Policy* (January 17, 2020), https://foreignpolicy.com/2020/01/17/socialist-us-foreign-policy-democratic-socialism/.

[28] Erik Olin-Wright, *Envisioning Real Utopias* (New York: Verso, 2010), pp. 336–65. Olin-Wright posited alternatives to symbiotic strategies of political change as interstitial (progressivism in spaces outside the reach of the state) and ruptural (violent revolution).

[29] As quoted in Maggie Astor, "What Is Democratic Socialism? Whose Version Are We Talking About?" *New York Times* (June 12, 2019), www.nytimes.com/2019/06/12/us/politics/democratic-socialism-facts-history.html. See also Bernie Sanders, "My Vision for Democratic Socialism in America," *In These Times* (November 19, 2015), https://inthesetimes.com/article/bernie-sanders-democratic-socialism-georgetown-speech.

[30] Geismer, *Left Behind*; Alexander Zevin, *Liberalism at Large: The World According to the Economist* (London: Verso, 2019), pp. 277–374.

[31] Gary Gerstle defines the neoliberal order as "grounded in the belief that market forces had to be liberated from government regulatory controls." Gary Gerstle, *The Rise and Fall of the Neoliberal Order: America and the World in the Free Market Era* (New York:

contrast, consisted of liberals who made common cause with leftists and radicals *against* the excesses of capitalism while not seeking to eliminate capitalism.[32] The left-liberal of old was an economic reformist antagonistic to laissez-faire thinking, individualism, monopolism, and corporate interests. Similarly, progressivism of the kind espoused by Sanders, Warren, Justice Democrats in the House of Representatives, and the Congressional Progressive Caucus is unambiguously anti-neoliberal. So categorizing left-liberals as economically liberal only makes sense if "economic liberalism" forecloses on neoliberalism. The sliding scale of progressivism at present ranges from estrangement to total vilification of neoliberalism.

The larger point, then, is that the way the "progressive" signifier floats reflects some combination of the user's reaction to current circumstances and the user's interpretive embrace of what progressivism meant in an earlier historical era. When someone identifies as progressive, or labels some policy or person "progressive," we cannot take for granted what aspect of the progressive tradition they are referring to. We must look at their reasons for invoking the term, and the genealogy to which they appeal. To that end, we need a working understanding of how progressivism related to liberal, radical, and socialist politics in different epochs.

## THE EVOLUTION OF PROGRESSIVE THOUGHT

The original progressive movement in the United States was a response to the conditions of the nineteenth-century Gilded Age – egregious corruption, dramatic economic inequality, imperialism (for some), and the social dislocations wrought by the industrial revolution. Because liberalism furnished the intellectual justification for the monopolies and laissez-faire economic policies that reformers and revolutionaries alike opposed, classical liberals were seen in opposition to what became the progressive cause. Leftist parties around the world came to be identified as the parties of labor – including, eventually, the Democratic Party in the United States – precisely because they were the party to take up the plight of (white male) working people against the interests of the "old" moneyed liberals.

---

Oxford University Press, 2022), p. 2. But this undersells the political work of neoliberalism, using policy to insulate capital from democratic demands. See especially Slobodian, *Globalists*.

[32] Rossinow, *Visions of Progress*, pp. 13–59.

## Early Reformist Progressivism

And yet, as much as leftists have associated liberalism with corporate power and even empire – linkages that are not wrong[33] – there was also an older elitist, Kantian liberalism in America that opposed war, militarism, and business corruption.[34] These attitudes endured among some liberals at the turn of the twentieth century, and for a while, allowed for congenial relations with both the socialistic left and reform-minded liberals.

That early Progressive Era, stretching from the 1890s through World War I, was a time of ideological promiscuity and fluid categories. Leonard Hobhouse's *Democracy and Reaction* hints at this with a claim Marx would have found risible – "The true Socialism," he said, "serves to complete rather than to destroy the leading Liberal ideals."[35] Whatever one thinks of the statement, it is indicative of just how much the era was one in which "men of advanced social opinions used the terms 'socialism,' 'radicalism,' 'liberalism,' and 'progressivism' with a certain disregard of their various shades of meaning."[36]

The ideas and interests of the progressive movement as such were a gumbo consisting of democratic socialism, reformist liberalism, labor unionism, anti-imperialism, religious pacifism, Fabianism, and farmer populism. The shared policy concerns of this milieu – parts of the progressive movement were also consumed by social transformations beyond policy – stressed anti-monopolism, improved wages and working conditions for the (white male) working class, anti-imperialism (though a cross-section of progressive liberals had imperialist leanings), opposition to the buildup of a large standing army and navy, and public ownership of "natural monopolies" (assets that existed primarily for the public good like railroads and utilities). Even though organizing on behalf of civil rights and feminism was part of this period – and notwithstanding the omnipresence of W.E.B. Du Bois and the prominent leadership of women's organizations in peace activism – racial and gender equality were simply not priorities for the progressive movement as a whole.[37] The color line, for instance, remained imprinted on labor unions through this period and women did not even gain the right to vote until 1920.

---

[33] On the relationship between liberalism and empire, see especially Morefield, *Empires Without Imperialism*.

[34] Rossinow, *Visions of Progress*, pp. 24–27.

[35] Leonard Hobhouse, *Democracy and Reaction* (London: Unwin, 1904), p. 229.

[36] Lasch, *The New Radicalism in America, 1889–1963*, p. 286.

[37] McKnight Nichols, *Promise and Peril*, p. 80.

In addition to Du Bois, the writings and activism of Henry George, Jane Addams, Charles Austin and Mary Beard, Randolph Bourne, Eugene Debs, John Dewey, muckrakers like Lincoln Steffens and Upton Sinclair, Mark Twain, Robert LaFollette, A.J. Muste, and Ida B. Wells were among those who comprised a coherent canon of progressive thought from that period. These voices and many more were in dialog with one another to varying degrees, and each emphasized certain aspects of the struggle for progressive change. Notably, they were all more socialistic than liberal, and yet, with the exception of Debs, were not socialists in any unqualified sense. Reform-minded liberals of this age were vehement critics of capitalism, and in American politics, it was far easier to be a proponent of socialist ideas (almost always within rather than against constitutional republicanism) than to be seen as a dogmatic adherent of Marx.

While there were always disagreements and differing priorities within this intellectually eclectic network, the first great intra-left rupture was brought on by World War I, and Woodrow Wilson's late-hour decision to intervene in 1917. American anti-imperialists, peace activists, socialists, some left-liberals, and even a number of conservatives sought until the end to keep the United States out of what they saw as a senseless war, worried about how militarism would infect American society and setback progressive reforms.[38] Wilson courted this peace constituency all the way up to his reelection in 1916, after which point he allowed the United States to be nudged into war by a series of smaller decisions. Crucially, many reformist progressives and philosophical pragmatists, such as John Dewey and Herbert Croley, lined up temporarily as Wilsonian liberals once the prospect of entering the war became politically feasible.

The pragmatist arguments of the time were that the war could be a forcing function for world democratization, that opposing the war had no prospect of bringing it to an end, and that the productive spirit of nationalism could accelerate domestic movements for political and economic equality.[39] Even Du Bois, who later became a socialist, briefly saw upsides to America's entry into World War I before eventually recoiling at what followed.[40]

---

[38] Christopher McKnight Nichols, *Promise and Peril: America at the Dawn of a Global Age* (Cambridge, MA: Harvard University Press, 2015), pp. 191–214; David Kennedy, *Over Here: The First World War and American Society* (New York: Oxford University Press, 1980), pp. 50–53; Kazin, *War against War*, pp. 146–86.

[39] Lasch, *The New Radicalism in America, 1889–1963*, pp. 200–2. Randolph Bourne, *The War and the Intellectuals* (New York: American Union against Militarism, 1917).

[40] Chad Williams, "World War I in the Historical Imagination of W.E.B. Du Bois," *Modern American History* Vol. 1, no. 1 (2018), pp. 3–22.

Socialists were divided on the war, with some seeking to compromise with Wilsonian liberals while others urged a staunch anti-imperialism and still others sought revolution.[41]

Wilson's entry into the war heightened the salience of ideological differences within the left, validating in the process some of the greatest worries that the peace activists and socialists in particular had expressed about joining the war. As soon as America entered the fray, Wilson and the Congress turned the home front into an illiberal nightmare.[42] The militarism in Germany that Wilson had condemned only one year earlier washed over American society. Mass conscription and the widespread forced sale of Liberty Bonds to fund the war meant that, one way or another, everyone felt pressure to tangibly back the slaughter going on in Europe. Even many registered conscientious objectors were pressed into service.[43] Free speech was the first casualty of the war. Through the newly passed Sedition Act and Espionage Act, newspapers were either censored, shutdown altogether, or turned into propaganda machines for the war. The government intimidated anyone who spoke out against the draft or Wilson's policies, some with arrest and prison. The infamous Palmer Raids, which was made possible by the war, jailed thousands of people and broke up union activity on the thinnest of pretexts. The Justice Department brought cases against peace activists for merely publicly opposing the war. Any argument favoring peace was quickly branded as working on behalf of the Kaiser. Anti-German racism spread throughout the country. The Federal Bureau of Investigation (FBI) deputized private citizens to act as vigilantes, terrorizing everyone from draft critics to labor organizers.[44] Even though black Americans enlisted in the war effort at scale, on the newly illiberal home front they were subjected to a surge of "racial terror – pogroms, mass murders, the renascence of the Ku Klux Klan."[45] And socialism and communism were so stigmatized that it produced the first "red scare" in 1919 and 1920 – a paranoid mood that conservative politicians actively created with the explicit goal

---

[41] On the American socialist divide in World War I, see especially Kazin, *War Against War*, pp. 155–8.

[42] For the full story on the anti-democratic consequences of entering the war, see Adam Hochschild, *American Midnight: The Great War, A Violent Peace, and Democracy's Forgotten Crisis* (New York: Mariner Books, 2022).

[43] Kazin, *War against War*, p. 206.

[44] Kazin, *War against War*, pp. 209–10.

[45] Adom Getachew, "The New Black Internationalism," *Dissent* (Fall 2021), www.dissentmagazine.org/article/the-new-black-internationalism. See also Scott Ellsworth, *The Ground Breaking: An American City and Its Search for Justice* (New York: Dutton, 2021).

of splitting the left and targeting political enemies. As a result, the federal government treated the more ideologically committed leftists in America as so many traitors to the nation, not only presaging the McCarthy era but giving it a how-to playbook.[46]

The climate of fear and oppression in America that accompanied its entanglement with World War I was not just a dark hour for American democracy, it dramatized the cleavage between anti-war leftists and Wilsonian liberals. Prior to 1917, liberal and progressive reformers had simpatico policy agendas with socialists. Ideology took a backseat to what a person actually wanted to get done.[47] But the war fractured solidarity between liberals and socialists in a way that tended to sort progressives more toward one side or the other, introducing antagonisms that would become an ineradicable feature of intra-left politics.

### New Deal and Anti-fascist Progressivism

Needless to say, liberalism had developed a bad rap on the left by the 1920s, and as a result the left did not function as a unified bloc but rather was divided among the Socialist Party, the independent and short-lived Progressive Party that ran Robert LaFollette as its nominee for the presidency in 1924, and a Democratic Party that had largely become the party of white supremacist Wilson. Journalist John Chamberlain channeled prominent leftist criticisms of the time in deriding "the unwillingness of the liberal to continue with analysis once the process of analysis had become uncomfortable."[48] He charged that "both conservatives and radicals know how capitalism works; it is only the liberal, who has mistaken an adjective for a credo, that is deluded."[49] He was of a class of intellectuals who blamed liberals for the Great Depression and for dragging America into World War I on the basis of a faulty worldview that refused to take seriously either the root causes of problems or the risks of their actions. These critical attitudes "helped forge an enduring leftist image of liberals as humanitarians whose cowardice in the face of criticism from the right literally defined them."[50]

---

[46] Michael Heale, *American Anticommunism: Combating the Enemy within, 1830–1970* (Baltimore: Johns Hopkins University Press, 1990), pp. 60–78.

[47] This was the larger message of Rossinow, *Visions of Progress.*

[48] John Chamberlain, *Farewell to Reform: The Rise, Life and Decay of the Progressive Mind in America* (New York: Quadrangle, 1965), pp. 304–5.

[49] Chamberlain, *Farewell to Reform*, p. viii.

[50] Rossinow, *Visions of Progress*, p. 99.

But the onset of the Great Depression in 1929 and the corresponding rise of fascism became new galvanizing forces for progressive politics which, by 1935, took the form of the Popular Front. The progressivism of the 1930s through World War II centered the working class far more than any prior point in US history, took up Keynesian political economy (government stimulus spending and national investment), and opposed excess concentrations of corporate power (especially monopolies). In these ways, Franklin Roosevelt's New Deal reforms were aimed at improving working and living conditions through greater economic employment and investment in nation-building at home – reforms that, for the first time, aligned labor with the Democratic Party.

The desperate conditions of the Great Depression led to calls for drastic measures. In 1931, the editor of *The New Republic*, Edmund Wilson, took to task his predecessors for having championed a progressivism that had been too gradual, too solicitous of power, and too ultimately conservative. His tone was remarkable because *The New Republic* had been a liberal magazine with a controversial history on the left. Although it was a champion of many reforms: it was firmly liberal in editorial outlook rather than socialist; it had become a cheerleader for Woodrow Wilson's entry into World War I; and, for a time, it repudiated the war's end and the League of Nations idea.[51]

Two years into the Great Depression though, with little hope of recovery on the horizon, Edmund Wilson stated with clarity what was needed and what progressivism ought to mean given the dire conditions of his time:

I believe that if the American radicals and progressives who repudiate the Marxian dogma and the strategy of the Communist party hope to accomplish anything valuable, they must take Communism away from the Communists, and take it without ambiguities or reservations, asserting emphatically that their ultimate goal is the ownership of the means of production by the government and an industrial rather than a regional representation.[52]

He wanted a socialism governed by constitutional republicanism – an economy embedded within society. In effect, a cooperative commonwealth. This was something that was perhaps different in degree but not kind from what many progressives had sought before and since. And while Roosevelt's New Deal reforms moved in this direction, many

---

[51] For a scathing leftist critique of *The New Republic*, see Lasch, *The New Radicalism in America, 1889–1963*, pp. 181–224.
[52] Wilson, "An Appeal to Progressives."

voices of the left – including John Dewey – rebuked its tepidity, its disproportionality between meager means and transformational ends. And despite the New Deal's lofty ambitions on behalf of the "common man," critics worried that the goal of economic growth would ultimately force Roosevelt into a hard right turn politically, allying with the nation's big corporate interests against workers.[53]

But the unifying driver of a coherent progressivism in this period was less the New Deal – which remained controversial – than opposition to fascism. Even the New Deal was not so much America-building for its own greatness as it was a national economic development agenda that would inoculate against the growing allure of fascism. Roosevelt himself recognized that economic depression was precisely the breeding ground from which extremism of all types were springing. The course of the Spanish Civil War from 1936 to 1939 had imprinted on Roosevelt the geopolitical threat of fascism and the imperative to oppose it.[54] When he made Henry Wallace his Vice President in 1940, it was because of his alignment with the Popular Front and his outspoken credentials as an anti-fascist.[55]

The Popular Front was a unified progressive movement that backed New Deal reforms but was to the left of both the reforms themselves and the Roosevelt administration. Seeing how fear-mongering of communism and socialism was an on-ramp to fascism in Europe, the Popular Front was determined to not only reject red-baiting entirely, but to improve upon the conditions of economic desperation that gave fuel to right-wing extremism.[56] It was also within the Popular Front that civil rights and feminism incubated as causes of the American left, because they were core to addressing the radical-right problem

[53] See, for example, Chamberlain, *Farewell to Reform*, p. xi.

[54] On Roosevelt's anti-fascist evolution as a result of the Spanish Civil War, see Dominic Tierney, *FDR and the Spanish Civil War: Neutrality and Commitment in the Struggle That Divided America* (Durham, NC: Duke University Press, 2007).

[55] Nichols, *The Fight for the Soul of the Democratic Party*, p. 27.

[56] On the anti-fascism of the Popular Front, and how that specifically required political *and* economic rights, see Brick and Phelps, *Radicals in America*, pp. 22–41; Doug Rossinow, "'The Model of a Model Fellow Traveler': Harry F. Ward, the American League for Peace & Democracy, and the 'Russian Question' in American Politics, 1933–56," *Peace and Change* Vol. 29, no. 2 (2004), pp. 177–220. For the Popular Front in a comparative context, see Herbert Lottman, *Left Bank: Writers, Artists, and Politics from the Popular Front to the Cold War* (Chicago: University of Chicago Press, 1982); David Blaazer, *The Popular Front and the Progressive Tradition: Socialists, Liberals, and the Quest for Unity, 1884–1939* (Cambridge: Cambridge University Press, 1992).

the country faced.[57] Popular Frontists understood fascism as "hyper-nationalistic racism with extreme political violence directed particularly at organized labor."[58] The movement's leaders remained white and mostly men, but its intellectuals, including Du Bois, portrayed America's history of racialized brutality – subjecting blacks and minorities in America to a violent oppression that was of a kind with the Jews' experience in Europe – as the American version of fascism.[59] The ultimate eradication of fascism required nothing less than political and economic democracy.

The controversy of the Popular Front eventually proved its undoing. In the name of opposing the right-wing power that showed risks of evolving into fascism, the Popular Front progressives were anti-anticommunist. From 1935 to 1939, and again from 1941 to 1946, American communists – on direction from the Communist International – cooperated with social democrats and liberals in the name of opposing right-wing demagogues.[60] Communists were among the most committed labor organizers during these periods, and had temporarily muted their revolutionary rhetoric in favor of American populism.[61] They were also an energetic ideological bloc when it came to racial justice, helping normalize demands for political equality within the Popular Front.[62]

But in a country where conservative politicians had a reliable track record of whipping up anti-communist hysteria, using the accusation of communist sympathy to discredit political opponents and worse, this unity with communists became the Popular Front's vulnerability. When Hitler and Stalin made their brief nonaggression pact in 1939,

---

[57] Naison, "Remaking America: Communists and Liberals in the Popular Front"; Rossinow, *Visions of Progress*, pp. 166–72. For a cultural history of the Popular Front and its pluralism, see Chris Vials, *Realism for the Masses: Aesthetics, Popular Front Pluralism, and U.S. Culture, 1935–1947* (Jackson: University Press of Mississippi, 2009).

[58] Rossinow, *Visions of Progress*, p. 166.

[59] Rossinow, *Visions of Progress*, pp. 166–72; Mark Naison, "Remaking America: Communists and Liberals in the Popular Front," in *New Studies in the Politics and Culture of U.S. Communism*, edited by Michael Brown, Randy Martin, Frank Rosengarten, and George Snedeker (New York: Monthly Review Press, 1993), pp. 45–74. See also Mark Naison, *Communists in Harlem during the Great Depression* (Urbana: University of Illinois Press, 2004), pp. 193–278; Harold Cruse, *The Crisis of the Negro Intellectual: A Historical Analysis of the Failure of Black Leadership* (New York: New York Review of Books, 2005).

[60] On the role of communists in the Popular Front, see Brick and Phelps, *Radicals in America*, pp. 22–5, 30; Maurice Isserman, *Which Side Were You On? The American Communist Party during the Second World War* (Urbana: University of Illinois Press, 1982).

[61] Naison, "Remaking America," pp. 45–7.

[62] Rossinow, *Visions of Progress*, p. 153; Naison, "Remaking America."

it deeply wounded the Popular Front, whose *raison d'etre* presented fascism as an existential threat that justified working with the communists. Suddenly the red-brown alliance contradicted that reality. And the Popular Front was already dealing with formidable headwinds. America's biggest corporations fought to subvert both the New Deal and the growing power of labor unions,[63] and in doing so had allies in not only anti-New Deal conservatives and Southern segregationists, but also progressives who had become so anti-Soviet that they were also anti-Popular Front.

The latter group – alienated, radically anti-Soviet liberals – were poison to the progressive movement. The investigations and hearings of the House Un-American Activities Committee (HUAC) in this period buoyed anti-communist sentiment, armed with arguments and moral support from newly forming civic associations like the Americans for Democratic Action (ADA) and the Committee for Cultural Freedom (CCF) – groups whose goals were to promote a liberal anti-communism in opposition to progressive Popular-Front politics.[64] It was these liberal anti-communist organizations that, throughout the 1940s, helped make Cold War liberalism the hegemonic reality of American politics.

The ascendance of Cold War liberalism on the back end of World War II quickly diverted America's attention from fascism to communism. In its domestic context, Cold War liberalism was a political project "determined to end all [liberal] cross-breeding with intellectual formations to their left."[65] Arthur Schlesinger's *The Vital Center*, which tried to position itself as the manifesto of Cold War liberalism, went to great rhetorical lengths to delegitimize progressivism and rally the nation to a "nonideological" hawkish liberalism as democracy's only chance of survival. Schlesinger spared no venom toward progressives. He mocked their discomfort with America's conquest of native Indian and Mexican

---

[63] Sally Denton, *The Plot against the President: FDR, a Nation in Crisis, and the Rise of the American Right* (New York: Bloomsbury, 2012); Jonathan Katz, *Gangsters of Capitalism: Smedley Butler, the Marines, and the Making and Breaking of America's Empire* (New York: MacMillan, 2022), pp. 305–44.

[64] Rossinow, *Visions of Progress*, pp. 162–5; Griffin Fariello, *Red Scare: Memories of the American Inquisition* (New York: W.W. Norton & Co., 1995), pp. 521–43; Heale, *American Anticommunism*, pp. 145–66. On the role of the CIA in backing various cultural, civic, and educational groups in the name of anticommunism, even at home, see Christopher Lasch, *The Agony of the American Left* (New York: Knopf, 1969), pp. 68–114.

[65] Thomas Meaney, "The Hagiography Factory," *London Review of Books* Vol. 40, no. 3 (2018), www.lrb.co.uk/the-paper/v40/no3/thomas-meaney/the-hagiography-factory.

lands – both of which he applauded as "fruits of victory."[66] And he remarked that progressives differed from communists mainly in that "the progressive is soft, not hard," and "His sentimentality has softened up the progressive for Communist permeation and conquest."[67] It was a caricature aimed at stigma in service of policing a new elite political consensus. The anti-communist actions of HUAC and the ADA, of which Schlesinger was also an active part, did much the same. Their collective efforts cemented an impression that progressives were either "democratic men with totalitarian principles" or else they had been infiltrated and compromised by evil communists.[68]

This polarization-turned-power consolidation was problematic for leftism generally, but especially because the Popular Front was the coalition explicitly championing political democracy and economic democracy. Delegitimizing progressivism in the name of Cold War liberalism – specifically "principles of internal stability, anti-communism, and a commitment to world hegemony without major war" – eliminated "economic democracy" from the Democratic Party's imagination and delayed meaningful social progress until Lyndon Johnson's "Great Society" legislation two decades later.[69]

When Roosevelt's former Vice President Henry Wallace decided to run for president against Harry Truman in 1948 as the candidate of the Progressive Party, the fate of the anti-fascist, pro-peace, anti-monopolist, racially just, and economically fair agenda that progressives spent the 1930s fighting for was on the line. But Wallace's progressive campaign was a disaster, marking the unceremonious death of Popular-Front progressivism.

Wallace had the civil rights vote, the feminist vote, some of the union vote, and the peace-activists' vote – essentially the hard core of the Popular Front coalition – but it was not nearly enough, because he also had the communist vote. Even if he had run a gaffe-free campaign – which was very far from what happened – Cold War liberals like Schlesinger painted Wallace as Stalin's stooge Manchurian candidate,

---

[66] Arthur Schlesinger, Jr., *The Vital Center: The Politics of Freedom* (Cambridge, MA: The Riverside Press, 1949), p. 43.

[67] Ibid., pp. 36–37.

[68] Ibid., p. 38.

[69] Marcus Raskin, *The Politics of National Security* (New Brunswick, NJ: Transaction Books, 1979), p. 47. For Cold War liberals like Schlesinger, Jr., discrediting New Deal politics and social democracy was part of the project. He says as much in Schlesinger, Jr., *The Vital Center*, p. 41.

and spread accusations far and wide that his campaign had been infiltrated by communist agents.[70] Sympathetic histories of Henry Wallace's campaign eschew the role of, and especially infiltration by, communists with a tether to Moscow.[71]

But new histories drawing on recently available archival material suggest the Soviets *were* trying to shape Wallace's campaign and its agents *had* infiltrated it.[72] Aside from Wallace's poor showing against Truman, "… the Progressive Party could not become the politically influential, broad-based organization that both Wallace and the Communists had envisioned because the basis of their alliance was fragile and negative and their ultimate ends incompatible."[73] It was simply unrealistic to succeed with a strategy that relied on working with communists in a country where mainstream politics treated communism as an existential threat.

### The Post-Progressive "New Left" and the Post-New Left Progressivism

After Wallace's poor showing for the presidency, the Progressive Party died, and New Deal politics along with it. The onset of the Cold War and Washington's new consensus of fear of the Soviet Union gave rise to blacklists and purges in government, Hollywood, and in unions on the basis of no more than innuendo. Anti-communist hatemongering by Senator Eugene McCarthy and his reactionary fellow travelers also led to an unprecedented degree of FBI surveillance of American citizens, congressional hearings that sometimes doubled as show trials, and a deeply reactionary militarism in foreign policy.[74] An entire generation of feminists, socialists, and civil rights activists in public service were purged from government.[75] In addition to delegitimizing communism – and

---

[70] Schlesinger, Jr., *The Vital Center*, pp. 117–20.

[71] For a thorough but favorable view of the Progressive Party's history and Wallace's 1948 campaign, see the three-volume history, Curtis McDougall, *Gideon's Army* (New York: Marzani and Munsell, 1965).

[72] Thomas Devine, *Henry Wallace's 1948 Presidential Campaign and the Future of Post-War Liberalism* (Durham: University of North Carolina Press, 2013).

[73] Devine, *Henry Wallace's 1948 Presidential Campaign and the Future of Post-War Liberalism*, p. 292.

[74] Heale, *American Anticommunism*; Regin Schmidt, *Red Scare: FBI and the Origins of Anticommunism in the United States, 1919–1943* (Copenhagen: Museum Tusculanum Press, 2004). See also Daniel Chard, *Nixon's War at Home: The FBI, Leftist Guerillas, and the Origins of Counterterrorism* (Chapel Hill: University of North Carolina Press, 2021).

[75] Landon Storrs, *The Second Red Scare and the Unmaking of the New Deal Left* (Princeton: Princeton University Press, 2013).

deliberately conflating socialism and communism – Cold War liberalism also abandoned indictments of capitalism, gradually co-opted the issue of racial equality from the Popular Front but in a narrowing way, and deactivated national concerns about fascism. *Progressive*, and much of what it signified, was squeezed out of the political lexicon, at least for a few decades. The left – having no real grip on power – increasingly identified as "radical," eventually becoming the New Left.

Although some of the intellectuals of the Popular Front survived into the 1950s and 1960s as voices of conscience,[76] the New Left's politics embodied a series of tensions that made it stunningly different from the "old left." C. Wright Mills urged the New Left to equally reject what he called "Vulgar Marxism" and Stalinism but also the vulgarity of Cold War liberalism.[77] The Students for a Democratic Society (SDS) – often presented as the centerpiece in histories of the New Left – adopted this view. So did the Institute for Policy Studies, a progressive think tank in all but name, founded in 1963 by staffers in the Kennedy administration who were disturbed by the reflexive militarism and censoriousness of Cold War liberalism.[78]

The New Left as a movement was "anti-imperialist, anti-capitalist, and opposed to war. Yet they were equally critical of communist totalitarianism, infringements on free speech, and the lack of democracy in Eastern Europe, the Soviet Union, and China."[79] For the New Left, Marxism was too doctrinaire, and communism too evidently brutal. The Soviets' violent crushing of Hungary's pro-democracy uprising in 1956 also proved disillusioning for the American left,[80] and somewhat discrediting to the peace movement that up to that point had targeted its condemnations disproportionately against the United States.

Still, the intellectual energy of the New Left derived from seeing Cold War liberalism as an ideological nemesis – as something between a well-intentioned project gone bad and an existential threat to democracy.[81] Validated by new interpretations of American history that acknowledged

[76] Maurice Isserman, *If I Had a Hammer: The Death of the Old Left and the Birth of the New Left* (New York: Basic Books, 1987).

[77] C. Wright Mills, "Letter to the New Left," *New Left Review* (July 4, 1960), p. 20.

[78] Mueller, *Democracy's Think Tank*.

[79] Petra Goedde, *The Politics of Peace: A Global Cold War History* (New York: Oxford University Press, 2019), p. 64.

[80] Because the Soviets rolled in tanks to crush Hungarian democracy, leftists who rationalized the Soviet Union's actions rather than opposed them were dubbed "tankies" – a term that now replies to leftists who apologize for autocracy and militarism abroad.

[81] Mueller, *Democracy's Think Tank*, pp. 17–53; Markus Raskin, *The Politics of National Security* (New Brunswick, NJ: Transaction Books, 1979), pp. 31–60.

its legacy of racism, violence, cruelty, and domination of others,[82] the left that operated outside the Democratic Party came to see the United States as a "liberal empire" and its brand of politics as "liberal authoritarian."[83] The black radicals of the time came to see their own treatment at the hands of police as the inward application of the national security state, a colonial existence within a self-proclaimed democracy. Nor was this view of America limited to the black radicals; in parts of the South, apartheid was an empirical fact prior to the 1970s.[84]

Much like the Popular Front and the earlier Progressive Era, the New Left was a multi-struggle coalition built on cross-class solidarity. The predominantly white student-led movement on college campuses demanding free speech and nuclear disarmament was but one current. Civil rights, black power, feminism, and the counter-culture "New Communalism" (which sought to transform the individual in a manner evoking the early Progressive Era attempts at social transformation) all comprised the New Left agenda and were not reducible to either whiteness or student leadership.

The civil rights movement in particular was not something that simply coincided with the New Left, but actively gave it life. It was the civil-rights activism in the South – the experience with frontal white supremacy and the tactics to protest it – that transmitted to college campuses as a means of demanding nuclear abolition, and eventually an end to the Vietnam War.[85] Consisting of multiple standpoints, the New Left settled into a mostly coherent set of political positions, but your entry point into the struggle affected which aspect of it you prioritized.[86] These positions bore a slight resemblance to progressivism's

[82] On the role of revisionist historians in girding the New Left, see James Morgan, *Into New Territory: American Historians and the Concept of US Imperialism* (Madison: University of Wisconsin Press, 2014).

[83] Marcus Raskin, *Being and Doing: An Inquiry into the Colonization, Decolonization and Reconstruction of American Society and Its State* (New York: RandomHouse, 1971), pp. xvi, 177–86.

[84] Robert Mickey, *Paths Out of Dixie: The Democratization of Authoritarian Enclaves in America's Deep South, 1944–1972* (Princeton: Princeton University Press, 2015), pp. 33–63.

[85] Howard Zinn documents this transmission or fusion of civil rights and anti-war politics in his memoir. Howard Zinn, *You Can't Be Neutral on a Moving Train: A Personal History* (Boston: Beacon Press, 2018). See also Goedde, *The Politics of Peace*, pp. 46–50, 61; Van Gosse, *Rethinking the New Left: An Interpretive History* (New York: Palgrave MacMillan, 2005), pp. 31–52.

[86] On the siloed treatment of issues within the New Left, and the halting efforts of the movement to overcome that reality, see Gosse, *Rethinking the New Left*.

earlier preoccupations with peace, economic equality, and anti-fascism. But they looked nothing like gradualism or a "golden mean" between socialism and plutocracy, and critiques of capitalism were more attitudinal than agenda-based.

The energy of the New Left gradually dissipated though. The withdrawal of American troops from Vietnam satisfied one of the student movement's most strident and politically popular demands. The counterculture strain of the movement transmogrified into a mix of libertarian politics and Silicon Valley techno-utopianism.[87] The nuclear abolitionists lived on, but by the 1980s had prioritized the far more realistic goal of a nuclear freeze and arms control, which they had more success with.[88] By the late 1970s, the Democratic Party had begun to internalize – and thereby mainstream – noneconomic aspects of the New Left agenda, including environmentalism, feminism, and elements of racial justice. And the rise of neoliberalism under Democratic President Jimmy Carter, which accelerated in the Reagan era, not only coincided with the decimation of labor unions but also depended on it.

The end of the Cold War – which appeared to eliminate the very political construct from which New Left politics arose – made neoliberal globalization the water in which the fish swam. "The end of ideology," which Daniel Bell had proclaimed in 1962 to imply no alternative to Cold War liberalism,[89] was, in so many words, being proclaimed again but for a post–Cold War unipolar liberalism. By the time Bill Clinton ran for president, this new, frothing, corporate-friendly economic dogma was washing over the Democratic Party. In this context, *progressive* came back into vogue, but not as an agenda or a theory of politics so much as a wistful rhetorical gesture at a solidarist past.[90]

That emptiness would only begin to change with the 2008 economic recession, a time when the left would rally enthusiastically around the presidency of Barack Obama. In the beginning, they called him "progressive" because he was an anti-war candidate, not because he challenged

---

[87] Fred Turner, *From Counterculture to Cyberculture: Stewart Brand, the Whole Earth Network, and the Rise of Digital Utopianism* (Chicago: University of Chicago Press, 2006).

[88] This was actually a fissure within the anti-nuclear movement. Some continued to believe arms control was anathema to disarmament. See Mueller, *Democracy's Think Tank*, pp. 195–218.

[89] Daniel Bell, *The End of Ideology: On the Exhaustion of Political Ideas in the Fifties* (Cambridge, MA: Harvard University Press, 1962).

[90] Geismer, *Left Behind*, pp. 112–13. Some Clintonite liberals resented bringing back *progressive*. See Wilentz, "Fighting Words."

economic orthodoxy (he did not).[91] Obama's track record in office gradually alienated the left though – the left by this time routinely referred
to as "progressive," in contrast with Obama's performance in office as a
liberal or a moderate.[92]

When Senator Bernie Sanders, a professed democratic socialist, ran for
the Democratic nomination for president against Senator Hillary Clinton
in 2016, he happily wore the label "progressive" as a contrast denoting
that he was to Clinton's left. From Sanders's 2016 run through the years
of the Trump presidency, *progressive* entered widespread use again as a
signifier of politics and foreign policy to the left of what had become the
centrist-liberal project of the mainstream Democratic Party.

Of the many Democratic candidates for president in 2020, the
media divided them into moderates and progressives (the latter referring to Sanders, Elizabeth Warren, Julian Castro, Jay Inslee, Marianne
Williamson, and sometimes Cory Booker – all of whom identified as
progressives). And the Justice Democrats who won races in the House
of Representatives in 2018 and 2020 – Alexandria Ocasio-Cortez, Ro
Khanna, Ilhan Omar, Ayanna Pressley, Rashida Tlaib, Pramila Jayapal,
and Raul Grijalva – were the "most progressive" of a much larger group
of fellow-traveling lawmakers known as the Congressional Progressive
Caucus. The politics of the Justice Democrats – who drew their base
of support from the activist grassroots that the Clinton-era Democratic
Party had largely forsaken – aligned closer to the Democratic Socialists
of America (DSA) than to the Democratic Party of the post–Cold War
generation. The Congressional Progressive Caucus mostly consisted of
left-liberals, but the kind who were in solidarity with Justice Democrats
and vice versa.

It is in this span of time since 2008, and especially since 2016, that
left-aligned activists and public intellectuals have rallied around the *progressive* signifier again, this time with greater meaning, louder voices, and
more concrete demands. There is no shortage of friction between socialists and liberals, or between the progressive wing of the Democratic Party
and the more moderate left-liberal wing. And as Chapters 5 through 7
make clear, there are numerous areas of disagreement on foreign policy

---

[91] On Obama's appeal to activists, see Michael Heaney and Fabio Rojas, *Party in the
Street: The Antiwar Movement and the Democratic Party after 9/11* (New York: Cambridge University Press, 2015), pp. 73–4.

[92] Obama's electoral success played a large role in both weakening the antiwar movement
and severing its ties to the Democratic Party. Heaney and Rojas, *Party in the Street.*

in particular. But there is also widespread dissatisfaction with the way things are. Widespread interest in rekindling something resembling the New Deal but for a new age.[93] And widespread desire for greater political *and* economic democracy, at home and abroad.

---

[93] There is a historically valid criticism that the New Deal order failed to address distributional problems within society and set the conditions for worker power to be sacrificed in favor of development, and eventually conservative interest groups. If a New Deal order were to be rekindled, it would need to grapple with that legacy of development trumping equality. See Erik Baker, "The People, It Depends," *N+1* (Summer 2021), www.nplusonemag.com/issue-40/reviews/the-people-it-depends-2/.

# 4

## Principles of Progressive Worldmaking

Since Bernie Sanders's rise to national prominence in 2016, there has been an outpouring of demands for a more explicitly progressive foreign policy. This book actually originated out of the need to make sense of the various and sundry claims progressives were making about how America ought to alter its global conduct. Across the many attempts by progressives to fashion a new foreign policy agenda and advance critiques of default liberal internationalism, there exists a common set of principles to guide the use/non-use of American power as part of a different way of interacting with the world – economic equality, anti-authoritarianism, and solidarity.

The discussion below surveys the principles that appear in the landscape of contemporary progressive-leftist thought about foreign policy, which includes not just references to left-leaning publications and the writings of self-identified progressive intellectuals but also speeches by progressive politicians, leftist multimedia (zines, blogs, newsletters, and podcasts), and the manifestos and calls to action of progressive organizations.[1] The fact that principles of economic equality,

---

[1] The most stable sources of progressive foreign policy thought since 2016 come from *Dissent, Jacobin, The Nation, Current Affairs, Boston Review, The Baffler, New Left Review*, and *N+1* – though there are numerous other places where progressives voiced their foreign policy preferences, including newsletters, blogs, podcasts, and obviously in books. I also surveyed *Monthly Review* and *Tempest*, though both are more revolutionary than progressive. It would be possible, though not worthwhile here, to conduct a content and network analysis, coding the frequency of concepts associated with consensus progressive principles and analyzing the content shared across (thus linking) prominent discursive sites on the left. Or you can just read what follows and track my reasoning.

anti-authoritarianism, and solidarity are not just discoverable but pervasive in leftist discourses about foreign policy should not be altogether surprising or novel given the historical context of Chapter 3. But these commitments require specifying here for several reasons. First, they have historical antecedents in earlier eras of leftist thought and there is value in making connections between how advocacy and analysis in the present echo that of the past. Second, these principles are susceptible to being interpreted or operationalized in ways that give rise to different theories of security and therefore different policy priorities. Being clear about why they matter to various constituencies within the left (and how they do not always mean the same thing to everyone) provides a basis for different progressive approaches to security, which I construct in Chapters 5–7 that follow. Third, because they have heuristic value, these principles represent what scholars of grand strategy would dispassionately describe as "national pathologies."[2] Everyone has analytical priors and value judgments that affect the color and frame imposed on world events. Transparency about what those priors are and where they come from gives us a basis for discerning how interpreting or prioritizing a common set of principles differently yields distinct models of foreign policy.

## ECONOMIC EQUALITY

Charles Tilly showed how all types of durable inequalities involve the same mechanisms – exploitation and opportunity hoarding – making inequality, once it arises, stubbornly path dependent.[3] In a broad sense, we might say this is why, for the past two centuries, inequality has not only tended to worsen over time, but also that it does not decrease either on its own or as a function of economic development.[4] In the span of human history, only "violent shocks" of war, pandemic, state collapse, and revolution have brought about deep, structural reductions in inequality.[5] These relatively recent analytical insights validate a much longer progressive tradition against laissez-faire economics and what we now describe as the neoliberal imperative to put public policy in service

[2] Balzacq, Dombrowski, and Reich, eds., *Comparative Grand Strategy*, pp. 10–14.
[3] Charles Tilly, *Durable Inequality* (Berkeley, CA: University of California Press, 1999), p. 10.
[4] Thomas Piketty, *Capital in the Twenty-First Century* (Cambridge, MA: Harvard University Press, 2017).
[5] Walter Scheidel, *The Great Leveler: Violence and the History of Inequality from the Stone Age to the Twenty-First Century* (Princeton, NJ: Princeton University Press, 2018).

of capital at the expense of labor.[6] The belief that politics must intervene directly to both redistribute capital and improve economic security for workers is core to progressives, and arguably *the* defining cleavage between progressivism and the economic liberalism that, prior to the Biden presidency, dominated the Democratic Party for decades.[7]

But the progressive demand for economic equality is not absolute or essential; material equality, or reductions in material inequality, matters to the extent that it facilitates human freedom.[8] In this way, economic equality as a priority does not only rest on a moral appeal, and progressivism's pursuit of equality as not just a political but also economic obligation arises from longstanding concerns about the myriad antidemocratic consequences of its absence – including monopoly and surveillance capitalism, white supremacy and neofascism, imperialism, kleptocracy, and the chronic impoverishment of the Global South. These are oppressive, freedom-depriving conditions favorable to violent instability within and between states.

### Imperialism

In the work of John Hobson and Rosa Luxembourg, imperialism abroad was born of domestic economic wealth disparities.[9] Owners needed to pay workers far less than the value of their labor to extract profits, but low-wage workers would then be unable to afford what they produced. Imperial political economy was the workaround; a way to keep factories

---

[6] As Karl Polanyi claimed, "man's economy, as a rule, is submerged in his social relationships." Karl Polanyi, *The Great Transformation: The Political and Economic Origins of Our Time* (Boston: Beacon, 2001), p. 48.

[7] Chapter 8 discusses progressive political economy in greater detail, but the Polanyi view of embedding the economy within society – an implicitly anti-neoliberal stance – is shared by liberals like John Ruggie, left-progressive political economists like Joseph Stiglitz and Mike Konczal, and anarcho-socialists like the late Dave Graeber. John Ruggie, "International Regimes, Transactions, and Change: Embedded Liberalism in the Postwar Economic Order," *International Organization* Vol. 36, no. 2 (1982), pp. 379–415; Joseph Stiglitz, "The Coming Great Transformation," *Journal of Policy Modeling* Vol. 39 (2017), pp. 625–38; Mike Konczal, *Freedom from the Market: America's Fight to Liberate Itself Form the Grip of the Invisible Hand* (New York: The New Press, 2021); David Graeber, *Debt: The First 5000 Years* (New York: Melville House, 2011).

[8] As Karl Kautsky argued, "It is not the freedom of labor, but the freedom from labor, which in a socialist society the use of machinery makes increasingly possible, that will bring to mankind freedom of life ..." Karl Kautsky, *The Socialist Republic*, trans. Daniel De Leon (New York: National Executive Committee Socialist Labor Party, 1918), p. 47.

[9] John Hobson, *Imperialism: A Study* (New York: James Pott & Co., 1902); Rosa Luxemburg, *The Accumulation of Capital* (Abingdon: Routledge Classics, 2003).

working when the population lacked the money to buy its outputs. Control of foreign markets not only afforded resource extraction opportunities but an outlet to absorb factory production that exceeded what the domestic population could consume. In this way, domestic inequality heightens global inequality, which in turn produces empires and the competition among them which then brought on World War I.[10] Some leftists have also characterized what they describe as the "new imperialism" of America's invasion of Iraq in 2003 – and twenty-first-century American militarism in general – as symptoms of the extreme inequities of American capitalism.[11]

## Monopolism

Many liberal progressives also see a threat in corporate monopolies, which spring from and reify inequality. Among the most visible political fights at the dawn of the twentieth century were the battles to break up monopoly control of "robber barons" in, for example, rail, steel, oil, and sugar – industries where trusts and vertically integrated companies used their size and market share to engage in anticompetitive (and ultimately antidemocratic) business practices, distorting public policy for their enrichment.[12] For Marxian analysts, moreover, monopoly capitalism itself represented a stage of capitalist development brought about by the tendency for the rate of profit to fall, leading to concentrations of wealth that lock in extreme inequality and convert to political power that in turn preserve rules that insulate and reproduce oligarchic

[10] Branco Milanovic, *Global Inequality: A New Approach to Globalization* (Cambridge, MA: Harvard University Press, 2016), pp. 94–95. The association between inequality and World War I was also tested in Branco Milanovic, "Inequality, Imperialism, and the Outbreak of World War I," in *The Economics of the Great War: A Centennial Perspective*, edited by Stephen Broadberry and Mark Harrison (London: CEPR Press, 2018), pp. 35–41.

[11] The best statement of this inequality-to-new imperialism view is David Harvey, *The New Imperialism* (Oxford: Oxford University Press, 2005). See also Michael Hardt and Antonio Negri, *Empire* (Cambridge, MA: Harvard University Press, 2001).

[12] On the de-skilling of workers problem under monopoly capitalism, see Harry Braverman, *Labor and Monopoly Capital: The Degradation of Work in the Twentieth Century* (New York: Monthly Review Press, 1974). On the problem that it exhibits and exacerbates an imbalance of class forces, see Paul Baran and Paul Sweezy, *Monopoly Capital* (New York: Monthly Review Press, 1966). See also Jeremiah Jenks, "Capitalistic Monopolies and Their Relation to the State," *Political Science Quarterly* Vol. 9, no. 3 (1894), pp. 486–509; Sam Gindin and Leo Panitch, *The Making of Global Capitalism: The Political Economy of American Empire* (New York: Verso, 2012), pp. 1–30.

(thus anti-majoritarian) class privileges, placing workers in an ever more desperate situation.[13] Herbert Marcuse, the "Father of the New Left," equated monopoly capitalism to totalitarianism, enslaving the masses through technological and cultural mechanisms of hegemonic control.[14] In the twenty-first century, these concentrations of corporate power have given rise to the system of surveillance capitalism within which society not only allows itself to be tracked and economically exploited but also permits the corporations that manage these systems of social surveillance (for example, Facebook/Meta, Apple, and Google) to accrue more political power than any other interest group in American politics.[15]

Of course, the kind of totalitarianism that Marxians and critical theorists see in monopoly capitalism is a very different problem set from something like a real-world industrial monopoly. Some have even argued that making the market more competitive and high-functioning is not actually in the left's interests.[16] But progressive activists recognize that it is not the size of a corporation that threatens but rather its ability to write punitive contracts, fix business rules in its favor, disempower workers, and influence politics.[17] As Henry Wallace wrote, "Monopolists who fear competition ... would like to secure their position against small and energetic enterprise. In an effort to eliminate the possibility of any rival growing up, some monopolists would sacrifice democracy itself."[18] Monopolism in this rendering is more than just a byproduct of inegalitarianism that reifies it; it is a threat to democracy. Seeing monopoly as a threat to society, not just markets, Senator Elizabeth Warren made breaking up Facebook and Amazon – and anti-trust enforcement

---

[13] Karl Marx, *Capital: A Critical Analysis of Capitalist Production* (New York: Humboldt Publishing Co., 1873), pp. 384–89; John Eatwell, Murray Milgate, and Peter Newman, eds., *Marxian Economics* (London: Palgrave MacMillan, 1990). Part of how monopoly capitalism precaritizes workers is through capital's constant pressure to make the skills of the worker obsolete. See especially Braverman, *Labor and Monopoly Capital*, pp. 3–4.

[14] Herbert Marcuse, *One-Dimensional Man* (New York: Beacon Press, 1964).

[15] Shoshanna Zuboff, *The Age of Surveillance Capitalism: The Fight for a Human Future at the New Frontier of Power* (New York: Profile Books, 2019); Virginia Eubanks, *Automating Inequality: How High-Tech Tools Profile, Police and Punish the Poor* (New York: St. Martin's Press, 2018); Stoller, *Goliath*.

[16] Henwood, "Why Socialists Should Distrust Antitrust"; Bruenig, "No, Small Isn't Beautiful".

[17] Zephyhr Teachout, "Look Out Big Tech, We're Coming For You," *New Republic* (December 11, 2021), https://newrepublic.com/article/164679/antitrust-break-up-big-tech?utm_source=newsletter&utm_medium=email&utm_campaign=tnr_daily.

[18] Henry Wallace, "The Dangers of American Fascism," *New York Times* (April 9, 1944), reprinted in *Truthout*, https://truthout.org/articles/the-dangers-of-american-fascism/.

generally – a focal point in her 2020 presidential campaign.[19] Progressive activists like Zephyr Teachout have lobbied for the same.[20] Sharing this sentiment, Senator Bernie Sanders claimed that without major economic reform to combat monopolist economics, the world was heading toward "a system in which a small number of billionaires and corporate interests have control our economic life, our political life, and our media."[21] Anti-monopolism has since become mainstream Democratic politics.[22]

## Kleptocracy

Opposition to corruption was among the earliest progressive priorities dating back to the nineteenth century. The concern that today's progressives evince about kleptocrats and oligarchs exploiting the global financial system can be understood as part of that historical through line. Kleptocracy is a form of direct political corruption (the word literally means "rule by thieves") that poses an underappreciated threat both to democracy and of conflict.[23] The neoliberal shift in the global economy starting in the 1970s made it possible for networks of dictators, political nepotists, and multinational corporations to plunder, and ultimately impoverish, societies around the world by laundering stolen money, avoiding taxes, and extracting private gain from public resources.[24] As Elizabeth Warren summarized, "Efforts to bring capitalism to the global stage unwittingly helped create the conditions for anti-democratic countries to rise up and lash out."[25] The politics that fueled globalization resulted in the most

[19] Elizabeth Warren as quoted in Nik DeCosta-Klipa, "Read the Transcript of Elizabeth Warren's Big Foreign Policy Speech," *Boston.com* (November 29, 2018), www.boston.com/news/politics/2018/11/29/elizabeth-warren-foreign-policy-speech-american-university.

[20] Zephyr Teachout, *Break 'Em Up: Recovering Our Freedom from Big Ag, Big Tech, and Big Money* (New York: All Points, 2020).

[21] Bernie Sanders, *Where We Go from Here* (New York: St. Martin's, 2018), p. 104.

[22] Centrist Democrat Senator Amy Klobuchar, for instance, wrote a book after her presidential run about challenging monopolies. Amy Klobuchar, *Antitrust: Taking on Monopoly Power from the Gilded Age to the Digital Age* (New York: Knopf, 2021).

[23] Sarah Chayes, *Thieves of State: Why Corruption Threatens Global Security* (New York: W.W. Norton & Co., 2015); Alexander Cooley and Daniel Nexon, "The Illiberal Tide," *Foreign Affairs* (March 26, 2021), www.foreignaffairs.com/articles/united-states/2021-03-26/illiberal-tide.

[24] See, for example, Alexander Cooley and John Heathershaw, *Dictators without Borders: Power and Money in Central Asia* (New Haven, CT: Yale University Press, 2017); J.C. Sharman, *The Despot's Guide to Wealth Management: On the International Campaign against Grand Corruption* (Ithaca, NY: Cornell University Press, 2017).

[25] Ibid.

gratuitously material form of "opportunity hoarding," locking in conditions that enabled extreme capital accumulation for a privileged few at the expense of societies.[26] Such inequality is reified and worsened in part by transnational corruption, which has allowed political elites to be "unaccountable for their financial crimes – from tax fraud to money laundering – and for their labor violations ... the same freedom from legal sanction that officials who commit torture or human rights abuses do ... illustrations of a corrosive political order that works on behalf of plutocracy."[27]

Progressives who see kleptocracy as a security threat believe "state violence and financial crime" are linked by the processes of globalization that produce and reinforce inequality.[28] This is why both the Sanders and Warren presidential campaigns centered their foreign policies on a premise that, as Sanders put it, "Inequality, corruption, oligarchy, and authoritarianism are inseparable ... [we face a] movement toward international oligarchy."[29] And although anti-kleptocracy has become a focal point for many on the left, it also now resonates as a mainstream security concern. The Biden administration, for instance, has incorporated anti-kleptocracy into its statecraft,[30] and in a May 2021 letter, Democratic representatives Tom Malinowski and Sheldon Whitehouse declared that "the threats presented to US national security by global corruption warrant a war-like footing" by the Treasury Department.[31]

## Neofascism and White Supremacy

Franklin Roosevelt had plenty of critics to his left in his time, but he summed up the essence of the economic-inequality challenge in a way that the left then and now cannot but endorse when he said, "necessitous men are not free men. People who are hungry and out of a job are

---

[26] Tilly, *Durable Inequality*, p. 10.

[27] Aziz Rana, "Renewing Working-Class Internationalism," *New Labor Forum* (2019), https://newlaborforum.cuny.edu/2019/01/25/working-class-internationalism/.

[28] Ibid.

[29] Bernie Sanders, *Where We Go from Here* (New York: St. Martin's, 2018), p. 104.

[30] Van Jackson, "NOW the White House Wants to Fight Kleptocracy," *Duck of Minerva* (December 10, 2021), www.duckofminerva.com/2021/12/now-the-white-house-wants-to-fight-kleptocracy.html; Nahal Toosi, "Going after the 'Achilles' Heel': Biden Charges into Global Anti-Corruption Fight," *Politico* (March 16, 2021), www.politico.com/news/2021/03/16/biden-global-anti-corruption-fight-476160.

[31] Tom Malinowski and Sheldon Whitehouse, *Letter to Secretary of the Treasury Janet Yellen* (May 3, 2021), https://malinowski.house.gov/sites/malinowski.house.gov/files/Malinowski%20Whitehouse%20Letter%20Yellen%20AML%5B1%5D.pdf.

the stuff out of which dictatorships are made."[32] If economic insecurity paved the road to fascism, then economic security was the obvious solution to it – "The fight of the progressive forces for full employment is at the same time a way of *preventing* the recurrence of fascism," observed Michal Kalecki.[33] Fascism of the European variety never reached a critical mass in the United States, but in the years of the Great Depression, it nevertheless enjoyed some popularity.[34] In addition, as mentioned in Chapter 3, an institutional and cultural white supremacy has always existed in America and it exercises itself in violent and terroristic ways that black radicals in particular have named as a distinctly American fascism.[35] While white supremacy and neofascism can be categorically distinct, they comprise a Venn diagram in practice; Hitler, after all, admired how the United States cordoned and exterminated Native Americans, and modeled Nazi anti-Semitic laws on Jim Crow.[36]

Economic dislocation and destitution, especially in co-existence with concentrated corporate wealth, are key ingredients that make and reify neofascism. As economic inequality grows, neofascism becomes, if not necessary, then at least a valuable way to protect systems of concentrating wealth against democratic political demands for redistribution.[37] This was why Henry Wallace touted policies of economic redistribution as the

---

[32] Franklin Roosevelt as quoted in Nichols, *The Fight for the Soul of the Democratic Party*, p. 3.

[33] Michael Kalecki, "Political Aspects of Full Employment," *The Political Quarterly* Vol. 14, no. 4 (1943), p. 331.

[34] Katy Hull, *The Machine Has a Soul: American Sympathy with Italian Fascism* (Princeton, NJ: Princeton University Press, 2021). For the story of how some American plutocrats were sympathetic to fascism and sought to overthrow Roosevelt, see Katz, *Gangsters of Capitalism*, pp. 305–44. See also John Huntington, *Far-Right Vanguard: The Radical Roots of Modern Conservatism* (Philadelphia: University of Pennsylvania Press, 2021), pp. 12–44; Michael Heale, *Franklin D. Roosevelt: The New Deal and War* (Abingdon: Routledge, 1999).

[35] On the black radical understanding of fascism, see especially Angela Davis, ed., *If They Come in the Morning ... Voices of Resistance* (New York: Verso, 2016); Alberto Toscano, "The Long Shadow of Racial Fascism," *Boston Review* (October 28, 2020), www.bostonreview.net/articles/alberto-toscano-tk/.

[36] James Whitman, *Hitler's American Model: The United States and the Making of Nazi Race Law* (Princeton: Princeton University Press, 2017); Alex Ross, "How American Racism Influenced Hitler," *New Yorker* (April 23, 2018), www.newyorker.com/magazine/2018/04/30/how-american-racism-influenced-hitler.

[37] The correlation between extreme inequality and fascism has been shown repeatedly in, for instance, Gregory Galofre Vila, Christopher Meissner, Martin McKee, and David Stuckler, "Austerity and the Rise of the Nazi Party," *Journal of Economic History* Vol. 81, no. 1 (2021), pp. 81–113; Barry Eichengreen, *The Populist Temptation: Economic Grievance and Political Reaction in the Modern Era* (Oxford: Oxford University Press,

only way that "Democracy can win the peace" after World War II.[38] There is also a "rational fascism" in which advocates of reactionary and racialized political violence put their power in service of corporate interests, making far-right politics a way of preserving systems of capital that are in crisis.[39] Bernie Sanders explained that without acknowledging America's failure to address poverty and inequality in America, "you can't understand why Donald Trump is president of the United States, you can't understand why most people in America are giving up on the political process."[40] At a global level, Sanders and progressive groups have tied inequality to the rising threat of a "nationalist international" – a perverse kind of solidarism among neofascists and right-wing demagogues.[41] Progressive political economists have similarly warned of something akin to fascism arising if the extreme inequities of an oligarchic system are allowed to persist and worsen.[42]

2018); Prabhir Vishnu Poruthiyil, "Big Business and Fascism: A Dangerous Collusion," *Journal of Business Ethics* Vol. 168, no. 1 (2019), pp. 121–35; Shane Burley, *Fascism Today: What It Is and How to End It* (Chico, CA: AK Press, 2017). The more important point here though is that progressives believe inequality creates conditions that make it possible for fascism to thrive and for white supremacy to strengthen. For a representative left perspective on the inequality-fascist linkage, see Prabhat Patnaik, "Why Neoliberals Need Neofascists," *Boston Review* (July 19, 2021), https://bostonreview.net/articles/why-neoliberalism-needs-neofascists/; Clara Mattei, *The Capital Order; How Economists Invented Austerity and Paved the Way to Fascism* (Chicago, IL: University of Chicago Press, 2022).

[38] Wallace, "The Dangers of American Fascism."

[39] Michael Parenti, *Blackshirts and Reds: Rational Fascism and the Overthrow of Communism* (San Francisco, CA: City Light Publishers, 1997).

[40] Bernie Sanders as quoted in "Deconstructed Podcast: We Need to Talk About Inequality (with Bernie Sanders)," *The Intercept* (March 23, 2018), https://theintercept.com/2018/03/23/deconstructed-podcast-we-need-to-talk-about-inequality-with-bernie-sanders/.

[41] For the general progressive worry about the nationalist international, see John Feffer, "The Far Right Continues to Build Its International," *Foreign Policy in Focus* (December 8, 2021), https://fpif.org/the-far-right-continues-to-build-its-international/?emci=76f83613-0a59-ec11-94f6-005of2e65e9b&emdi=4a9a6236-1f59-ec11-94f6-005of2e65e9b&ceid=8751633. For Sanders's take specifically, see Bernie Sanders, "A New Authoritarian Axis Demands an International Progressive Front," *The Guardian* (September 13, 2018), www.theguardian.com/commentisfree/ng-interactive/2018/sep/13/bernie-sanders-international-progressive-front.

[42] Joseph Stiglitz, *People, Power, and Profits: Progressive Capitalism for an Age of Discontent* (New York: Norton, 2019), pp. 14–20; Robert Reich, *The System: Who Rigged It, How We Fix It* (New York: Vintage, 2021), pp. 91–152; Robert Reich, "The American Fascist," *RobertReich.org* (March 8, 2016), https://robertreich.org/post/140705539195; Robert Reich Tweet, @RBReich (December 6, 2021), https://twitter.com/RBReich/status/1467661526756741123; Paul Krugman, "Why It Can Happen Here," *New York Times* (August 27, 2018), www.nytimes.com/2018/08/27/opinion/trump-republican-party-authoritarianism.html.

The Capitol Insurrection on January 6, 2021, illustrates the point. The attack on the US Capitol had many causes; it is not enough to recognize it as seeking to preserve a white supremacist order because, while true enough, that racial order has always existed in America and has a class dimension. Only 7 percent of those involved were unemployed, yet more than half had a troubled financial history.[43] Those data points actually tell the same story – precarity – if you understand the attack as a proto-fascist spasm aimed at preventing economic dispossession in a nation of growing economic desperation and precarity. As Robert Reich put it,

The despair Trump has channeled is ... connected to a profound loss of identity, dignity and purpose, especially among Americans who have been left behind .... The wages of these Americans has not risen in 40 years ... even though the economy is now three times larger. The norm of upward mobility has been shattered ... This part of America yearns for a strongman to deliver it from despair.[44]

## Oppressing the Global South

Since the early twentieth century, a cross-section of progressives has also seen inequality as a problem of relations between the Global North and South. Anti-colonialist Frantz Fanon popularized what is today a commonly held view on the left that "The wealth of the imperialist nations is also our wealth ... Europe is literally a creation of the Third World."[45] On these grounds, during the Cold War, many newly independent states

---

[43] Barton Gellman, "Trump's Next Coup Has Already Begun," *The Atlantic* (December 7, 2021), www.theatlantic.com/magazine/archive/2022/01/january-6-insurrection-trump-coup-2024-election/620843/?fbclid=IwAR2xF1LPBOlmTFhClpPx9PVACQtn9mRSlQn oKZLEw7B2S4q7LdbjbNl4iGg; Todd Frankel, "A Majority of the People Arrested for Capitol Riot Had a History of Financial Trouble," *Washington Post* (February 10, 2021), www.washingtonpost.com/business/2021/02/10/capitol-insurrectionists-jenna-ryan-financial-problems/.

[44] Robert Reich, "What Is the Real Meaning of January 6?" *Robert Reich Substack* (December 29, 2021), https://robertreich.substack.com/p/real-meaning-jan-6?token=eyJ1c2Vy X2lkIjozNDczMTU2LCJwb3N0X2lkIjooNjIyMjkwNSwiXyI6IlNjeTA5Iiwia WFoIjoxNjQwOTcoMTg5LCJleHAiOjE2NDA5Nzc3ODksImlzcyI6InB1YiozNjUo MjIiLCJzdWIiOiJwb3N0LXJlYWNoaW9uIn0.3wbpVwTkaju8Yt9mS_snoBeIMhq QATGhh58ZDQTV-EQ.

[45] Frantz Fanon, *The Wretched of the Earth* (New York: Grove Press, 1961), p. 58. Fanon was a militant radical but his thought is an anchor of the black radical tradition that Johan Galtung drew on to conceptualize "structural violence," which is a central problem in progressive thought. Johan Galtung, "Violence, Peace, and Peace Research," *Journal of Peace Research* Vol. 6, no. 3 (1969), 167–91. For more popular contemporary renderings of Fanon, see Hickel, *The Divide*; Utsa Patnaik and Prabhat Patnaik, *A Theory of Imperialism* (New York: Oxford University Press, 2016).

in the Third World tried to enact a New International Economic Order (NIEO) that would have imposed obligations on the United States in particular to not simply provide aid to developing nations but craft policies to rectify historical imbalances in the global economy that systematically disadvantaged the developing world.[46] Since the Cold War's end, progressives and heterodox political economists have called for policies that slow and ideally reverse the Global North's enrichment at the Global South's expense. Proposals to achieve this range from de-growth in the North and a global labor movement to "progressive globalization" (diverting investment capital rather than aid to the Global South) and a Global Green New Deal that redresses North-South inequities through climate action (all of which are discussed hereafter).[47] This is not just penance for centuries of colonial exploitation and oppression; it ameliorates the conditions that spur civil and ethnic conflict, which occur disproportionately in the Global South. Moreover, progressives generally understand that, much like the civil rights movement followed the New Deal era, "shared prosperity [that brings North and South into balance] is the terrain on which battles for the entire range of democratizing, progressive reforms become winnable."[48] Reducing the gap between North and South creates a more favorable environment for realizing progressive foreign policy preferences generally.

Remedying inequality, in sum, matters in all manner of cross-cutting ways. The larger point not to be missed though is that seeking economic equality necessarily means opposing economic neoliberalism. The renaissance in what might be called progressive political economy in recent years, which I discuss in Chapter 8, fuses progressives' ongoing resistance critiques against neoliberalism with the palpable failures of austerity and the sovereignty of capital to move freely around the world at the expense of democracy.

---

[46] For a review of how "liberal" scholars found the NIEO demands of the Third World confounding because they transgressed against classical economic dogma, see Craig Murphy, "What the Third World Wants: An Interpretation of the Development and Meaning of the New International Economic Order Ideology," *International Studies Quarterly* Vol. 27, no. 1 (1983), pp. 55–76.

[47] Tobita Chow, Michael Collins, and Jake Werner, *The Movement We Need: Think Strategically, Act Strategically* (Chicago, IL: Center for Progressive Strategy and Research, 2016); Ying Cheng and An Li, "Global Green New Deal: A Global South Perspective," *Economic and Labor Relations Review* Vol. 32, no. 2 (2021), pp. 170–89; Jason Hickel, "The Anti-Colonial Politics of Degrowth," *Political Geography* Vol. 88 (June 2021), www.sciencedirect.com/science/article/pii/S0962629821000640.

[48] Jake Werner, as quoted in Eric Levitz, "Only the Left Can Save Globalization Now," *New York Magazine* (February 9, 2021), https://nymag.com/intelligencer/2021/02/only-the-left-can-save-globalization-now.html.

## ANTI-AUTHORITARIANISM

Pragmatism, a philosophy strongly associated with progressive thought,[49] is inherently anti-authoritarian. Some progressives believe anti-authoritarianism is pragmatism's highest value because it is only by escaping authority without consent that we can realize the Enlightenment's promise of human emancipation.[50] Although dictatorships are intrinsically antagonistic to projects of participatory and majoritarian democracy, progressive anti-authoritarianism is expressed in sometimes conflicting ways depending on one's priors and the historical analogy most prized to make sense of the present. Some are concerned foremost with forms of fascism and eth-nonationalism, while others posture against what they see as Western/American imperialism. Before World War II, the original anti-fascists were often communists, militant in their defense of a utopian vision of democracy. Around 70 percent of American volunteers in the International Brigades of the Spanish Civil War, for example, were members of the Communist Party.[51] While fascism had much greater traction in America than did communism (even among some union members, awkwardly),[52] the Popular Front coalition that included American socialists, labor leaders, civil rights activists, and left-liberals saw the rise of fascism in Europe as a danger to democracy – and worried about its spread to the United

---

[49] Socialists have often portrayed pragmatism as a liberal ideology, which, depending on how you understand liberalism, is true. But pragmatist philosophy has also been central to progressive politics throughout the twentieth century, and that politics, as the previous chapter explained, was not just liberal. Pragmatist John Dewey criticized the New Deal for not being progressive enough, routinely decried the many travesties of capitalism, supported socialist Eugene Debs, and defended Leon Trotsky against Stalin. Richard Rorty, though stridently anti-communist, considered himself both a disciple of Dewey and a progressive. Pragmatist philosophy, moreover, influenced both the Students for a Democratic Society in the 1960s, and the founders of the Institute for Policy Studies who rejected Cold War liberalism and became intellectual beacons of the New Left. For the left's conflicted legacy on interpreting Dewey, see Alexander Livingston and Ed Quish, "John Dewey's Experiments in Democratic Socialism," *Jacobin Magazine* (January 8, 2018), https://jacobinmag.com/2018/01/john-dewey-democratic-socialism-liberalism. On pragmatism in progressive politics and the New Left, see Mueller, *Democracy's Think Tank*, pp. 9–10, 39–41, 45, 51–53.

[50] Richard Rorty, *Pragmatism as Anti-Authoritarianism* (Cambridge, MA: Harvard University Press, 2021), pp. 144–58.

[51] Giles Tremlett, *The International Brigades: Fascism, Freedom and the Spanish Civil War* (New York: Bloomsbury, 2020), p. 231. On the unsullied idealism of pre–Cold War American communism, see Vivian Gornick, *The Romance of American Communism* (New York: Basic Books, 1977).

[52] Hull, *The Machine Has a Soul.*

States – well before the Roosevelt administration mobilized against Hitler and Mussolini.[53] As mentioned in Chapter 3, some within the Popular Front even made the case that a more indigenous brand of fascism was already rooted in America and need not migrate from Europe.

With the onset of the Cold War though, anti-communist liberals sided with conservatives to shift Washington's focus from anti-fascism to anti-communism, which had the effect of splitting the American left.[54] Some became Cold War liberals worried foremost about "totalitarianism."[55] Others, including progenitors of critical theory who were normally pre-occupied with exposing rather than exercising power,[56] treated resistance against right-wing extremism and fascism as a categorical imperative.[57] Still other leftists, meanwhile, became preoccupied with what they considered imperialism in a liberal disguise.

From the late nineteenth century through World War I – a period when the United States was acquiring its own empire – America's anti-imperialist movement was at its height. William Appleman Williams later popularized the critical interpretation that had underwritten an earlier generation of anti-imperialists – that American foreign policy had long been and remains deeply imperialistic not only because of the formal colonies it held but because it came to control much of the western United States itself through settler colonialism.[58] Socialists had always viewed capitalist foreign policies in imperial terms, but by the 1960s, non-socialists aligned with the New Left also routinely employed *empire* or *liberal authoritarian* as terms of abuse critiquing US foreign policy.[59]

---

[53] See, for example, John Diggins, "The Italo-American Anti-Fascist Opposition," *Journal of American History* Vol. 54, no. 3 (1967), pp. 579–98; Rick Baldoz, *The Third Asiatic Invasion: Empire and Migration in Filipino America, 1898–1946* (New York: NYU Press, 2011), pp. 194–236; Daniel Geary, "Carey McWilliams and Antifascism, 1934–1943," *Journal of American History* Vol. 90, no. 3 (2003), pp. 912–34.

[54] In addition to the previous chapter, see Christopher Lasch, *The Agony of the American Left* (New York: Knopf, 1969), pp. 61–114.

[55] Kevin Mattson, "Virtues of Cold War Liberalism: A Response to Michael Brenes and Daniel Steinmetz-Jenkins," *Dissent Magazine* (March 29, 2021), www.dissentmagazine .org/online_articles/virtues-of-cold-war-liberalism.

[56] For example, Theodor Adorno, *Negative Dialectics* (Abingdon: Routledge, 2003), p. 365.

[57] As late as 1967 Adorno warned about the fascist tendencies of the then-modern far right. See Theodor Adorno, *Aspects of the New Right-Wing Extremism* (Cambridge, UK: Polity Press, 2020).

[58] William Appleman Williams, *Tragedy of American Diplomacy* (New York: W.W. Norton & Co., 1959); William Appleman Williams, *The Contours of American History* (New York: Verso, 2011).

[59] See especially Raskin, *Being and Doing*, pp. xvi, 177–86.

This nested well with the black radical view of America as already colonizing African-American communities.[60]

While the America-as-liberal-authoritarian-empire narrative survives today and, in some ways, has become more salient than it was at the end of the Cold War,[61] its applicability to twenty-first-century America is highly contested. Many leftists either identify as explicitly anti-imperialist or freely describe American foreign policy in imperial terms (often both). So doing signifies that the greater threat they see is not the character of foreign actors and foreign behavior but rather the character of the United States and what it does – an anti-authoritarianism that looks inward.

But some leftists have argued that, while the Cold War *was* a competition of US and Soviet imperialisms, the post–Cold War neoliberal order per se *is not* imperialist, however unfair it may be on its own terms.[62] Still others align with interventions by Daniel Nexon – a scholar of imperial orders who also happened to have served as an informal adviser to Bernie Sanders's 2016 presidential campaign. Nexon clarified that contemporary US foreign relations has imperial attributes but only sporadically, like Guam or the post-war administration of Iraq. What self-identified anti-imperialists decry as imperialism today tends to actually be US liberal hegemony – that is, American domination tends to be mediated by a degree of consent, consensus, and multilateral institutionalism.[63] It is easy to see though how an anti-authoritarianism that only looks outward, beyond borders, could become imperialistic when shorn of anti-militarism or a principle like solidarity. For instance, neoconservatism, a hawkish variation of liberal internationalism, is more prone to an

---

[60] Mickey, *Paths Out of Dixie*, pp. 33–63; Angela Davis, ed., *If They Come in the Morning ... Voices of Resistance* (New York: Verso, 2016).

[61] For thoughtful depictions of the empire narrative during the unipolar era, see especially Perry Anderson, *American Foreign Policy and Its Thinkers* (New York: Verso, 2015). For a contemporary account of American empire past and present, see Daniel Immerwahr, *How to Hide an Empire: A History of the Greater United States* (New York: Farrar, Straus, Giroux, 2019).

[62] Rohini Hensman, *Indefensible: Democracy, Counter-Revolution, and the Rhetoric of Anti-Imperialism* (Chicago, IL: Haymarket Books, 2018), pp. 39–41. See also Panitch and Gindin, *The Making of Global Capitalism*.

[63] Daniel Nexon, "Toward a Neo-Progressive Foreign Policy," *Foreign Affairs* (September 4, 2018), www.foreignaffairs.com/articles/united-states/2018-09-04/toward-neo-progressive-foreign-policy; Daniel Nexon and Thomas Wright, "What's at Stake in the American Empire Debate," *American Political Science Review* Vol. 101, no. 2 (2007), pp. 253–71. Some Marxian analysis has also adopted this view. See Panitch and Gindin, *The Making of Global Capitalism*.

imperial impulse than other permutations of liberalism.[64] It follows that the degree to which US foreign policy dominates and oppresses depends on who is conducting it at any given time.

These differences of emphasis within a shared commitment to anti-authoritarianism matter a great deal in today's left. For some, it manifests as prioritizing opposition to American liberal hegemony rather than Russian, Chinese, or Turkish revanchist authoritarianism. The magnitude of threat posed by foreign "imperialism" does not hold a candle to that of the United States – "few dictators match [American] imperialists in humanitarian garb for downright viciousness."[65] This is also why some leftists were reluctant to recognize Donald Trump as fascist or anything remotely comparable. It was sometimes argued that fascism must be understood as a political form more or less unique to a specific moment in history (the 1930s).[66]

But during the Trump years, the more prevalent perspective on the left was a cynical one, that "the force involved in calling something fascist is heavily about the kinds of oppositional politics that can then be demanded ... Popular Frontism ... the emergence of the alarm of fascism is usually a call to assemble as broad a resistance as possible."[67] In this view, recognizing fascism either at home or abroad amounts to a calculated move by liberals to defer progressive political projects in favor of a unified loyalty by invoking an immediate threat.[68]

By contrast, some of the progressive movement's leading voices – including Sanders and Warren, as well as their surrogates – show greater concern about the threat to democracy posed by both the global far right and statist autocrats abroad. Opposing authoritarianism globally is necessary

---

[64] Hensman, *Indefensible*, pp. 40–45; Daniel Nexon and Paul Musgrave, "American Liberalism and Imperial Temptation," in *Empire and International Order*, edited by Noel Parker (London: Ashgate, 2013), pp. 131–48.

[65] Richard Seymour, *American Insurgents: A Brief History of American Anti-Imperialism* (Chicago, IL: Haymarket Books, 2012), p. xxiv.

[66] Jennifer Szalai, "The Debate over the Word 'Fascism' Takes a New Turn," *New York Times* (June 10, 2020), www.nytimes.com/2020/06/10/books/fascism-debate-donald-trump.html; Udi Greenberg, "What Was the Fascism Debate?" *Dissent* (Summer 2021), www.dissentmagazine.org/article/what-was-the-fascism-debate.

[67] Nikhil Pal Singh and Richard Seymour, "Twenty-First Century Fascism in the US," *Haymarket Books Podcast* (June 24, 2021), www.youtube.com/watch?v=QsZ4nxytAUQ.

[68] The irony, of course, is that not only did the Popular Front make greater economic demands than the New Deal delivered, but it was also the engine behind both the later civil rights and feminist movements in the United States. The Popular Front was the first American progressive movement as such to take political and economic equality seriously.

because "unless we support democracy in other countries, we will face the right-wing backlash in our own."[69] That Russia invaded Ukraine in 2014 is not a trivial problem, but the greater threat is that "the Kremlin has inserted itself into a number of transnational right-wing networks, and marketed itself as a cultural beacon for illiberal parties and movements."[70] As I discuss at greater depth in Chapter 5, Russia is actively nurturing a global far right – the "nationalist international" about which Bernie Sanders and others warned.[71] China, meanwhile, is not only hostile to democracy at an ideological level,[72] but also in practice with its genocide in Xinjiang, large-scale domestic repression, the re-colonization of Hong Kong, and unilateral military occupation and claim to 90 percent of the South China Sea – all of which Sanders and Warren have criticized and promised to combat, along with most congressional democrats.[73]

## SOLIDARITY

The principle of solidarity, that is, empathic collective action across borders and categories, has always been vital to the progressive tradition. The politics of the early Progressive Era were built on cross-class solidarity. The politics of the Popular Front made cross-class, cross-race, and cross-ideological solidarity a goal and a strategy. And the same could be said of the eclecticism of the New Left as a movement of movements stressing racial and gender unity far more (and more successfully) than previous generations of leftists. Looking back, progressivism itself seemed to be at its most vibrant and broad based in moments when leftists of a wide range of ideological priors were willing to blur boundaries among them in favor of a common cause.

Solidarity has thus been the watchword of progressive thought from its inception. American socialist Eugene Debs made the ultimate statement

---

[69] Hensman, *Indefensible*, p. 290.

[70] Cooley and Nexon, *Exit from Hegemony*, p. 139.

[71] Bernie Sanders, "A New Authoritarian Axis Demands an International Progressive Front" *The Guardian* (September 13, 2018), www.theguardian.com/commentisfree/ng-interactive/2018/sep/13/bernie-sanders-international-progressive-front.

[72] "Communique on the Current State of the Ideological Sphere," A Notice from the Central Committee of the Communist Party of China's General Office (April 22, 2013), www.chinafile.com/document-9-chinafile-translation.

[73] Elizabeth Warren, "It's Time for the United States to Stand Up to China in Hong Kong," *Foreign Policy* (October 3, 2019), https://foreignpolicy.com/2019/10/03/it-is-time-for-the-united-states-to-stand-up-to-china-in-hong-kong/; "Bernie Sanders: Candidates Answer CFR's Questions," *CFR Blog* (July 30, 2019), www.cfr.org/article/bernie-sanders.

of solidarity at his sentencing hearing for illegally protesting US involvement in World War I in 1918: "... while there is a lower class, I am in it, and while there is a criminal element, I am of it, and while there is a soul in prison, I am not free."[74] The civil rights movement and the black radical tradition also both sought solidarities across identity categories. As Martin Luther King, Jr. extolled, "Injustice anywhere is a threat to justice everywhere."[75] Similarly, Fred Hampton, a leader of the Black Panther Party (BPP), said "We say you don't fight racism with racism – we fight racism with solidarity."[76] The BPP subsequently not only formed a Rainbow Coalition with minority groups like the United Farm Workers,[77] they also forged ties to Third-World revolutionaries in Africa, China, and even North Korea.[78] In the context of labor unions, solidarity once meant transnational coordinated action – a response to "the diagnosis that capital's ability to relocate across borders had pitted countries against each other."[79] Cosmopolitanism too, which identifies with an ideal of political (but not necessarily economic) equality that transcends the nation, espouses a kind of international solidarity in its concept that there can be "global citizens" that transcend national identity.[80]

Today, this same rationale exists in transnational galvanization linking Black Lives Matter to Palestinian justice, and climate activism to the Hong Kong pro-democracy movement.[81] As scholar-activist Angela

---

[74] As quoted in Ron Grossman, "Long Before Bernie Sanders, There Was Eugene Debs," *Chicago Tribune* (January 27, 2016), www.chicagotribune.com/opinion/commentary/ct-eugene-debs-socialist-bernie-sanders-per-flashback-0131-20160127-column.html.

[75] Martin Luther King, Jr., "Letter From a Birmingham Jail" (April 16, 1963), www.africa.upenn.edu/Articles_Gen/Letter_Birmingham.html.

[76] Fred Hampton, "Power Anywhere Where There's People!" Speech delivered at Olivet Church, Illinois (1969), www.marxists.org/archive/hampton/1969/misc/power-anywhere-where-theres-people.htm.

[77] Lauren Araiza, *To March for Others: The Black Freedom Struggle and the United Farm Workers* (Philadelphia, PA: University of Pennsylvania Press, 2013).

[78] Joshua Bloom and Waldo Martin, Jr., *Black against Empire: The History and Politics of the Black Panther Party* (Berkeley, CA: University of California Press, 2013); Sean Malloy, *Out of Oakland: Black Panther Party Internationalism during the Cold War* (Ithaca, NY: Cornell University Press, 2017).

[79] Caleb Weaver, "Policy from the People, Part 2," *Fellow Travelers Blog* (November 12, 2018), https://fellowtravelersblog.com/2018/11/12/policy-from-the-people-part-2/. See also Daniel Rodgers, *Atlantic Crossings: Social Politics in a Progressive Age* (Cambridge, MA: Harvard University Press, 2000).

[80] Martha Nussbaum, "Kant and Stoic Cosmopolitanism," *Journal of Political Philosophy* Vol. 5, no. 1 (1997), pp. 1–25; Kwame Anthony Appiah, *Cosmopolitanism: Ethics in a World of Strangers* (New York: W.W. Norton & Co., 2007).

[81] Angela Davis, *Freedom is a Constant Struggle: Ferguson, Palestine, and the Foundations of a Movement* (Chicago, IL: Haymarket Books, 2016); Joshua Wong, "Hong Kong's International Front Line," *Journal of International Affairs* Vol. 73, no. 2 (2020), p. 264.

Davis has argued, the failure to see and act as if such disparate issues are indeed closely linked is a failure of solidarity.[82] Solidarity with oppressed peoples everywhere is "Our deepest commitment" on the left.[83] Noam Chomsky declared that "… international solidarity, particularly in a globalized world where many face similar threats to decent existence," is the only way to address the twin existential threats of climate change and nuclear weapons.[84] Bernie Sanders urged for human solidarity to be the core principle of "a genuinely progressive global order."[85] Jason Hickel similarly asked, "what is the point of a progressive politics in the North that is not aligned with the struggle for decolonization in the South … solidarity with the South requires degrowth in the North."[86] Progressive International, a leftist foreign policy network launched in 2018 in partnership with the Sanders Institute, identifies solidarism as core to its vision of normative international relations. And Kate Kizer, a leading anti-war activist, wrote that solidarity imposes the duty to bridge and broker "U.S. grassroots movements and others around the world … to achieve mutual goals of dignity, liberation, and self-determination."[87]

Solidarism, in other words, is an end and means of progressive politics that precludes devil's bargains, especially ones that would render other peoples as objects. It is the binding logic of "chain-of-equivalence" strategies that predominate in left activist circles.[88] And it differentiates the committed anti-imperialist from the pathology of "campism," a perspective that "so fixates on the role of imperialism and places so much emphasis on its 'anti-imperialist camp' that it ends up taking a very forgiving view of oppressive regimes."[89]

[82] Davis, *Freedom Is a Constant Struggle*, pp. 129–45.

[83] Michael Walzer, *A Foreign Policy for the Left* (New Haven, CT: Yale University Press, 2018), p. 8.

[84] Noam Chomsky, *Internationalism or Extinction* (Abingdon: Routledge, 2020), pp. 42, 80.

[85] Sanders, "A New Authoritarian Axis Demands an International Progressive Front."

[86] Hickel, "The Anti-Colonial Politics of Degrowth."

[87] Kate Kizer, *A U.S. Grand Strategy for a Values-Driven Foreign Policy* (Washington, DC: Center for a New American Security, 2019), pp. 41–42.

[88] I mention this in the introductory chapter for this book, but chains of equivalence are simultaneously a belief in the indivisibility of justice under conditions of shared hegemonic subordination and a strategy for building mass movements via coalitions. See Laclau and Mouffe, *Hegemony and Socialist Strategy*, pp. 113–131.

[89] John Clarke, "The US Left, China, Internationalism & Campism: When Your Enemy's Enemy Is Not a Friend," *Global Dialogue* (March 3, 2021), https://globaldialogue .online/ally-en/2021/the-us-left-china-internationalism-campism-when-your-enemys-enemy-is-not-a-friend/.

As with other principles, disagreement among progressives is not about whether solidarity matters but rather how to operationalize it. Socialists and many who identify as anti-imperialists believe the solidarity that matters most bonds class, not governments or nations.[90] But a more conventional anti-authoritarianism sees alliance bonds between democratic governments facing foreign aggression as the vital test of solidarity. Alternatively, still others insist that intra-elite policy bargains made at the expense of civil societies are not just morally wrong, but strategically counterproductive – "resulting in anti-American sentiment and the loss of U.S. credibility on human rights" in addition to "harmed local reform efforts."[91] This interpretation of solidarism, in other words, suggests a grand strategy cannot claim to be progressive if it achieves security for itself "by way of directing precarity at others" regardless of the class or regime to which the others belong.[92] In essence, all progressives claim to be global solidarists with an at least thinly cosmopolitan outlook, but that conviction can be directed narrowly at democratic governments, selectively at the working class, or universally at human beings.

### GETTING SORTED

Three things should be evident by now. First, principles of economic equality, anti-authoritarianism, and solidarity are central to the progressive project today and connect to leftist demands and beliefs that reach back as far as the nineteenth century. These principles are values, and in that sense, it would not be wrong to say that a progressive foreign policy is a values-based foreign policy. But the sub-text of that characterization is wrong because progressive principles are values founded in structural analysis, embedded in lived experience and observation of the real world (i.e., not an alternative to reality but a response to reality). They also do not preclude acknowledging the world as it is but rather condition how we ought to make sense of and respond to the world as we find it. And to the extent that they make recurring appearances in contemporary left discourses *and* nobody who identifies with progressive politics would repudiate any of these principles, we can infer that they approximate a consensus.

---

[90] DSA's call for US withdrawal from NATO invoked solidarity with the Ukrainian and Russian working class as the reason. See "On Russia's Invasion of Ukraine."
[91] Kizer, *A U.S. Grand Strategy for a Values-Driven Foreign Policy*, pp. 41–42.
[92] Olufemi Taiwo, "Who Gets to Feel Secure?" *Aeon* (October 30, 2020), https://aeon.co/essays/on-liberty-security-and-our-system-of-racial-capitalism.

Second, however, progressives do not embrace these principles based on the same analysis or understanding. Authoritarianism abroad, for example, must be compared with not just authoritarian practices at home, but America's illiberal conduct abroad – *whose* authoritarianism deserves priority redress is a major cleavage within the progressive movement. Similarly, the reasons for remedying economic inequality could range from forestalling the rise of fascism to making capitalism more sustainable (by rebalancing the power of labor in relation to capital) to ending capitalism altogether. It follows that the preferred method for reducing inequality may differ depending on the reason for reducing it. For example, the classical Marxist view that ending imperialism, born of capitalism, was the only way to realize peace contrasts with the American New Left, which saw peace as the means of unlocking a truly progressive politics grounded in participatory democracy and economic equality.[93] Both were trying to reach a place of economic egalitarianism, but thought about the causal process in opposing ways. And these orientations differ still from those who see anti-monopolism and anti-corruption as priority methods for unlocking a more just and stable world.

Finally, it is unrealistic to value each principle with equal weight, even if a chain-of-equivalence strategy tells us we should treat them as equal. If a democratic ally of the US government gets militarily invaded, an appeal to solidarity, and perhaps moral responsibility, may imply US military support. But that same scenario may not arouse a committed anti-militarist who finds no peace in violence, or a leftist who comes to the question not via Deweyan pragmatism but rather Marxian anti-imperialism. Similarly, anti-authoritarianism sometimes clashes with the search for economic equality. Fighting kleptocracy requires America exploiting its power within the global political economy whereas an inward looking anti-authoritarian commitment requires bridling or diluting American power in all its forms.

It is these observations that make Chapters 5–7 essential. Leftists can interpret and sort progressive principles in more than one way. In practice they do. And in so doing, competing agendas, priorities, and disagreements within the left arise, as Table 4.1 draws out.

What follows are individual chapters dedicated to unpacking three different internally coherent modes of reasoning based on privileging (and understanding) these principles in different ways. They present

---

[93] See especially Petra Goedde, *The Politics of Peace: A Global Cold War History* (New York: Oxford University Press, 2019), pp. 39–66.

TABLE 4.1 *The diverging agendas of progressive grand strategies*

| | Progressive pragmatism | Anti-hegemonism | Peacemaking |
|---|---|---|---|
| Sources of security | -Reducing inequality/precarity<br>-Supporting democracies | -Reducing military presence and operations<br>-Accommodating adversaries | -Disarming gradually<br>-Building inclusive societies |
| Most compatible defense strategy | -Forward balancing | -Offshore balancing<br>-Garrison defense | |
| Use of force | -Multilateral defense of democratic allies | -Direct self-defense | -Constabulary/peacekeeping<br>-Peace enforcement |
| Answer to great power politics | -Democratic power balancing<br>-Multilateralism<br>-Economic rivalry | -Sphere-of-influence diplomacy<br>-Costly reassurance signaling | -Cooperative security<br>-Mutual threat reduction |
| Answer to terrorism | -Reducing economic precarity prevents terrorist radicalization | -Ending War on Terror and US basing reduces terrorist grievances | -Grassroots peacebuilding stabilizes societies |
| Answer to climate change | -Site of rebalancing Global North-South inequity<br>-Means of starving petro-dictators | -Site for great-power cooperation | -Site of local peacebuilding |
| Principal risks | -Eroding economic interdependence<br>-Entanglement<br>-"Nationalist security" tools<br>-Fracturing economic order | -Arms-racing<br>-Spread of illiberalism<br>-Adversary emboldenment | -Vulnerability to predation<br>-Autocratic interference in democracies<br>-"Peacewashing" oppression |

distinct approaches to a grand strategy that would ultimately seek security within a context of greater political and economic democracy. Advancing the former without advancing the latter is, for progressives today, Sisyphean; without improvements in political and economic democracy, security will always prove illusory or fleeting. Progressive pragmatism, anti-hegemonism, and peacemaking can be understood as individual "schools of thought" in the sense that each is a logically consistent, fully formulated way of thinking about the world and how to orient the power of the state in relation to it. Each privileges and interprets the progressive principles from this chapter in different ways, accepting different configurations of assumptions, wagers (a proposed relationship between policy choices and expected outcomes in the world), and risks.

In depicting and analyzing these schools, I draw as much as possible from specific language in left and progressive discourses. The reason for this is not to suggest that the actor whose words and ideas I cite always belongs to this or that school of progressive thought, but rather to show that these ways of thinking are active and real, not just abstract. These ideal-type categories or "schools" are organizing the discourse as it exists, especially since the 2016 presidential election (when the *progressive* signifier came back into vogue). It would lose the plot to say that someone like Alexandria Ocasio-Cortez is a progressive pragmatist or an anti-hegemonist or a peacemaker in all instances when in fact she can toggle among these ways of thinking depending on the issue and context. And while it might be desirable for all progressive principles to be valued equally and interpreted from the same standpoint, progressives tend not to do that. As these next chapters make clear, depending on how you apply progressive principles to the real world, it is not always possible to value them equally at any rate.

# 5

# Progressive Pragmatism as
# a Progressive Grand Strategy

This chapter gives an accounting of *progressive pragmatism*, elements of which are sometimes described interchangeably as *progressive internationalism*. I avoid the latter label because its meaning has been substantially diluted – both liberal internationalist hawks and a transnational post-capitalist movement on the left have occasionally embraced the term while obviously meaning very different things by it.[1] As constructed here, progressive pragmatism builds on what Daniel Nexon called *neo-progressivism*, a foreign policy alternative to both the liberal internationalism discussed in Chapter 2 and the anti-hegemonism discussed in Chapter 6.[2]

The progressive pragmatist approach to worldmaking relies foremost on political economy, prioritizing the principle of economic equality as a preferred means of realizing democracy and peace. As the most self-consciously "anti-fascist" of the three approaches to progressive foreign policy, its diagnosis of insecurity in the world is best understood as a corrective to the faults of liberal internationalism (rather than a total overturning of it), which placed too much emphasis on military power and not enough on the impact of globalization and the way dictators thrived off of the structure of the global economic order.[3] As such, it advocates for sustaining international

---

[1] For liberal internationalist hawk usage, see especially *Progressive Internationalism: A Democratic National Security Strategy* (Washington, DC: Progressive Policy Institute, 2003). The post-capitalist movement calls itself Progressive International, co-founded in 2018 by the Sanders Institute and Yanis Varoufakis.

[2] Nexon, "Toward a Neo-Progressive Foreign Policy."

[3] Ganesh Sitaraman, a former policy adviser to Elizabeth Warren, makes this point explicitly in an interview with *Vox*. See Beauchamp, "What Should a Left Foreign Policy Look Like?" See also Moyn, "Beyond Liberal Internationalism."

commitments to fellow democracies (but not to autocratic regimes) while focusing on system-level changes to the prevailing political-economic order. These wagers aim to inhibit and dilute gratuitous concentrations of wealth in the Global North, reduce structural violence in the Global South, resist (and ideally prevent) military aggression against democracies, and deprive dictators and oligarchs – including in China, Russia, and the United States – of the means to enrich themselves and exploit others. This way of reasoning necessarily takes an adversarial view of both traditional autocratic regimes and the global far right as a movement.

## ASSUMPTIONS

Progressive pragmatism rests on three primary assumptions: (1) extreme concentrations of wealth and political corruption, which tend to coincide, are endemic sources of insecurity; (2) democracy is facing the resurgent threat of neofascism and right-wing authoritarianism as a result of economic dislocation and the shadow of personal insecurity it casts; and (3) American power, whether via international regimes or reforms to its domestic economy, is necessary to remedy both the underlying causes of insecurity and the more proximate symptoms of injustice like military aggression. These assumptions follow from structural analysis; they are not myths pulled from thin air. But I identify them as assumptions (as opposed to proofs or facts or something else) because they are premises that you must accept to make sense of the policy wager-risk propositions of progressive pragmatism.

### Oligarchic and Kleptocratic Authoritarianism

Antidemocratic political formations, which threaten progressive commitments whether they occur within or outside democracies, are blurrily bound up with extreme concentrations of ill-gotten wealth – corruption is both a tactic oligarchs use to preserve their advantages and a strategy of kleptocrats to sustain their regimes.[4] Bernie Sanders's 2020 presidential campaign repeatedly hit the theme that "authoritarianism feeds off of corruption, inequality, and oligarchy."[5] Elizabeth Warren and

---

[4] On corruption as a tactic of oligarchy, see Robert Reich, *The System: Who Rigged It, How We Fix It* (New York: Vintage, 2020), pp. 166–79.

[5] As quoted in Michael Hirsch, "Berned beyond Recognition: How Sanders's Rise Changes U.S. Foreign Policy," *Foreign Policy* (February 3, 2020), https://foreignpolicy.com/2020/02/03/berned-beyond-recognition-how-sanders-rise-changes-u-s-foreign-policy/.

Julian Castro, both of whom ran for president as progressives in 2020, advanced similar stories about how oligarchs and their political nepotists gave rise to and exacerbated the trend of growing authoritarianism and neofascism.[6] Increasingly, progressives have also coalesced around the idea that climate change belongs in this matrix of oligarchy-induced insecurity as a structural pressure that amplifies preexisting distributional conflicts, from political representation to wealth and pandemic vaccine hoarding.[7]

The diagnosis that inequality molests democracy and breeds violent reactionary politics is inherently transnational in scope because "The ability of politicians and oligarchs to hide money offshore … helps entrench undemocratic and kleptocratic regimes."[8] Dictators use access to foreign markets and international financial institutions to launder illegally obtained currency, divert government funding into personal accounts, and fund patronage networks.[9] These practices, made possible by the global financial system, make it harder to dislodge authoritarianism wherever it takes hold. Not only do corrupt politicians – often legally – weaken democratic governance, and ultimately secure regime loyalty, they also make autocrats less vulnerable to international sanctions.[10] As a matter of course, such practices also commit structural violence against civil society, making the corruption-inequality nexus a

---

[6] Elizabeth Warren, "A Foreign Policy for All," *Foreign Affairs* (January/February 2019), www.foreignaffairs.com/articles/2018-11-29/foreign-policy-all; Julian Castro, "The Future of American Leadership," Remarks delivered at Stanford University (December 5, 2019), https://medium.com/castro2020/the-future-of-american-leadership-3abd32aeco5a.

[7] See, for example, Christian Parenti, *Tropic of Chaos: Climate Change and the New Geography of Violence* (New York: Bold Type Books, 2012); Mike Davis, *Late Victorian Holocausts: El Nino, Famines, and the Making of the Third World* (New York: Verso, 2017); Albena Azmanova and James Galbraith, "Disaster Capitalism or the Green New Deal," *Progressive International* (May 15, 2020), https://progressive.international/blueprint/8b29fc89-4ac5-4f16-aa82-848f354383dd-azmanova-galbraith-disaster-capitalism-or-the-green-new-deal/en.

[8] Patrick Iber, "Patrick Iber: Five Principles," *Fellow Travelers Blog* (October 23, 2018), https://fellowtravelersblog.com/2018/10/23/patrick-iber-five-principles/.

[9] Alexander Cooley and John Heathershaw, *Dictators without Borders: Power and Money in Central Asia* (New Haven, CT: Yale University Press, 2017); J.C. Sharman, *The Despot's Guide to Wealth Management: On the International Campaign against Grand Corruption* (Ithaca, NY: Cornell University Press, 2017).

[10] Trevor Sutton and Ben Judah, *Turning the Tide on Dirty Money: Why the World's Democracies Need a Global Kleptocracy Initiative* (Washington, DC: Center for American Progress, 2021), pp. 10–11; Ben Judah and Belinda Li, *Money Laundering for Twenty-First Century Authoritarianism: Western Enablement of Kleptocracy* (Washington, DC: Hudson Institute, 2017).

major risk factor for violent radicalization, political extremism, and civil wars.[11] And as "Kleptocratic networks ... undermine the economic diversity of their countries ... Economic opportunities dry up. Unemployment rises. And the distortions that result can have destabilizing impacts."[12] This was the dynamic that led to the Arab Spring in 2011 which, at root, was a popular revolt against kleptocracy.[13]

The threat posed by the Communist Party of China manifests this problematique in a unique way. The cycle of elite capital accumulation, deepening political corruption, and worker precaritization fueling varieties of authoritarianism is a general story of neoliberal globalization, but in China is entwined with a larger project of displacing American influence and consolidating asymmetric bilateral relationships in a manner that undermines democracy.[14] The owner-managerial class in China, rather than paying its workers enough so that domestic demand can satisfy its manufacturing output, captures the surplus value of Chinese labor and offshores it, sometimes in foreign real estate or financial instruments like US debt, but increasingly in the cultivation of foreign markets in developing nations. In this light, the ambitious Belt and Road Initiative (BRI) is a problem not because it stands as proof that China seeks to create an illiberal global hegemonic order but because it promotes illiberalism, corruption, and structural violence all the same as a byproduct of its economic policies. Smaller BRI member countries are a dumping ground for "excess Chinese capacity, especially in its construction sector."[15] The way BRI allocates capital – via state-backed firms

---

[11] Mary Caprioli, "Primed for Violence: The Role of Gender Inequality in Predicting Internal Conflict," *International Studies Quarterly* Vol. 49, no. 2 (2005), pp. 161–78; James D. Fearon and David D. Laitin, "Ethnicity, Insurgency and Civil War," *American Political Science Review* Vol. 97, no. 1 (2003), pp. 75–90; William J. Linehan, "Political Instability and Economic Inequality: Some Conceptual Clarifications," *Journal of Peace Science* no. 4 (Spring 1980), pp. 134–139; James Piazza, "Rooted in Poverty? Terrorism, Poor Economic Development, and Social Cleavages," *Terrorism and Political Violence* Vol. 18, no. 1 (2006), pp. 159–77.

[12] Sarah Chayes, *Thieves of State: Why Corruption Threatens Global Security* (New York: W.W. Norton, 2015), p. 186.

[13] Chayes, *Thieves of State*, pp. 180–87. See also Yassin Al-Haj Saleh, *The Impossible Revolution: Making Sense of the Syrian Tragedy* (Chicago, IL: Haymarket Books, 2017).

[14] Tobita Chow and Jake Werner, "The US, China, and the Left," *Socialist Forum* (Fall 2021), https://socialistforum.dsausa.org/issues/fall-2021/the-us-china-and-the-left/.

[15] Alexander Cooley and Daniel Nexon, "To Re-Establish U.S. Influence, Biden Should Play Rope-a-Dope, Not Compete Globally," *National Interest* (January 31, 2021), https://nationalinterest.org/blog/buzz/re-establish-us-influence-biden-should-play-rope-dope-not-compete-globally-177380.

with opaque lending criteria and political fealty to the CCP – distorts local economies, helps suppress domestic Chinese wages and precaritizes its workforce, and heightens both political corruption and environmental degradation.[16] And politically, the process of party-friendly oligarchs siphoning away capital that could reduce domestic inequality perpetuates a cycle of insecurity by empowering reactionaries and oligarchs in China, in the United States, and in the fragile governments that absorb China's capital excess.[17] Empowered reactionaries, in turn, draw political vitality from appeals to ethnonationalism and jingoism, which ultimately play out as military competition and transgressive moves like China's de facto colonization of Hong Kong in 2019.[18]

## The Global Far Right

While the inequities of oligarchy and kleptocracy increase elite impunity and risks of civil conflict, they can manifest even worse political formations too: "The far right's metastatic growth represents a grave threat to the prospects of global peace, to the human rights of marginalized groups – and to the very foundations of multiracial democracy itself."[19] Martin Luther King, Jr. characterized the Reconstruction Era as one in which "The Southern aristocracy took the world and gave the poor white man Jim Crow."[20] A racist, reactionary political order, King argued, ensured the survival of extreme wealth hoarding and entrenched privilege. During Reconstruction, oligarchy needed white supremacy. Today, as progressive economist Robert Reich diagnosed, oligarchs need Trumpists in one form or another – "[Trump] stokes divisiveness in ways that keep the bottom 90 percent from seeing how the oligarchy has taken

---

[16] Matthew Klein and Michael Pettis, *Trade Wars Are Class Wars: How Rising Inequality Distorts the Global Economy and Threatens International Peace* (New Haven, CT: Yale University Press, 2020), pp. 124–6; Van Jackson, "New Perspectives on China's Ambitions in the Pacific," *Global Asia* Vol. 16, no. 3 (2021), pp. 114–17; Ho Fung-hung, "Repressing Labor, Empowering China," *Phenomenal World* (July 2, 2021), www.phenomenalworld.org/analysis/repressing-labor-empowering-china/.

[17] Chow and Werner, "The US, China, and the Left."

[18] Ho-fung Hung, *Hong Kong under Chinese Rule* (New York: Cambridge University Press, 2022).

[19] Tobita Chow and Ben Lorber, "Tucker Carlson's Flip-Flops on Russia Mask a Deep Militarism," *The Nation* (March 28, 2022), www.thenation.com/article/politics/carlson-russia-nationalism-far-right/.

[20] "Our God is Marching On!" Speech by Martin Luther King, Jr., Montgomery, Alabama (March 25, 1965), https://kinginstitute.stanford.edu/our-god-marching; Reich, *The System*, p. 180.

over the reins of government, twisted government to its benefit, and siphoned off the economy's benefits."[21]

This American turn toward a far-right populism that works (wittingly or not) on behalf of oligarchic interests intersects with the evolving threat of the global far right or "nationalist international,"[22] which is both a deliberate project of reactionary opportunists and a transnational coalition that shares ideological affinity. By their very existence, oligarchs and kleptocrats create conditions of economic desperation that incubate right-wing extremism – which includes militias, terrorists, and insurgents with racist motivations.[23] But extremist violence is not just a byproduct of durable inequality, it becomes a tool of it. The progressive pragmatist perspective holds that "At the root has been the right wing's capacity to harness people's sense of alienation – the discontents of globalization."[24] In the Trump years and since, reactionary militants and more politically subtle corporate oligarchs have formed an "alliance of extreme right, radical right, populists, and mainstream conservatives" within and across national borders.[25] Well-heeled authoritarians manage this bridging feat by blurring their ideological differences with right-wing extremists and accommodating a narrative that is both anti-globalization and racist – "the 'great replacement' ... minorities and immigrants, with help from 'globalists,' are 'stealing' the privileges of the dominant group."[26] Put simply, reactionary cultural and identity narratives bridge differentiated coalitions that makeup the global far right.[27] Oligarchs and kleptocrats have thrived within an economic order that encourages loose capital controls, austerity

---

[21] Reich, *The System*, pp. 180–81.

[22] Bernie Sanders and Yanis Varoufakis have used this term repeatedly, but so have other progressive movements and organizations.

[23] This is not to say that white supremacy is economically motivated, but rather that race and class as categorical inequalities reify and exacerbate each other regardless of which basis of differentiation is at the root of the problem.

[24] Fiona Dove as quoted in Feffer, *Right across the World*, p. 23.

[25] John Feffer, *Right across the World: The Global Networking of the Far-Right and the Left Response* (London: Pluto Press, 2021), p. 13.

[26] Feffer, *Right across the World*, pp. 12–13. On the narrative tactic of ideological blurring, see Cynthia Miller-Idriss and Brian Hughes, "Blurry Ideologies and Strange Coalitions: The Evolving Landscape of Domestic Extremism," *Lawfare* (December 19, 2021), www.lawfareblog.com/blurry-ideologies-and-strange-coalitions-evolving-landscape-domestic-extremism?fbclid=IwAR2shrPS5DPHmZd7j31h8qTC22zMZbpnFI5lJFkvMiscprFtyy9UFq2pkFM.

[27] Kathryn Joyce, "The New Right's Grim, Increasingly Popular Fantasies of an Internationalist Nationalism," *The New Republic* (January 7, 2022), https://newrepublic.com/article/164441/conservative-inspiration-orban-hungary-poland?utm_source=newsletter&utm_medium=email&utm_campaign=tnr_daily.

politics, and deregulation. The conditions this order has wrought – wage suppression, financial crises, and precaritized economic life for workers – embolden the radical right and prime globalization's victims to seek alternatives, which include demagogic strongman politics that indulge racist scapegoating and forge ties to far-right movements in other countries.

The irony of neofascism, then, is that the discontented who react against the inequities of oligarchic order become allies (or handmaidens) of the oligarchic interests that produced that loathed order in the first place; ideologies of hate mute class conflict (from below; class war from above proceeds) and preserve societal imbalances of power.[28] And through mutual identification with a global far right, local right-wing projects in individual countries can access the promise of symbolic (legitimating, normalizing) resources and material ones (tactical best practices for disinformation, weapons, and financing).

### American Power as a Solution

The other assumption on which progressive pragmatism relies is the necessity of American power, albeit militarily circumscribed. Nexon's manifesto for neo-progressivism rested on a premise that, "The United States, especially in concert with Europe and Japan, still has the financial and economic power to address the globalization of oligarchy and kleptocracy."[29] The United States has an ability unique among national governments to change how the global economy works. US defense commitments to democratic allies give it a basis for coordinated action against autocrats and the inequalities that leaven their bread. The role of the US dollar as the global reserve currency gives the United States the incomparable power to punish others through sanctions, blacklists, asset freezes, and financial surveillance.[30]

---

[28] See especially Arlie Hochschild, *Strangers in Their Own Land: Anger and Mourning on the American Right* (New York: New Press, 2016). But also Reich, *The System*; Feffer, *Right across the World*; Cynthia Miller-Idriss, *Hate in the Homeland: The New Global Far Right* (Princeton, NJ: Princeton University Press, 2020); Walden Bello, *Counter Revolution: The Global Rise of the Far Right* (Manitoba: Fernwood Publishing, 2019).

[29] Nexon, "Toward a Neo-Progressive Foreign Policy."

[30] Edoardo Saravelle, "The Watchful Eye of the U.S. Dollar," *Alchemist Magazine* (May 19, 2021), www.alchemistmag.com/past-editions/the-watchful-eye-of-the-us-dollar; Joshua Zoffer, "The Dollar and the United States' Exorbitant Power to Sanction," *American Journal of International Law* Vol. 113 (2019), pp. 152–56; Henry Farrell and Abraham Newman, "Weaponized Interdependence: How Global Economic Networks Shape State Coercion," *International Security* Vol. 44, no. 1 (2019), pp. 42–79.

Most global economic transactions are denominated in US dollars and rely on intermediary institutions (third-party correspondent banks) based disproportionately in New York – an artifact of the liberal economic order that makes it possible for the United States to monitor economic flows and intervene as desired to disrupt them.[31] With the 2008 global financial crisis, the Federal Reserve Bank (Fed) also made US dollars available to foreign entities that needed them, providing liquidity necessary to keep the global banking system from collapsing. Since then, the Fed has normalized coordination with other central banks around the world, making its ability to direct fiscal interventions a potential source of leverage. And the size of the American consumer market for finished goods combined with America's disproportionate voting share within international financial institutions (IFIs) gives it, in principle, the ability to shape the rules of global finance and trade. All of these advantages put the United States in a better position to tackle global inequality and its symptoms (war, societal conflict, and authoritarianism) than any other individual government, and progressives who evince a pragmatist logic advocate for precisely that.[32]

## ANALYTICAL WAGERS

Elizabeth Warren's policy director during the 2020 presidential campaign, Jon Donenberg, once explained that most of Warren's progressive plans were part of a singular bet: "we're only trying to solve one problem .... It's the corrupt government and economy that only benefits those at the top. Every solution flows from that."[33] Similarly, the two broad wagers for how progressive pragmatism proposes to realize

---

[31] The "pipes" of international banking that empower the United States go well beyond correspondent banks. For a cataloging, see Pierre Hughes-Verdier, *Global Banks on Trial: U.S. Prosecutions and the Remaking of International Finance* (New York: Oxford University Press, 2020).

[32] The progressive case for American economic power is most explicit in Joshua Zoffer, "To End Forever War, Keep the Dollar Globally Dominant," *The New Republic* (February 4, 2020), https://newrepublic.com/article/156417/end-forever-war-keep-dollar-globally-dominant. Alex Cooley and Dan Nexon also speculate that the inequities of the existing order will worsen if Washington "does not use its economic power to tackle corruption and money laundering." Alexander Cooley and Daniel Nexon, *Exit from Hegemony: The Unraveling of the American Global Order* (New York: Oxford University Press, 2019), p. 196.

[33] As quoted in Paul Blumenthal and Kevin Robillard, "This Was Elizabeth Warren's Plan All Along" *HuffPost* (July 17, 2019), www.huffpost.com/entry/elizabeth-warren-has-a-plan-for-that_n_5d279e9ee4b0060b11e9a22e.

security are (1) sustaining alliance commitments to democratic allies only (which backs into an embrace of balance-of-power reasoning) and (2) reforming the global economic order to make it more egalitarian and less corrupt. Every progressive pragmatist solution flows from those bids, which present the global far right and autocratic regimes resting on oligarchic, kleptocratic, or ethnonationalist foundations as priority threats.

### Democratic Power Balancing

Progressive pragmatism's power-balancing wager, which entails confronting dictators who wield their influence in ways that impose violence or propagate despotism, has political-economic and military dimensions. Virtually all progressives critiquing liberal internationalism challenge the merits of American military primacy, which can be translated narrowly as enough raw power to overmatch all plausible adversaries in war.[34] As an aim that justifies arms racing and fails to put upper limits on America's peacetime military buildup, military superiority of this sort is utterly at odds with a commitment to anti-militarism.

But "If not military primacy, then what" can only be answered with reference to some kind of concept that puts the means of militarized violence in service of societal ends, not just military objectives. The answer that the logic of progressive pragmatism furnishes is to preserve regional balances of power (i.e., balancing as equilibrium, not favorable imbalances of power) in a manner that reduces both defense spending and the role of the military in foreign policy, but only amends (rather than eliminates) US security commitments.[35] The imperative to oppose authoritarianism and extreme inequality does not justify simply building a war machine made for unilaterally overmatching other great powers' militaries in large-scale conventional conflicts – because buildups at such a level come at the expense of a democratic society and encourage adversaries to mirror image us. It does, however, presuppose global engagement and

---

[34] Jackson, "American Military Superiority and the Pacific Primacy Myth."

[35] See, for instance, Jackson, "Wagering on a Progressive versus Liberal Theory of National Security"; Adam Mount, "Principles for a Progressive Defense Policy," *Texas National Security Review* (December 2018), https://tnsr.org/roundtable/policy-roundtable-the-future-of-progressive-foreign-policy/#essay3; Robert Farley, "What if a Progressive President Cut U.S. Defense Spending Dramatically," *The National Interest* (November 29, 2019), https://nationalinterest.org/blog/buzz/what-if-progressive-president-cut-us-defense-spending-dramatically-99937.

fidelity to democratic institutions and regimes abroad. While the balance of international engagement ought to be via non-military means (like those in the next section), outright military retrenchment does more harm than good. Not only would shedding the bulk of US security and political commitments abroad reduce the means by which the United States could influence international politics, it would also leave a political vacuum that autocrats could fill.[36] And to the extent that America's security commitments to democratic allies had been deterring authoritarian predations against them, withdrawing those commitments will make them more vulnerable.

This all describes perfectly Bernie Sanders's stance on defense policy during the 2020 president campaign. Sanders declared support for North Atlantic Treaty Organization (NATO) and select East Asian allies while also calling for substantial military withdrawal from the Middle East and an end to the Global War on Terror.[37] He signaled a willingness to cutoff support for Saudi Arabia while decrying Trump's abrupt withdrawal of US forces that were effectively protecting the Kurdish (social democratic) territory of Rohava from Turkish military incursions. And he voiced support for measures to deter a Chinese invasion of Taiwan despite calls for reducing the size of the military.[38] Putting anti-authoritarianism into practice, these tailored commitments accord with the political character of the international counterpart – undemocratic entities meet presumptive skepticism or opposition while democratic actors elicit presumptive solidarity.

These positions also implicitly describe a forward-balancing defense strategy in which the United States preserves alliances and forward presence for the purpose of maintaining regional balances of power through *multilateral* coalitions vis-à-vis Russia and China rather than the traditional pursuit of a favorable imbalance that requires *unilateral* military superiority.[39] Elizabeth Warren and Congressman Julian Castro both

---

[36] Jackson, "Wagering on a Progressive versus Liberal Theory of National Security," p. 181.

[37] Uri Friedman, "The Sanders Doctrine," *The Atlantic* (February 11, 2020), www.theatlantic.com/politics/archive/2020/02/bernie-sanders-doctrine-america-military-foreign-policy/606364/.

[38] Annie Grayer, "Sanders Says He'd Meet with Kim Jong Un as President and Would Take Action if China Invaded Taiwan," *CNN.com* (February 23, 2020), www.cnn.com/2020/02/23/politics/bernie-sanders-north-korea-meeting-military-force-china-taiwan/index.html.

[39] Forward balancing, a defense posture of restraint that still seeks a balance of power in Asia and Europe, is summarized in Van Jackson, "Defense Strategy for a Post-Trump World," *War on the Rocks* (January 15, 2020), https://warontherocks.com/2020/01/

endorsed a similar pro-democracy, anti-authoritarian, and militarily multilateralist security agenda during their respective 2020 presidential campaigns.[40] The Center for International Policy (CIP), a left-aligned think tank established in response to the Vietnam War, has additionally produced multiple proposals for this approach to defense through its recurring Sustainable Defense Task Force.[41] The defense budget CIP advocates for endorses the logic of security through forward-balancing and limited military presence in Asia and Europe, but only as part of a more variegated approach to foreign policy (not as a primary feature) that substantially reduces US military capability and capacity.

Because progressive pragmatism prioritizes economic inequality and authoritarianism as the animating causes of insecurity, Russia and China persist as threats to be countered but less because of their military capabilities than their role in worsening global corruption and oligarchy. CIP's defense proposals, for example, are explicit that "The challenge posed by China is primarily political and economic, not military," and that "Russia does not represent a traditional military challenge … it can be more than adequately addressed through increased security and diplomatic cooperation on the part of European nations … with the United States in a limited, supporting role."[42]

Weakening Vladimir Putin's kleptocracy, from the progressive pragmatist perspective, ought to be done in terms commensurate with the problem, which means upholding but not expanding NATO, imposing a "foreign direct product rule" that would limit Russia's access to any technology that relies on US parts or software, undermining the hydrocarbon market on which Russia relies, cracking down on Russian investment via shell companies and tax havens, and "attacking the nodes of the illicit finance network" that enrich Russian oligarchs.[43] In response

---

defense-strategy-for-a-post-trump-world/. For variations on forward balancing, see William Hartung and Ben Freeman, *Sustainable Defense: A Pentagon Spending Plan for 2021 and Beyond* (Washington, DC: Center for International Policy, 2020), https://3ba8a190-62da-4c98-86d2-893079d87083.usrfiles.com/ugd/3ba8a1_84180a1b3cdf478f8023d8ca96cb682a.pdf; Michael Swaine, Jessica Lee, and Rachel Esplin Odell, "Toward an Inclusive and Balanced Regional Order: A New U.S. Strategy in East Asia," *Quincy Paper Number 5* (Washington, DC: Quincy Institute for Responsible Statecraft, 2021), https://quincyinst.org/wp-content/uploads/2021/02/A-New-U.S.-Strategy-in-East-Asia.pdf.

[40] Warren, "A Foreign Policy for All"; Castro, "The Future of American Leadership."

[41] Hartung and Freeman, *Sustainable Defense*.

[42] Ibid.

[43] David Adler and Ben Judah, "Hawks Say Sanders Will Be Weak on Russia. But Putin Should Fear a President Bernie," *The Guardian* (February 20, 2020),

to Russia's 2022 invasion of Ukraine, Sanders adviser Matt Duss argued that the Biden administration's near-term focus on squeezing Putin's oligarchs, sanctioning the Russian economy, and providing military support to Ukraine without engaging in combat operations was the right immediate course, noting, "a responsible progressive position on Ukraine is basically what Biden is doing right now."[44] But a tactical military answer to Putin's invasion is only worthwhile if accompanied by some effort to deliver a cure, not just a treatment of the symptom, which is why the progressive pragmatist wagers toward Russia must involve larger structural changes discussed hereafter.

China's illiberal conduct, similarly, must be met with a combination of human rights-based sanctions, consistent public condemnation, economic decoupling from Chinese firms in security-relevant technology areas, and commitments to defend against outright military aggression (to the extent such commitments prevent war).[45] As Sanders adviser Matt Duss explained in response to what he characterized as a genocide in Xinjiang, the United States should use statecraft to "mobilize international pressure ... use our influence to build consensus ... sanctions on individual human rights abusers ... underlying all of this, we are going to be more effective in making the case for human rights if we are protecting them at home."[46] Elizabeth Warren had made identical commitments, adding that China in particular was emblematic of a trend in which "economic gains legitimize oppression,"[47] suggesting that US policies ought to make China choose between economic growth or human-rights abuses on the presumption that sharpening the choice will push it toward the

---

www.theguardian.com/commentisfree/2020/feb/20/bernie-sanders-russia-putin-kremlin; Ellen Nakashima and Jeanne Whalen, "U.S. Threatens Use of Novel Export Control to Damage Russia's Strategic Industries if Moscow Invades Ukraine," *Washington Post* (January 23, 2022), www.washingtonpost.com/national-security/2022/01/23/russia-ukraine-sanctions-export-controls/?utm_campaign=wp_todays_worldview&utm_medium=email&utm_source=newsletter&wpisrc=nl_todayworld&carta-url=https%3A%2F%2Fs2.washingtonpost.com%2Fcar-ln-tr%2F35d76cd%2F61ee338f9d2fda14d705a14c%2F59 6a389e9bbc0f0e09e85d78%2F27%2F55%2F61ee338f9d2fda14d705a14c.

44  @Mattduss (March 21, 2022), https://twitter.com/mattduss/status/1505597725932343298.

45  There is a view within "establishment Washington" that peace and war prevention in key regions are not the highest priorities – US primacy is. But for progressives, military commitments are difficult to justify unless they are part of a theory of war prevention. On peace as a secondary concern in Washington, see Van Jackson, *Pacific Power Paradox: American Statecraft and the Fate of the Asian Peace* (New Haven, CT: Yale University Press, 2023).

46  Matt Duss as quoted in "The Bernie Sanders Doctrine on Foreign Policy."

47  Ibid.

former. The rationale for confronting China and Russia in these ways extends to other autocratic regimes too, withholding "support for governments that use resources to repress their own citizens."[48] This would lead to targeted sanctions against, and the suspension of military aid for, regimes like Saudi Arabia, Hungary, and the Philippines.[49] These kinds of directly adversarial moves, particularly against Russia and China, impose costs on them that narrow their opportunity space for illiberal conduct (thereby making it less prevalent), dissuade them from outright aggression, and prevent moral hazard effects (i.e., not imposing costs would further empower them).

### Reforming the International Economic Order

But frontally addressing the threat of revisionist and authoritarian regimes through sanctions and alliance commitments is insufficient for securing democracy and reducing risks of war longer term. The greater security comes from using American power to realize structural economic transformation. China, for instance, has undertaken constructing an exclusionary sphere of influence in its geographic periphery not by military conquest but rather via practices of settler colonialism, corruption-intensifying political quid pro quos, and the export of technologies that aid authoritarian control, all of which amounts to a pattern of informal imperialism.[50] For some on the left, the regime governing China is, without qualification, an imperialist power.[51] While sanctions

[48] Timothy Gill, "Towards a Democratic Socialist Foreign Policy," *Current Affairs* (October 22, 2019), www.currentaffairs.org/2019/10/towards-a-democratic-socialist-foreign-policy.

[49] Ibid.

[50] Robert Barnett, "China Is Building Entire Villages in Another Country's Territory," *Foreign Policy* (May 7, 2021), https://foreignpolicy.com/2021/05/07/china-bhutan-border-villages-security-forces/; Darren Byler, *In the Camps: China's High-Tech Penal Colony* (New York: Columbia Global Reports, 2021); Eyck Freymann, *One Belt One Road: Chinese Power Meets the World* (Cambridge, MA: Harvard University East Asia Center, 2020); Van Jackson, "Understanding Spheres of Influence in International Politics," *European Journal of International Security* Vol. 5, no. 3 (2020), pp. 270–73; Matt Schrader, "China Is Weaponizing Globalization," *Foreign Policy* (June 5, 2020), https://foreignpolicy.com/2021/05/07/china-bhutan-border-villages-security-forces/. See also "Godfather of Progressive Foreign Policy Part II: Interview w/ Dr. Daniel Nexon," *The Un-Diplomatic Podcast* (February 4, 2020), https://podcasts.apple.com/us/podcast/godfather-progressive-foreign-policy-part-ii-interview/id1480597540?i=1000464492879.

[51] For a discussion justifying this distinct leftist view, see Travis S., "Building a Mass Movement with No Apologism," *Tempest* (December 24, 2021),

and deterrence might be necessary on occasion to meet the world (and China) as it is, relying entirely on such confrontational tools would only incentivize China to intensify this revisionism, thereby heightening geopolitical rivalry and empowering reactionary forces in societies everywhere. Progressive pragmatism's answer to this aspect of the China challenge instead lay primarily in subsuming the problem set itself into a reformation of the global economic order – fight imperialism by making more equality, not more threats.

A foreign policy project of protecting democracy must at some level also mean protecting "the world from the excesses of capitalism and counteract[ing] the violent implosions that US policies and interventions around the world have all too often oxygenated, if not ignited."[52] American influence must directly intervene to change global distributions of wealth and how the regime of economic globalization functions.

### Monetary Policy

Since monetary policy set by the Federal Reserve in coordination with other central banks has made economic inequality worse for decades,[53] it might also be used to reduce inequality and set more favorable conditions for democracy.[54] The Federal Reserve has a unique form of state power in its ability to manipulate interest rates and conduct QE or "quantitative easing" (i.e., creating money to purchase securities from commercial banks). These tools can make capital cheaper or more expensive, dilute the value of the dollar through inflation, and influence where foreign holders of capital re-invest their riches. The progressive monetary solution encourages central banks to use monetary policy for the common good. This means that interest rates can rise gradually, but only in tandem with targeted price controls, restructuring unpayable public

www.tempestmag.org/2021/12/building-a-mass-movement-with-no-apologism/?utm_source=rss&utm_medium=rss&utm_campaign=building-a-mass-movement-with-no-apologism.

[52] Meaney, "What U.S Foreign Policy Will Look Like under Socialism."

[53] "Diversity and Inclusion in Economics, Finance, and Central Banking," Speech by Isabel Schnabel, Member of the Executive Board of the ECB (November 9, 2021), www.ecb.europa.eu/press/key/date/2021/html/ecb.sp211109_2~cca25b0a68.en.html.

[54] See, for example, Yanis Varoufakis, "A Progressive Monetary Policy Is the Only Alternative," *Project Syndicate* (October 28, 2021), www.project-syndicate.org/commentary/progressive-recipe-for-monetary-policy-tightening-by-yanis-varoufakis-2021-10; "A Socialist Primer on Monetary Policy and Inflation," Daniel Denver interview with Tim Barker, *Jacobin Magazine* (September 19, 2021), www.jacobinmag.com/2021/09/socialist-primer-monetary-policy-inflation-federal-reserve-volcker-shock-class-tim-barker-interview.

debt (discussed below), and repurposing QE so that the paper it produces would not only go to commercial banks but also public investment banks that could finance green energy transitions, subsidize floor wages for certain sectors of the economy, and furnish basic income.[55] Some progressives have even argued that US monetary coordination could be leveraged to empower European Union (EU) members to avoid austerity measures and instead spend more on fiscal stimulus and Europe's Just Transition Fund (which pays for carbon emission reductions).[56] An increase in European productivity from Keynesianism would in turn correct for decades of austerity-induced, artificially low European demand for American goods and services.[57] At a minimum, US monetary policy can encourage other central banks not to punish their own nations' economies for wage growth – effectively a defensive rear-guard consideration to ensure monetary policy and central banks abroad work with rather than against efforts to reduce inequality in their own countries.

### Democratizing International Financial Institutions

Globalization processes and IFIs that support the worst of transnational capital (plutocracy, corruption, and ultimately authoritarianism) constitute an architecture of insecurity that transcends individual actors. Whatever the benefits of the world that liberal internationalism built, "the contemporary liberal order works better for authoritarian regimes than it does for liberal democracies."[58] It thus follows that policy solutions must target deficiencies in global governance broadly understood. Ameliorating a structural threat of this kind requires reforming institutions and practices that liberal internationalism either takes for granted or treats as beneficial.

Put differently, it is not enough to simply do multilateralism; global institutions and rules are necessary for security, but the distribution of benefits and whom they serve matters. Sanders has said that "we have got to help lead the struggle to defend and expand a

---

[55] Varoufakis, "A Progressive Monetary Policy Is the Only Alternative"; Edoardo Saravelle and Ben Judah, "Trans-Atlantic Ties Should Put Finance, Not Security, First," *Foreign Policy* (July 30, 2020), https://foreignpolicy.com/2020/07/30/transatlantic-us-nato-germany-finance-security-biden/.

[56] Saravelle and Judah, "Trans-Atlantic Ties Should Put Finance, Not Security, First."

[57] Klein and Pettis, *Trade Wars Are Class Wars*, pp. 148–73, 228–32.

[58] Alexander Cooley and Daniel Nexon, "The Real Crisis of Global Order," *Foreign Affairs* (January/February 2022), www.foreignaffairs.com/articles/world/2021-12-14/illiberalism-real-crisis-global-order.

rules-based international order in which, law, not might, makes right."[59] Michael Walzer has similarly argued to neither uncritically accept nor destroy IFIs, stating, "We still need global regulation by social-democratic versions of the International Monetary Fund and World Trade Organization."[60] At an institutional level, the power of the World Bank, International Monetary Fund (IMF), and World Trade Organization (WTO) must be democratized. Proposals toward that end include eliminating America's veto rights at the World Bank and the IMF, recalculating the basis of voting rights at the World Bank and IMF to favor Global South economies (e.g., indexing voting share to the size of country populations rather than country financial contribution), prohibiting the imposition of structural adjustment conditions on World Bank and IMF loan recipients, mandating public transparency in WTO trade negotiations and tribunal rulings, requiring labor representation at the WTO as a condition of membership, and creating a general fund to equalize access to technical staff and support so that poorer members are not "out-litigated" by richer ones.[61] Whatever the specific measures though, their collective role is to "begin to dismantle the architecture of upward redistribution that defines the world system."[62] Over time, these changes should help produce more equitable economic outcomes globally and give IFIs greater political legitimacy than they have had in recent decades.

### A Just Economic Order

But reforming formal institutional power, while necessary, is insufficient for remedying the inequities of neoliberal globalization that have fueled reactionary movements and demagogues both directly (in the form of kleptocratic governance within the global economy) and indirectly (in the form of the global far right and oligarchy-neofascist coalitions).

---

[59] Sanders, *Where We Go from Here*, p. 98.

[60] Michael Walzer, *A Foreign Policy for the Left*, p. 48.

[61] For a catalog of various democratic reforms to IFIs, see especially Hickel, *The Divide*, pp. 240–51; "Reform the IMF and World Bank to Re-Build Better from Covid-19," International Trade Union Confederation (undated), www.ituc-csi.org/reform-imf-word-bank-covid-19; *Adding Fuel to the Fire: How IMF Demands for Austerity Will Drive Up Inequality Worldwide* (Oxford: Oxfam, 2021), https://reliefweb.int/sites/reliefweb.int/files/resources/bp-covid-loans-imf-austerity-110821-en.pdf; Crystal Simeoni and Miriam Brett, "Take Back Our Institutions," *Progressive International* (May 16, 2021), https://progressive.international/blueprint/98bf6846-33cd-45ea-ae9f-575d6e0c18dc-take-back-our-institutions/en.

[62] Hickel, *The Divide*, p. 244.

Making the economic order less accommodating to kleptocrats, pluto-crats, and dark money generally requires a multinational regime, which some have described as a "Global Kleptocracy Initiative" focused on the Global North (where most dark money ends up).[63] Under President Biden, the US national security state began mobilizing against corruption, tax evasion, and money laundering as a "priority national security threat." Its approach relied heavily on exercising informal US influence with Europe in particular – which presupposes a US security commitment to the continent – to more stringently enforce a bevy of existing anti-corruption and anti-trust laws, as well as expanding staff for "financial intelligence units" to analyze flows of data.[64] The Biden administration also used its economic clout to pursue a global minimum tax regime, which would satisfy a longstanding progressive demand for corporations to pay taxes in the places where their money is earned, not parked.[65] But these efforts do not, collectively or indi-vidually, deal with the enormous political influence of Big Tech firms and plutocrats. Neither do they stop nepotists working on behalf of dictators and oligarchs from taking money stolen from the public or from workers and laundering it in luxury real estate or US debt instruments. Reforming the global economy according to an anti-corruption logic also requires a role for civil society (proposals for which exist),[66] more rigorous screening of foreign investment, and something like a global minimum wage (not just a global minimum tax). The United States would also need to improve the conditions that would help other nations implement progressive tax poli-cies by, for instance, creating a public registry that ends the practice of both anonymizing the beneficiaries from corporate profits and ending the use of anonymous shell corporations to avoid taxation.[67]

But the most dramatic shift in the global economy would come from an economic statecraft that tries to do right by the Global South by reduc-ing forms of impoverishment and worker precarity there. Progressives with an anti-colonial sensibility have rejected foreign aid and the

[63] Sutton and Judah, *Turning the Tide on Dirty Money*.

[64] *United States Strategy on Countering Corruption* (Washington, DC: The White House, 2021), www.whitehouse.gov/wp-content/uploads/2021/12/United-States-Strategy-on-Countering-Corruption.pdf. For Europe's importance to anti-corruption, see Sutton and Judah, *Turning the Tide on Dirty Money*.

[65] Max Fraser, "Soak the Rich," *New Labor Forum* Vol. 31, no. 1 (2022), pp. 91–93.

[66] Gabe Lezra and Jenna Grande, "Real Anti-Corruption Reform Requires a Role for Civil Society," *Just Security* (December 23, 2021), www.justsecurity.org/79643/real-anti-corruption-reform-requires-a-role-for-civil-society/.

[67] Thomas Piketty, *Time for Socialism: Dispatches from a World on Fire, 2016–2021* (New Haven, CT: Yale University Press, 2021), pp. 305–9.

"international development paradigm" as the method of reducing inequities in the Global South because they have not worked and in many cases have promoted a system that continues to benefit the Global North at the South's expense. A wide range of alternative approaches have instead been proposed to realize these ends. In addition to introducing a global corporate minimum tax and global minimum wage, advocates have argued for encouraging greater capital controls to prevent financial crises, writing off "odious" debt, initiating "green sanctions" and social dumping tariffs, reducing Global-North domestic subsidies in commodities that Global-South economies rely on, negotiating floor wages for textile manufacturers, permitting trade imbalances and keeping the US dollar strong to enable export-oriented growth strategies, incentivizing indigenous wage growth in the Global South, subsidizing green energy production in the South through a Global Green New Deal, coordinating price stability and increases in commodities the South exports, permitting the strategic incubation of "infant industries" as part of a right to development, creating Global-North incentives to invest capital in the South, negotiating trade deals that disincentivize multinational firms from exploiting economies with weak labor protections, making US corporations legally responsible for their global supply chains, and more.[68] Plans for these initiatives already exist at varying levels of detail, and it is the art of economic statecraft to weigh the merits and tradeoffs among them (discussed in Chapter 8) given the political context. And it was adjudicating and implementing such wide-spanning measures that led Elizabeth Warren to propose establishing a Department of Economic Development, because the existing bureaucracy is not positioned to coordinate economic statecraft in this way.[69] What these numerous initiatives have in common though is adapting the architecture of world politics to

---

[68] Most of these proposals are descendants of the "New International Economic Order" during the postcolonial era of the Cold War. See Nils Gilman, "The New International Economic Order: A Reintroduction," *Humanity* (Spring 2015), pp. 1–15. For the modern versions, see Erik Loomis, "A Left Vision for Trade," *Dissent* (2017), www .dissentmagazine.org/article/left-vision-trade-tpp-isds-international-law; Chayes, *Thieves of State*, pp. 184–204; Klein and Pettis, *Trade Wars are Class Wars*, pp. 226–8; Chow, Collins, and Werner, *The Movement We Need*; Ha-Joon Chang, *Kicking Away the Ladder: Development Strategy in Historical Perspective* (London: Anthem Press, 2002), pp. 125–42; Jason Hickel, *The Divide: Global Inequality from Conquest to Free Markets* (New York: W.W. Norton & Co., 2017), pp. 239–59; Nicholas Mulder, "Can 'Climate Sanctions' Save the Planet?" *The Nation* (November 18, 2019), www.thenation.com/ article/archive/climate-green-new-deal/.

[69] Elizabeth Warren, "A Plan for Economic Patriotism," *Team Warren* (June 5, 2019), https://medium.com/@teamwarren/a-plan-for-economic-patriotism-13b879f4cfc7; Henry

serve the interests of greater equality, anti-corruption, and environmental protection. They enhance worker power and well-being in the Global South, which tamps down on radical political pressures and reduces the need for developing nations to secure the dubious bargains from Chinese state-backed firms that would otherwise risk exploiting them and the environment while cohering an illiberal Sino-centric order.

### Green Reparations Fight Petro-Dictators

Finally, progressive pragmatism's political economy approach to security places importance on the climate crisis in two ways. One is that climate action – through, for example, a Global Green New Deal[70] – is a vital way of rebalancing the inequities between the Global North and South. Massive financial outlays for a green energy transition in the Global South would reduce carbon emissions and serve as climate reparations for a history of Northern colonial exploitation.[71] This could include debt restructuring, intellectual property waivers and technology transfers that make it easier to sustain economic growth without fossil fuels, and subsidy offsets for green manufacturing exports (all of which are taken up in Chapter 8). Since the Global South accounts for most carbon emissions, it makes environmental sense to support their shift to an ecologically sustainable economy, and so doing would reduce global inequality.

The second way the climate crisis proves instrumental to the progressive pragmatist wager is as an empowering front in the fight against oligarchy and kleptocracy. Bernie Sanders responded to Putin's 2022 invasion of Ukraine by not simply supporting sanctions that would cutoff Putin's inner circle from the global economy, he also urged the United States to accelerate the fight against climate change because it would "deny authoritarian petrostates the revenues they require to survive."[72] Both volatile and sustained high oil prices make resource-rich autocrats more

Farrell, "Elizabeth Warren Has a Plan for the Nation's Approach to Trade," *Washington Post* (June 4, 2019), www.washingtonpost.com/politics/2019/06/04/elizabeth-warren-has-plan-nations-approach-trade/; Astead Herndon and Patricia Cohen, "Elizabeth Warren Proposes 'Aggressive Intervention' to Create Jobs," *New York Times* (June 4, 2019), www.nytimes.com/2019/06/04/us/politics/elizabeth-warren-economy-jobs.html.

[70] Noam Chomsky and Robert Pollin, with C.J. Polychroniou, *Climate Crisis and the Global Green New Deal: The Political Economy of Saving the Planet* (London: Verso, 2020).

[71] Olufemi Taiwo, *Reconsidering Reparations* (New York: Oxford University Press, 2022), pp. 149–90.

[72] "Sanders Statement on U.S. Response to Russia," *Common Dreams* (February 22, 2022), www.commondreams.org/newswire/2022/02/22/sanders-statement-us-response-russia.

likely to engage in militarized conflict.[73] Not only does capturing wealth from fossil fuels give oil oligarchs the financing for military action, it also emboldens them to do it knowing that resource scarcity limits the kinds of financial punishment they will face, building up foreign exchange reserves to insulate them from sanctions in the meantime.[74] Because an "economy that runs on fossil fuels is at the mercy of authoritarian aggression," fighting climate change *is* fighting petro-dictators.[75]

In sum, the wagers of progressive pragmatism include (1) maintaining regional balances of power via democratic alliance coalitions – not unilaterally – and (2) reforming the international political economic order to make life harder for autocrats and reduce inequality both between the Global North and South and within individual Global North countries. This prioritizes policy measures that reduce military spending but preserve democratic military commitments, handcuff the political influence of autocrats, return maximum amounts of government funds to civil society, and steer flows of capital based on how it affects democratic governance and economic equality at home and abroad with a prejudice toward investing in the Global South. Reforming the global economic order in this implicitly more social democratic direction constrains rather than empowers kleptocrats and oligarchs, including in Russia and China, respectively. It makes offshoring ill-gotten wealth harder. It reduces the dependency of Global South economies on politically corrosive capital from authoritarian economies. And it incentivizes state-backed Chinese firms and those in resource-rich autocratic regimes to reinvest capital domestically, thereby reducing inequality in those countries. And drawing down inequalities within functional oligarchies reduces the need for regime elites to stoke the ethnonationalism that fuels geopolitical competition.[76] All of this, in turn, reduces terrorism in the long run far better than the Global War on Terror (GWOT) since 2001. Addressing precarity and economic dislocation "before these conditions give rise to conflict

[73] Rupert Russell, *Price Wars: How the Commodities Markets Made Our Chaotic World* (New York: Penguin RandomHouse, 2022), pp. 103–29.

[74] Russell, *Price Wars*; Cullin Hendrix, "Oil Prices and Interstate Conflict," *Conflict Management and Peace Science* Vol. 34, no. 6 (2015), pp. 575–96.

[75] "Investing in Clean Energy Is the Key to Energy Independence," *Climate Power Message Guidance* (February 24, 2022), https://docs.google.com/document/d/123naAPF4j_WgtkYiP64TSptR8aEu4QJfPJp4QrCztAg/edit.

[76] Fertik, "Geopolitics for the Left"; Klein and Pettis, *Trade Wars Are Class Wars*; Bernie Sanders, "Washington's Dangerous New Consensus on China," *Foreign Affairs* (June 17, 2021), www.foreignaffairs.com/articles/china/2021-06-17/washingtons-dangerous-new-consensus-china.

can eliminate the need to address them militarily in the future."[77] Making workers more economically secure and enhancing their relative power is the only real safeguard against the political forces of reaction.

RISKS

Four major risks arise from the bets of progressive pragmatism: an erosion of economic interdependence; a courting of the problems of strategic entanglement; the construction of "nationalist security" tools for the American far right; and a Balkanization of the global economic system.

## The Economic-Peace Question

For decades, US liberal internationalism has embraced the reasoning of economic interdependence, particularly in justifying deep economic ties to China.[78] Among its proponents, the "capitalist peace" is a way of accounting for the absence of great-power wars and conflicts between democracies.[79] The mechanisms by which economic interdependence is thought to attenuate conflict pressures include businesses that lobby to avoid war because of the opportunity cost,[80] the role of capital markets as a means of "competition and communication for states that might otherwise be forced to fight,"[81] dense contractual ties across borders that inhibit politician imprudence and suborn decisions to the rule of law,[82] and the restraining effects of domestic institutions that accompany a capitalist economy.[83] Whether economic interdependence is in fact the

[77] Bernie Sanders, "Ending America's Endless War," *Foreign Affairs* (June 24, 2019), www.foreignaffairs.com/articles/2019-06-24/ending-americas-endless-war.

[78] For the role of economic interdependence in strategic relations with China, see especially James Mann, *About Face: A History of America's Curious Relationship with China, from Nixon to Clinton* (New York: Vintage, 2000); Tom Fingar and Fan Jishe, "Ties that Bind: Strategic Stability in the U.S.-China Relationship," *Washington Quarterly* Vol. 36, no. 4 (2013), pp. 125–38.

[79] Erik Gartzke, "The Capitalist Peace," *American Journal of Political Science* Vol. 51, no. 1 (2007), pp. 166–91.

[80] Edward Mansfield and Brian Pollins, "The Study of Interdependence and Conflict: Recent Advances, Open Questions, and Directions for Future Research," *Journal of Conflict Resolution* Vol. 45, no. 6 (2001), pp. 834–59.

[81] Gartzke, "The Capitalist Peace," p. 166.

[82] Michael Mousseau, "Market Prosperity, Democratic Consolidation, and Democratic Peace," *Journal of Conflict Resolution* Vol. 44, no. 4 (2000), pp. 472–507.

[83] Patrick McDonald, *The Invisible Hand of Peace: Capitalism, the War Machine, and International Relations Theory* (Cambridge: Cambridge University Press, 2009).

best explanation for the absence of great power and intra-democracy conflicts is contested,[84] and there can be no certainty about its effects on state behavior given that the economic order has co-varied with US military dominance, the institutionalization of world politics, durable alliances, and other conflict-shaping factors. What is more, the ongoing Sino-US rivalry is a contest happening within capitalism,[85] even because of capitalism,[86] which should induce caution about the supposed virtues of a capitalist peace that the field of international relations once took as gospel. But it is possible to accept a circumscribed version of the capitalist peace that assumes global capital has a dampening effect on interstate conflict in a world free of dirty money and shuttered tax havens. Nevertheless, the point of foregrounding risks is to consider what could logically be, not insist on an objective truth about how the world works. Shaping and shoving trade ties and capital flows in various principled ways accept the risk of international conflicts that might have otherwise been suppressed by capitalist-peace mechanisms.

## Entanglement Dilemmas

A second security risk of a progressive pragmatist approach comes in the form of strategic entanglement. Entanglement is a "process whereby a state is compelled to aid an ally in a costly and unprofitable enterprise because of the alliance."[87] Preserving US commitments to democratic allies means that the United States risks becoming involved in peripheral crises or conflicts that would not otherwise compel participation in the form of US military operations. Because a progressive pragmatist foreign policy would only retain security commitments to democratic allies – circumscribing or conditionalizing commitments to illiberal regimes – its commitments would be presumptively fewer in number than those of a

---

[84] Allan Dafoe and Bruce Russett, "Does Capitalism Account for the Democratic Peace? The Evidence Still Says No," in *Assessing the Capitalist Peace*, edited by Gerald Schneider and Nils Petter Gleditsch (New York: Routledge, 2013), pp. 110–26.

[85] Jackson, *Pacific Power Paradox*, pp. 142–55, 177–83; Jake Werner, "Why Did the US-China Relationship Collapse, and Can It Be Repaired?" *The Nation* (November 21, 2022), www.thenation.com/article/world/china-biden-taiwan-democracy/.

[86] Kanishka Jayasuriya, "The Age of Political Disincorporation: Geo-Capitalist Conflict and the Politics of Authoritarian Statism," *Journal of Contemporary Asia* Vol. 53, no. 1 (2022), pp. 165–78.

[87] Tongfi Kim, "Why Alliances Entangle but Seldom Entrap States," *Security Studies* Vol. 20, no. 3 (2011), p. 355.

default liberal internationalism that has long positioned the United States as the global "security provider of choice" regardless of regime type.[88] Yet this raises several potential problems.

First, limiting alliances and security cooperation to democratic governments may be insufficient to prevent the regional hegemonic or imperial ambitions of revisionist powers. To the extent rising powers like China are also revisionist states, their antidemocratic ambitions may not be capable of being countered unless the United States is willing to partner with undemocratic forces in the world. Progressive pragmatists do not reject the logic of balancing as a basis for stability, yet balance-of-power reasoning does not discriminate by regime type.

The second problem is that progressive pragmatism also rejects military superiority, which in liberal internationalism underwrites alliance commitments. Preserving commitments without the underlying ability to uphold them with unilateral war-winning capabilities may increase upper-end costs the United States suffers in the event a conflict actually ensues in defense of an ally. Having less than the necessary capability to prevail in such a worst-case scenario means more destruction and more lives lost, to say nothing of the survival of the client state.

The third problem is that allies and adversaries may see a less capable US commitment – that is, a US commitment underwritten by a no-longer-dominant US military – and react as if it is incredible. With adversaries emboldened and allies pursuing unilateral alternative recourse to security (such as nuclear weapons or offensive military postures), the United States risks becoming ensnared in circumstances that might have been avoided altogether if only the United States retained greater military power or jettisoned the commitment in the first place.

## Building Nationalist Security Tools for the Far Right

Even though progressive pragmatism would de-center the role of the military and furnish it with far fewer resources than it has enjoyed since World War II, it is nevertheless an approach to foreign policy that requires building up the capacity of the national security state. Eliminating tax havens, cracking down on money laundering, sanctioning individuals

---

[88] This phrase is uniquely linked to the US role in sustaining the "liberal international order." See, for example, Daniel Twining, "The G-7 Must Rescue the Liberal World Order," *Foreign Policy* (May 23, 2016), https://foreignpolicy.com/2016/05/23/the-g-7-must-rescue-the-liberal-world-order/.

and firms, and surveilling financial flows exploit, rather than restrain, US power and influence. This could prove problematic because, from China to Brazil, and from Russia to Hungary, anti-corruption has been the banner under which right-wing despots have used the power of the state to selectively target opposition politicians and critics. Elevating the threat of corruption and kleptocracy to the level of a "vital national security interest" inevitably legitimates future autocrats doing the same but implementing their anti-corruption agenda in ways that erode rather than protect democracy. Worse, there is real risk that as the United States and Global North countries build an apparatus akin to the Global War on Terror to fight kleptocracy and tax evasion, they simply end up creating authorities and resources that reactionary politicians will use to eliminate their political enemies.[89] Building national security tools only makes sense if the tools can be rationalized as serving democratic ends. But given the political volatility in Global-North democracies, and in the United States in particular, it is now just as likely that they will eventually serve reactionary nationalist ends at odds with democracy. Even the 1/6 Capitol Insurrection, which involved right-wing mobs trying to overturn the US presidential election, has been used to build up the domestic surveillance state, harass leftist organizers, and introduce legislation that makes it easier for law enforcement to shutdown protests across the country.[90] This is consistent with the historical precedents suggesting national security and reactionary, undemocratic politics are ultimately symbiotic. If that is true, then any policy measures that expand national security power also empower the forces that oppose democracy.

## Fracturing the Global Economic Order

Progressive pragmatists want to change how the global economy works, effectively disrupting patterns of transnational behavior by the world's political and economic actors. It stands to reason that both dictators and self-interested globalized economies – those who simultaneously benefit from the international order as currently constructed and would be harmed by progressive, egalitarian reforms to it – would try to stymie US efforts and build alternative forms of economic order suited to their

[89] Jackson, "NOW the White House Wants to Fight Kleptocracy."
[90] Branco Marcetic, "How January 6 Is Being Used to Crush Dissent on the Left," *In These Times* (January 6, 2022), https://inthesetimes.com/article/january-6-capitol-riot-trump-anti-protest-left.

purposes. Oligarchy and kleptocracy are ongoing features of the liberal international order that may globalize and intensify if economic actors (states, oligarchs, and multinational corporations) that resent America's exercise of de facto economic hegemony opt to balance, subvert, or otherwise route around it as a result.[91] In effect, US attempts to purge corruption and inequality from the global economy could induce forms of "soft balancing" against it that lead to the fracturing of the global economic order as it has existed since the 1970s.[92] This would be a case of the lion that is American hegemony (or what remains of it) eating its own tail. The exercise of American economic power may have diminishing returns that eventually hit a point of disrupting the economic order on which it relies. Already Russia, China, and Europe have shown signs of challenging US dollar supremacy and creating alternate systems of economic transaction that circumvent the US-controlled Society for Worldwide Interbank Financial Telecommunication (SWIFT) system.[93] Notably, these challenges predate US attempts to crackdown on oligarchy and kleptocracy and were explicitly intended to counteract US financial power. If they persist or accelerate, they could insulate the worst of the current economic order from America's reach.

---

[91] Cooley and Nexon, *Exit from Hegemony*, pp. 196–200.
[92] The literature on soft balancing is massive, but for a review that situates it as a type of balancing within a literature on balancing that has other merits and drawbacks, see Daniel Nexon, "The Balance of Power in the Balance," *World Politics* Vol. 61, no. 2 (2009), pp. 330–59.
[93] Stephanie Zable, "Instex: A Blow to US Sanctions?" *Lawfare* (March 6, 2019), www .lawfareblog.com/instex-blow-us-sanctions; Wang Xu and Xin Zhiming, "Hu Urges Revamp of Finance System," *People's Daily*, November 17, 2008, www.chinadaily .com.cn/china/2008-11/17/content_7208992.htm.

# 6

## Anti-hegemonism as a Progressive Grand Strategy

Progressive pragmatism challenges liberal internationalism in many ways, but it seeks its reformation rather than a total jettisoning of it. Anti-hegemonism, by contrast, is a more radical break. The anti-hegemonist attitude toward the United States shares something with the slaves who revolted against their oppressors in the Haitian Revolution – "they were seeking their salvation in the most obvious way, the destruction of what they knew was the cause of their sufferings."[1] One of the progressive co-founders of the Quincy Institute for Responsible Statecraft, a transpartisan anti-war think tank launched in 2019, acknowledged at the outset that "addressing climate change, reducing global poverty and inequality, and combating transnational corruption and money laundering ... are not Quincy's top priorities."[2] These issues – which are the core wagers of progressive pragmatism – are not necessary for an anti-hegemonist grand strategy because they are not resolvable until American power is put in check.

Much of the thinking portrayed in this chapter appears in left discourses as references to "anti-imperialism," which is sometimes a reasonable alternative description of anti-hegemonism. I use "anti-hegemonism" though for two reasons. First, the term "empire" is often wielded as an emotion-laden pejorative and people should be able to identify with this form of reasoning separate from the pathos commonly attached to it. Second, the crux of the problem for anti-hegemonists is often American

---

[1] C.L.R. James, *The Black Jacobins: Toussant L'Ouverture and the San Domingo Revolution* (New York: Vintage, 1989), p. 88.
[2] David Klion, "Can a New Think Tank End Endless War?" *The Nation* (July 29, 2019), www.thenation.com/article/archive/quincy-institute-responsible-statecraft-think-tank/.

power itself. In an analytical sense, using the term "anti-imperialism" opens you up to litigating the extent to which US foreign policy fits ideal-type standards of imperialism, which would be an unproductive line of argumentation given that much of the US behavior at issue is harmful or unjust without technically being imperial.

The logic of anti-hegemonism is one of robust restraint. It is built on the principle of anti-authoritarianism, but the interpretation of it concerns foremost the undemocratic character of American power abroad; an inward-looking anti-authoritarianism. Whereas progressive pragmatism seeks large structural changes in the global political economy that will require wielding American power, the anti-hegemonist position seeks to inhibit it, as a consequence of making different assumptions that prioritize different threats. Seeing liberalism per se as the underlying source of insecurity because it gives rise to imperialistic foreign policy (which some but not all leftists believe is the case) means that the global far right, dictatorships abroad, and kleptocracy are downstream of liberal elite unaccountability.[3] For anti-hegemonists, it is not durable inequalities driving insecurity but rather the military and economic power of the United States – the biggest liberal capitalist of all. The answer for how to approach foreign policy, accordingly, is to prioritize restraining and checking American power over fighting global corruption or oligarchy. It is not that the latter issues are not problems, but that they are symptoms of a deeper rot in the way the American national security state thinks and acts. The wagers of this view include strategically accommodating the interests of other great powers and reducing US coercive power by cutting US commitments abroad [including to North Atlantic Treaty Organization (NATO)], de-centering the United States in the global economic order, and dramatically reducing the military's global presence (especially in the Middle East), as well as the size of the US military (including, potentially, nuclear weapons). These steps will help restore American democracy, and in so doing will create more favorable conditions for peace and open the possibility of seeking economic equality.

---

[3] The degree to which leftists in an anti-hegemonic mode are hostile toward liberalism varies. While most embrace the New Left genealogy, for example, it is also common to hear some leftists criticize the activism of the New Left anti-war movement – mostly on the grounds that it was excessively bourgeoisie in origin and consequence. It is this view that leads to casual assertions that, for example, Donald Trump was not much worse than Barack Obama. See, for example, "Episode 235: The Sorkin Effect," *Nostalgia Trap podcast* (December 1, 2020), www.nostalgiatrap.com/episodes/2020/12/1/episode-225-the-sorkin-effect-w-jon-wiener-and-danny-bessner.

## ASSUMPTIONS

Anti-hegemonist foreign policy is built on three interlocking assumptions: (1) US policy is militarist and undemocratic (whether characterized as imperial, hegemonic, or oligarchic), (2) America's elites inflate the threat posed by competitors that are more or less defensive, status quo states, and (3) the use and threat of military force play a negative role in resolving political problems other than direct self-defense.

### America's Militarist Empire

For anti-hegemonists, militarism and US imperialism are so entwined as to verge on mutual constitution. This fusion appears in the work of historian Charles Austin Beard in the late Progressive Era, as well as the Wisconsin School of critical historians and eventually the anti-imperialist cross-section of New Left intellectualism.[4] By casting US foreign policy in imperial terms, US military interventions become a "fruit of the poisonous tree" problem – the use of force becomes prima facie illegitimate. Any democracy worthy of its name cannot be engaged in imperial conduct, and the fact that so many have (including the United States) is something that requires reckoning, not eliding. Consequently, the diagnosis of militarist imperialism has usually given rise to a "non-interventionist" posture on defense issues. Taken to its extreme, some in this school have been critical even of US involvement in World War II.[5]

Anti-hegemonists are the intellectual heirs to this historical non-interventionism. Understanding the sum of US foreign policy as a project to sustain political and military dominance over the world necessarily means that the notion of American exceptionalism – or the "liberal international order" that US commitments are supposed to underpin – amounts to so much rhetoric justifying undemocratic control of foreign territories.[6] It is Washington's unwillingness to acknowledge that to this day it maintains a

---

[4] On Charles Beard specifically, see Charles A. Beard, *President Roosevelt and the Coming of the War, 1941: A Study in Appearances and Reality* (New Haven, CT: Yale University Press, 1948); Richard Drake, *Charles Austin Beard: The Return of the Master Historian of American Imperialism* (Ithaca, NY: Cornell University Press, 2019). On the anti-imperialism and anti-militarism of the New Left, see James G. Morgan, *Into New Territory: American Historians and the Concept of U.S. Imperialism* (Madison: University of Wisconsin Press, 2014).

[5] Beard, *President Roosevelt and the Coming of the War, 1941*.

[6] Stephen Wertheim, "The Price of Primacy: Why America Shouldn't Dominate the World," *Foreign Affairs* Vol. 99, no. 2 (2020), pp. 19–29.

"pointillist empire,"[7] or that "they search for peace by warlike means,"[8] or that it has been continuously fighting in foreign wars for more than a century,[9] that enables it to sustain its long history of wielding militarized violence abroad whatever the circumstances it actually faces in the world.

### Elites Inflate Threats

The second assumption, that elites engage in threat inflation, implies that America's adversaries are less revisionist than policymakers often claim. As C. Wright Mills excoriated the United States and the Soviet Union, "Each defines his own nation's reality in terms of his own nation's favourite proclamations; each defines the reality of the other nation in terms of its worst decisions and actions."[10] Analytically, anti-hegemonists treat foreign actors as presumptively status quo states that do not seek to use force as a method of territorial conquest, order-building, or self-aggrandizement. As such, the global problems facing the United States are not existential but "politicians have inflated international threats to justify military adventurism, boost military spending, increase domestic surveillance and campaign on a politics of fear."[11]

This assumption has two implications. One is that the continued pursuit of military power is inherently illegitimate if it is predicated on an overhyped matrix of threats. Given the first assumption above – that military operations are fruit from the poisonous tree – the illegitimacy of America's exercise of military power is overdetermined. The other implication is that adversaries can be mollified. If other states in the international system are security-seeking rather than revisionist actors, then the aggression and coercion they exhibit are more likely to stem from their insecurity (implicitly in reaction to US policy). The political grievances of Russia, China, Iran, and even North Korea can be accommodated and resolved without the threat or use of force. To the extent adversaries' behavior stems from them needing to balance against US power, it stands to reason that reducing or otherwise checking the US power that they find threatening will prevent their undesirable behavior. In essence,

[7] Immerwahr, *How to Hide an Empire*, p. 18.
[8] Mills, *The Causes of World War Three*, p. 61.
[9] Bradley and Dudziak, eds., *Making the Forever War*, pp. 123–36.
[10] Mills, *The Causes of World War Three*, p. 61.
[11] Daniel Bessner, "What Does Alexandria Ocasio-Cortez Think about the South China Sea?" *New York Times* (September 17, 2018), www.nytimes.com/2018/09/17/opinion/democratic-party-cortez-foreign-policy.html.

the world is a security dilemma and, for analytical purposes, the United States is the only actor with sufficient agency to actually change it.

But the assumption that US national security elites overhype the threat posed by international actors does not mean that anti-hegemonism rejects balance-of-power logic entirely or embraces prefigurative reasoning. To the contrary, anti-hegemonists advocate a very steely eyed power politics; it just targets America with its gunsights rather than foreign regimes. Indeed, on the extreme edges of anti-imperialist movements, there is a long tradition of accepting amoral means to realize the principled ends of opposing American militarism.[12]

At least one pundit imagining a socialist foreign policy suggested that the left could support US forces going "to war to protect the environment from climate chauvinists, slave states, or other enemies of a social democratic global order .... There is no reason why a left administration should not demand the best possible military technology in the world."[13] To believe this while also believing that US power is the priority threat has everything to do with its encasement within the illiberalism of liberal internationalism, not simply the fact of America (or any other country) having power. Stephen Wertheim said of the Quincy Institute's rationale of allying progressives with non-progressive forces who share their restraint agenda, "It takes power to beat power."[14] Quincy Institute Chair of the Board Suzanne DiMaggio stressed at the time of the think tank's founding that it was "not a pacifist organization."[15] As Daniel Bessner explains, "... social movements are unable to have a particularly restraining effect on the use of US power – particularly military power – abroad ... the American left ... will thus need to ... manipulate power within a status quo."[16]

---

[12] For leftist critiques of anti-imperialism turned campism, see Gilbert Achcar, "How to Avoid the Anti-Imperialism of Fools," *The Nation* (April 6, 2021), www.thenation .com/article/politics/anti-imperialism-syria-progressive/; Jason Schulman and Dan La Botz, "Against Campism, For International Working Class Solidarity," *Socialist Forum* (Winter 2020), https://socialistforum.dsausa.org/issues/winter-2020/against-campism-for-international-working-class-solidarity/.

[13] Meaney, "What U.S. Foreign Policy Will Look Like under Socialism."

[14] Daniel Bessner, "Can We Democratize Foreign Policy?" *Dissent Magazine* (December 4, 2019), www.dissentmagazine.org/online_articles/foreign-policy-quincy-institute-antiim perialism.

[15] "Engage the Enemy: Interview with Suzanne DiMaggio," *The Un-Diplomatic Podcast* (November 8, 2019), https://podcasts.apple.com/us/podcast/engage-enemy-interview-suzanne-dimaggio-presidential/id1480597540?i=1000456192269.

[16] Conversation with Kelsey Atherton and Daniel Bessner, "The Quartermaster's Tools and the Quartermaster's House," *Fellow Travelers Blog* (August 7, 2019), https://fellowtravelersblog .com/2019/08/07/the-quartermasters-tools-and-the-quartermasters-house/#more-678.

These statements portray anti-hegemonism as not inherently anti-power. As radical as it seems relative to liberal internationalism, it is thoroughly pragmatic when indexed against how it sees the distribution of power and threats in world politics. Believing US foreign policy elites are engaged in simultaneous threat inflation and imperialism in a world of basically defensive regimes is the premise that security practitioners and defense intellectuals would see as the radical departure, but the actions and prescriptions based on that belief (discussed below) are just realpolitik instrumental reasoning.

### Militarism Makes Threats Worse

The third assumption – that the deployment, threat, or use of force is counterproductive – presumes that, in the final analysis, adversaries cannot be cowed with violence or its shadow, and attempts to influence or destroy others with such methods risk blowback.[17] International actors will inevitably resist US pressure "so long as the United States continues to seek military dominance across the globe. Dominance, assumed to ensure peace, in fact guarantees war."[18] Marcus Raskin, a co-founder of the Institute for Policy Studies, called national security during the Cold War a "dance of death" in which "armaments themselves increase anxiety, distort the value and priority structure within the arming nation, and ultimately cause an inter-dependent link between military bureaucracies of opposing sides who use each other to rationalize their commitment to arming."[19]

Many of today's progressives make modern versions of this critique. The global war on terror "perpetuates itself by producing new enemies," which is literally true.[20] America's "empire of global military bases … make wars more likely … and in many countries they fortify authoritarian governments."[21] Congressman Ro Khanna, a Justice Democrat, has repeatedly argued that US support for the Saudi war against Houthi rebels in Yemen has deepened US rivalry with Iran while strengthening Al

---

[17] Chalmers Johnson, *Blowback: The Costs and Consequences of American Empire* (New York: Henry Holt and Co., 2001).

[18] Stephen Wertheim, "The Only Way to End 'Endless War'," *New York Times* (September 14, 2019), www.nytimes.com/2019/09/14/opinion/sunday/endless-war-america.html.

[19] Marcus Raskin, *The Politics of National Security* (New Brunswick, NJ: Transaction Books, 1979), p. 115.

[20] Wertheim, "The Price of Primacy," p. 25.

[21] Richard Lachmann, "How to Build a Socialist Foreign Policy," *Jacobin Magazine* (February 27, 2019), www.jacobinmag.com/2019/02/socialist-foreign-policy-bernie-sanders-us-military.

Qaeda's position, all while civilians in Yemen blame the United States for the Saudi war.[22] Senator Chris Murphy, a proponent of progressive foreign policy, lamented that the Trump administration's assassination of Iranian General Qasem Soleimani in January 2020 "didn't restore deterrence [as expected] because the Iranians launched a [retaliatory] strike against US assets in Iraq … We set in motion a series of events that almost got perhaps 100 Americans killed."[23] US nuclear policy goads China into modernizing its nuclear force, and the latter's nuclear expansion has been "clearly a response to the gratuitous, unrestrained nuclear policies of the Trump administration."[24] And ultimately, the most compelling arguments against a Cold War with China have been not geopolitical but politically existential – Sino-US rivalry risks eroding civil liberties, empowering ethnonationalists in both countries, and diverting domestic investment into arms races.[25] A core belief in anti-hegemonism is, quite simply, that "The logic of absolute war harms American democracy."[26] Believing that the military can be a remedy to the world's ills requires believing that war can protect democracy when America's own history with war suggests it often emaciates and imperils it.

Paradoxically, then, it is US overreliance on the tools of national security that produce US insecurity: "When America tries to solve the nation's security problems by exercising its power or using force, it *tends to produce resistance and backlash* [italics added] that leaves the country bereft of authority, isolated, and ultimately more insecure than it was before it acted."[27] Even the international norm of the responsibility to protect is

---

22 Gould, "Ro Khanna and Progressive Democrats Hope 'Blue Wave' Shakes Up American Defense Policy"; Rand Paul and Ro Khanna, "The Case for Restraint in American Foreign Policy."

23 Jake Tapper interview with Senator Chris Murphy, *The Lead with Jake Tapper* (January 13, 2020), www.cnn.com/TRANSCRIPTS/2001/13/cg.03.html.

24 Van Jackson, "America Is Turning Asia into a Powder Keg," *Foreign Affairs* (October 22, 2021), www.foreignaffairs.com/articles/asia/2021-10-22/america-turning-asia-powder-keg. See also Van Jackson, "Who's Afraid of China's Nukes?" *Duck of Minerva* (November 22, 2021), www.duckofminerva.com/2021/11/whos-afraid-of-chinas-nukes.html.

25 Jackson, *Pacific Power Paradox*; Ted Fertik, "Co-Existence or Carnage," *Dissent* (Spring 2022), www.dissentmagazine.org/article/coexistence-or-carnage.

26 Bessner, "A Very High Degree of Certainty in Future Military Operations."

27 Curiously, this quote comes from Ikenberry. At a conceptual level, restraint – a chief wager of anti-hegemonism – was both an outcome and a mechanism of liberal order as he theorized it. The rupture with anti-hegemonism has to do with both the larger political project that liberal strategic restraint is attached to and the way liberal practice diverges from liberal theory. G. John Ikenberry, "The Security Trap," *Democracy: A Journal of Ideas* No. 2 (2006), https://democracyjournal.org/magazine/2/the-security-trap/.

inadequate to justify military interventions to disrupt ethnic cleansing and other mass humanitarian disasters because of the expected effect: "in most cases, any form of explicitly militarist intervention would spell disaster."[28]

## ANALYTICAL WAGERS

Given these assumptions, anti-hegemonism wagers that US security derives from reducing its coercive (military and economic) power, disentangling the military from international commitments, and accommodating rivals' apparently revisionist ambitions via spheres of influence rather than contesting them via geopolitical competition or arms racing.

## Curbing US Coercive Power

The imperative to dramatically curb US power may seem counterintuitive as a positive wager, particularly for anyone socialized into seeing the world through the lens of liberal internationalism, but it follows logically from the diagnostic assumptions above.

### *In Defense, of Restraint*

Anti-hegemonists would have the United States act on the belief that "The immediate cause of World War III is the preparation for it."[29] Demilitarizing US foreign policy and unwinding the activities and commitments anti-hegemonists deem imperial are the primary means of ending the generations-long cycle of responding to the world in ways that perpetuate threats to the United States. In this, anti-hegemonists find overlapping interests with the "restraint" school of foreign policy – a broad and eclectic movement that believes America's approach to security would yield better outcomes if it was not so heavily militarized.[30] Anti-hegemonists desire to do less militarily because military operations abroad tend to produce endlessly self-generating security threats,

---

[28] Meaney, "What U.S. Foreign Policy Will Look Like under Socialism."

[29] Mills, *The Causes of World War Three*, p. 59.

[30] It is worth repeating that all forms of progressive worldmaking are forms of restraint, but anti-hegemonism most aligns with the connotation of restraint in mainstream policy discourse. On restraint and its effects, see Brent Steele, *Restraint in International Politics* (New York: Cambridge University Press, 2019). On restraint as grand strategy, see Barry Posen, *Restraint: A New Foundation for U.S. Grand Strategy* (Ithaca, NY: Cornell University Press, 2014); Emma Ashford, "Strategies of Restraint," *Foreign Affairs* (September/October 2021), www.foreignaffairs.com/articles/united-states/2021-08-24/strategies-restraint.

including the rise of right-wing extremism.[31] This do-less wager takes multiple forms – shrinking the size of the military and its global presence, disentangling the United States from risky security commitments, and adopting a non-interventionist defense posture in general but toward hot spots like Ukraine and Taiwan in particular.

Anti-hegemonist opposition to military superiority means a rejection of both the Pentagon's prevailing force structure standard that justifies the annual defense budget and the global force posture that puts that capability out in the world for various uses. An anti-hegemonist grand strategy is compatible with either an offshore balancing defense strategy or a garrison defense strategy (i.e., keeping a force that mostly limits itself to US territory and relies primarily on missiles and systems that can deliver nuclear warheads). The United States does not need to be engaged in a Global War on Terror, should not have any military presence in the Middle East or Africa, and does not need a force designed to conduct stabilization operations or counterterrorism missions. This is not an argument that terrorism does not threaten Americans, but rather that counterterrorism is no kind of answer because military operations worsen the problem, as evidenced by the fourfold increase in the number of Salafi-Jihadist militants globally since 2001.[32] The United States does not need a large army for a ground war contingency on the Korean Peninsula, and the removal of the 28,000 troops permanently positioned there would actually facilitate a peace process between North and South Korea. It should not be arms-racing China and should not be aroused by China's nuclear and naval expansion continuing for some time given America's massive numerical and qualitative advantage (as of 2022, the United States had some 3,750 warheads while China had at most 350. If China continued building nuclear weapons at a breakneck pace through 2030, it would still only have at most 1,000 warheads).[33] And it should not build any forces that presuppose forward military presence, like intermediate-range ground-launched cruise missiles.

---

[31] Stephen Wertheim, "The Only Way to End 'Endless War'," *New York Times* (September 14, 2019), www.nytimes.com/2019/09/14/opinion/sunday/endless-war-america.html; Van Jackson, "The Liberal Internationalist Origins of Right-Wing Insurrection," *Inkstick Media* (January 11, 2021), https://inkstickmedia.com/the-liberal-internationalist-origins-of-right-wing-insurrection/; Jonathan Katz, "It Happened Here," *Foreign Policy* (January 9, 2021), https://foreignpolicy.com/2021/01/09/capitol-riot-united-states-imperialism-trump/.

[32] Jones, Newlee, and Harrington, *The Evolution of the Salafi-Jihadist Threat.*

[33] Jackson, "Who's Afraid of China's Nukes?"

But focusing on what to do with defense policy in a positive sense sells short the larger proposition here – standing down America's role as the world's police and reducing the US military's menacing potential (as well as omnipresence) promises to alleviate geopolitical tension and arms-racing pressures, and thereby risks of conflict.

A second component of the military-restraint wager is disentanglement, or distancing the United States from commitments that would chain-gang it into conflicts that would not otherwise threaten US territory. Channeling a common sentiment among Justice Democrats, Ro Khanna has bemoaned that the US military is "entangled in places we don't need to be. And I'd like that to be part of a Democratic strategy to bring more restraint for foreign policy."[34] Since "Russia and China's military ... do not pose a threat to this country,"[35] the United States does not need military alliances to counter them. To the extent they are threats at all, they exist only as the counterpoint to American empire in the first place. Unilateral demilitarization and base closures – especially in the Middle East – removes a catalyst for future terrorism.[36] It also reduces the likelihood that the United States becomes embroiled in costly peripheral conflicts that do not directly threaten US existence. The United States should therefore logically end the provision of extended nuclear deterrence commitments to allies, given that US extended deterrence promises create commitment traps that increase the likelihood that the United States becomes a party to a future nuclear war. Additionally, the United States should preemptively foreclose on troop deployments or "tripwire" forces in geopolitical flashpoints like Ukraine and Taiwan. And, most controversially, it should consider ending its entire system of bilateral military alliances globally, but at a minimum gradually withdraw from the NATO, if necessary by facilitating Europe's transition to a European Union force. Some argue that "An argument for NATO is an argument for empire, pure and simple."[37] But the most generous thing that can be

---

[34] As quoted in Joe Gould, "Ro Khanna and Progressive Democrats Hope 'Blue Wave' Shakes Up American Defense Policy," *Defense News* (October 30, 2018), www.defensenews .com/congress/2018/10/30/ro-khanna-and-progressive-democrats-hope-blue-wave-will-shake-up-american-national-defense-policy/.

[35] Lachmann, "How to Build a Socialist Foreign Policy."

[36] Wertheim, "The Price of Primacy," p. 26. It is worth remembering that Osama bin Laden's primary grievances against the United States were its military bases in Saudi Arabia; the attacks of 9/11 might not have happened if there had not been a military presence in the Middle East.

[37] Daniel Bessner, @dbessner (June 15, 2021), https://twitter.com/dbessner/status/1404464 174084902917.

said analytically, from the anti-hegemonist view, is that "NATO now largely exists to manage the risks created by its existence."[38] Winding down its existence, therefore, is the only sustainable security solution.

A third element of the anti-hegemonist's military restraint wager is non-interventionism, raising the threshold and narrowing the conditions for offering security assistance to foreign actors and deploying forces abroad. Whereas progressive pragmatism would halt weapons sales and military training for dictatorships as well as for societies in turmoil, the anti-hegemonist call would be to end such forms of assistance everywhere except where it facilitates drawing down from an existing commitment or supports a quid pro quo with foreign actors (discussed below). And whereas progressive pragmatism would intervene militarily to support a fellow democracy under direct attack, the anti-hegemonist would not. As such, the United States should end its "qualitative military edge" policy that commits to always ensuring Israel has superior military technology over its Arab neighbors,[39] but ought also to wind down security assistance activities in the Middle East generally. It should not intervene in the affairs of the Korean Peninsula, and instead allow South Korea to defend itself. And it should not defend Ukraine from Russia, or Taiwan from China. The threat Russia poses to Ukraine – specifically the prospect of a formal armed invasion – has occurred because "[US] flirting with a security commitment for Ukraine helped bring that country under threat."[40] Russian aggression against Ukraine since 2014 arose from a context in which the United States signaled "the possibility of Ukraine's close alignment with the West," which in Vladimir Putin's imagination always posed a geopolitical threat to Moscow.[41] The surest way to prevent war with

---

[38] Katrina vanden Heuvel, "What a Sensible Ukraine Policy Should Look Like," *Washington Post* (January 5, 2022), www.washingtonpost.com/opinions/2022/01/04/biden-putin-ukraine-russia-nato/?utm_campaign=wp_opinions&utm_medium=social&utm_source=twitter.

[39] Euan Harlow-Lawrence, "The Progressive Peace Movement and the 2020 Democratic Platform," *Massachusetts Peace Action* (September 21, 2020), https://masspeaceaction .org/the-progressive-peace-movement-the-2020-democratic-platform/; Eric Cortellessa, "Bernie Sanders Says He Would 'Absolutely' Mull Cutting Aid to Pressure Israel," *Times of Israel* (July 28, 2019), www.timesofisrael.com/bernie-sanders-says-he-would-absolutely-mull-cutting-aid-to-leverage-israel/; Catie Edmondson, "Sanders Introduces Legislation to Block a $735 Million Arms Sale Package to Israel," *New York Times* (May 20, 2021), www.nytimes.com/2021/05/20/us/politics/bernie-sanders-israel-arms-sale.html.

[40] Joshua Shifrinson and Stephen Wertheim, "Acting Too Aggressively on Ukraine May Endanger It – and Taiwan," *Washington Post* (December 23, 2021), www.washingtonpost .com/outlook/2021/12/23/ukraine-taiwan-red-lines/.

[41] Ibid.

Russia would thus be for the United States to "agree not to place troops in Ukraine," state publicly that Ukraine will not join NATO, and limit the kinds of security assistance it provides to Ukraine to professionalization training. Those moves might have prevented Putin's invasion, and even if Putin had invaded anyway, they "would nevertheless disentangle the United States from the conflict and help avoid the outcome truly unacceptable ... a war with Russia."[42] Similarly, anti-hegemonists have argued that defense of Taiwan against Chinese invasion is not acceptable because of the cost war would entail. US force posture in Asia, and especially US defense cooperation with and arms sales to Taiwan, appears to China as military encirclement on an issue (unification with Taiwan) that it views as its "core interest."[43] US military support for Taiwan, in this view, actually makes its invasion more likely. And even if China invades Taiwan despite US restraint, the anti-hegemonist position would not be to rush in with counter-insurgency or blockade or some third measure of militarized solidarity, but instead only to take in Taiwans as refugees; military involvement is not an option.[44]

There is also a counter-intuitive linkage logic at play in dealings with Russia and China. If the United States were to respond to Russia's war against Ukraine with US troop deployments or US combat operations, China could be pushed to accelerate its campaign against Taiwan because it would "see Washington pushing to revise geopolitical arrangements without regard for the vital interests of other powers."[45] American policymakers have a habit of worrying about how adversaries see US resolve, but rarely stop to ponder how US demonstrations of resolve confirm the worst interpretations about American revisionist intentions.[46] Even in a narrow coercive bargaining frame, resolve only matters as part

---

[42] Ibid.

[43] Michael Klare, "Containment on Steroids: Pentagon's 2022 Budget Seeks China's Encirclement," *Committee for a Sane U.S.-China Policy* (December 31, 2021); Lyle Goldstein, "Eerie Similarities Link the Ukraine Taiwan Situations," *The Hill* (December 27, 2021), https://thehill.com/opinion/national-security/586949-eerie-similarities-link-the-ukraine-and-taiwan-situations?rl=1.

[44] "Episode 157: Imperial Rollback with Daniel Bessner," *Left Anchor podcast* (September 29, 2020), https://leftanchor.podbean.com/e/episode-157-imperial-rollback-with-daniel-bessner/.

[45] Shifrinson and Wertheim, "Acting Too Aggressively on Ukraine May Endanger It – and Taiwan."

[46] Van Jackson, "America Is the Preeminent Revisionist Power," *Duck of Minerva* (January 1, 2023), www.duckofminerva.com/2023/01/america-is-the-preeminent-revisionist-power.html.

of a relative balance with the other side; if US demonstrations of resolve strengthen the resolve of the adversary, they undermine the very purpose of US resolve.

### Choosing Democracy over Economic Primacy

This argument against American power extends to political economy as well. Anti-hegemonists are champions of the campaign for Washington to "take the profits out of war" by making the defense industry a government monopoly.[47] Since the government determines demand for national security resources, it should also be able to determine price controls and other methods that would disembowel the defense lobby, preventing it from distorting US foreign policy in the direction of war and military buildups. This line of reasoning dates back more than a century, to America's arms manufacturers allying with Teddy Roosevelt because he supported literal imperial adventures and argued for war "preparedness" (a term he coined to justify building a large standing military).[48] Ultimately it was businessmen who stood to benefit from war that lobbied publicly and privately for the United States to enter World War I, financing a public campaign against the anti-war movement.[49] Today, echoing then, "Coziness between defense lobbyists, Congress, and the Pentagon tilts countless decisions away from national security interests and toward the desires of giant corporations."[50] Taking the profits out of war is the surest way to prevent lobbyist pressure favoring military buildups and arms-racing.

The democratization of international financial institutions (IFIs) that progressive pragmatists seek may also further the anti-hegemonist project of checking US power. Strictly speaking, the logic of anti-hegemonism does not require IFIs, and the anti-liberal strand of thinking that runs through it implies skepticism about the necessity of IFIs given their track record of serving global capital at labor's expense. But IFIs and other forms of multilateralism may be instrumentally useful if they comprise one in a series of moves meant to check US influence.

---

[47] There is a century-long tradition of anti-imperialists from the left and right making this argument.

[48] Ian Toll, *Pacific Crucible: War at Sea in the Pacific, 1941–1942* (New York: W.W. Norton & Co., 2012), p. xxxv.

[49] This was why opponents of war called to "take the profits out of war" and remove the "economic causes" of war. See Kazin, *War against War*, pp. 5, 28, 43,121–2.

[50] Elizabeth Warren, "Reducing Corporate Influence at the Pentagon," *Warren Democrats* (May 16, 2019), https://elizabethwarren.com/plans/corporate-influence-pentagon.

Beyond democratizing IFIs and taking the profits out of war, anti-hegemonists propose reforming the economic order in a manner that primarily bridles the United States – inhibiting America's use of economic sanctions and replacing the US dollar as the world's reserve currency with a basket of currencies that would redistribute the balance of global financial power.

For anti-hegemonists, economic sanctions represent the most directly harmful and self-damaging instrument of the national security state other than the military. Noam Chomsky has been among those who question the right of the United States to sanction foreign governments, and especially as long as it simultaneously supports authoritarian regimes and illiberal democratic practices, such as Israel's ongoing oppression of Palestinians.[51] But the analytical problem with sanctions is that they "fail much more often than they succeed," "their unintended consequences are rarely worth the meager gains," and "the overuse of sanctions has become a major source of international instability."[52] All of America's purported adversaries in the international system – Russia, China, North Korea, and Iran in particular – have retaliated in one form or another against US sanctions, sometimes with tariffs and counter sanctions (as China has done), and sometimes with threats of war and defiant acceleration of nuclear weapons expansion (as North Korea has done).

Sanctions have become a habit that perpetuates conditions of security precarity because, for America's rivals, they are signals of antagonism and cost imposition, sometimes equated to acts of war themselves.[53] In this way, they are not the alternative to war that they were originally intended to be, but rather steps on a path to war; mechanisms locking in rivalry and triggering crises that end up increasing Washington's perceived need to rely on a coercive, zero-sum frame of militarized geopolitics.[54] This represents a more pernicious dilemma than just "blowback" or "ineffective" sanctions. Whether any individual set of sanctions work or not, they set conditions that naturalize a militarist foreign policy, perpetually tilting the terrain of policy debates toward arguments that eternalize

---

[51] C.J. Polychroniou, "Noam Chomsky: Trump's Economic Boom Is a Sham," *Global Policy* (June 3, 2019), www.globalpolicyjournal.com/blog/03/06/2019/noam-chomsky-trumps-economic-boom-sham. See also Mark Lamont-Hill and Mitchell Plitnick, *Except for Palestine: The Limits of Progressive Politics* (New York: The New Press, 2021).

[52] Nicholas Mulder, "A Leftist Foreign Policy Should Reject Economic Sanctions," *The Nation* (November 20, 2018), www.thenation.com/article/archive/sanctions-economy-foreign-policy/.

[53] Mulder, "A Leftist Foreign Policy Should Reject Economic Sanctions."

[54] Nicholas Mulder, *The Economic Weapon: The Rise of Sanctions as a Tool of Modern War* (New Haven, CT: Yale University Press, 2022).

insecurity in the world. The solution, then, is to pursue sanctions more sparingly, and remove some of the sanctions that are already imposed on rivals. This would unlock the possibility of arms control agreements, lessen geopolitical tensions, and indirectly reduce some of the risks of interstate conflict.[55]

In addition to restraining US sanctions practices, anti-hegemonists seek to end America's "exorbitant privilege" of printing the world's reserve currency.[56] The argument for dollar multilateralism and against dollar hegemony – that is, replacing the US dollar as reserve currency with a basket of currencies or an International Monetary Fund (IMF)-backed supernote – is a strategically motivated frontal attack on US centrality in the global economic system. The thinking goes that because the United States has abused its economic power in the form of sanctions overuse and running deficits to fund military superiority, part of the restraint project should undermine the US ability to pursue imperialism and militarism in the first place – "We have an obligation ... to tie the hands of future American presidents ... we need to make it harder, not easier, to wage war."[57] Ending dollar hegemony unwinds the system that gives America unrivaled ability to impose unilateral sanctions on others. It limits America's ability to finance the Pentagon's largesse and global force posture, making it a costly "hand-tying" signal toward adversaries about America's non-aggressive intentions.[58] And it lowers the likelihood of US-driven financial crises. The process of deficit financing large military buildups and wars of choice (which dollar supremacy made possible) created the conditions for US fiscal crisis in the 1960s, 1980s, and in 2008.[59]

---

[55] This logic is most thoroughly developed on North Korea but extends to all US rivals. For discussions in the North Korea context, see Van Jackson, *Risk Realism: The Arms Control Endgame for North Korea Policy* (Washington, DC: Center for a New American Security, 2019); Tobias Harris, Abigail Bard, and Haneul Lee, *Prospects for Diplomacy with North Korea* (Washington, DC: Center for American Progress, 2021); Catherine Killough, *Begun Is Half Done: Prospects for US-North Korea Nuclear Diplomacy* (Washington, DC: Ploughshares Fund, 2019).

[56] David Adler and Daniel Bessner, "To End Forever War, End the Dollar's Global Dominance," *New Republic* (January 29, 2020), https://newrepublic.com/article/156325/end-forever-war-end-dollars-global-dominance.

[57] Van Jackson, as quoted in Laicie Heeley, *Things That Go Boom podcast* (December 4, 2020), www.pri.org/programs/inkstick-media/special-episode-things-go-boom-blob.

[58] On costly signaling, see especially James Fearon, "Signaling Foreign Policy Interests: Tying Hands Versus Sinking Costs," *Journal of Conflict Resolution* Vol. 41, no. 1 (1997), pp. 68–90. Robert Jervis parsed credibility by distinguishing signals from "indices." Robert Jervis, *The Logic of Images in International Relations* (New York: Columbia University Press, 1970).

[59] Thomas Oatley, *A Political Economy of American Hegemony: Buildups, Booms, and Busts* (New York: Cambridge University Press, 2015).

## Accommodating Spheres of Influence

The other distinct wager that follows from the priorities of anti-hegemonism is the strategic accommodation of rivals' foreign policy ambitions. Every autocratic great power is not Nazi Germany. In fact, none are. Geopolitical appeasement, therefore, should be a legitimate policy option for promoting global stability and reducing the pressures of militarism. Anti-hegemonists have explicitly urged granting or acknowledging regional spheres of influence that would implicitly permit great powers like China and Russia to exercise exclusionary control of foreign territories in the manner that the United States exercises exclusionary control over several territories in the Pacific.[60] Former progressive presidential candidate Henry Wallace urged a sphere-of-influence bargain in the Soviet context of the early Cold War, saying "We should recognize that we have no more business in the political affairs of Eastern Europe than Russia has in the political affairs of Latin America, Western Europe and the United States. Whether we like it or not, the Russians will try to socialize their sphere of influence just as we try to democratize our sphere of influence."[61] Although Wallace later repudiated that call for sphere-of-influence compromise as being premised on his misjudgment of Soviet intentions,[62] anti-hegemonists today see spheres of influence as a commendable alternative to power-balancing rivalries and the risks of conflict they entail.[63]

Buttressing the rationale that retrenchment and restraint would benefit US security, anti-hegemonists also explicitly call for accepting or granting exclusionary spheres of influence to authoritarian great powers – specifically Russia and China – that may permit them to exercise illiberal influence over the political life of those states and territories within an agreed

---

[60] US foreign policy does not acknowledge it, but the United States retains a formal, codified sphere of influence over Guam, American Samoa, the Northern Mariana Islands, the Marshall Islands, the Federated States of Micronesia, and Palau. See Jackson, "Trapped by Empire"; Jackson, "Understanding Spheres of Influence in International Politics."

[61] As quoted in US House of Representatives, "The Cold War: Origins and Developments," Hearings before the Subcommittee on Europe of the Committee on Foreign Affairs, 92nd Congress, First Session (Washington, DC: U.S. Government Printing Office, 1971), p. 217.

[62] Steven O'Brien, *American Political Leaders: From Colonial Times to the Present* (Santa Barbara, CA: ABC-CLIO, 1991), p. 425.

[63] Peter Beinart, "Bernie Sanders Offers a Foreign Policy for the Common Man," *The Atlantic* (October 15, 2018), www.theatlantic.com/ideas/archive/2018/10/bernie-sanders-and-end-american-century/573001/.

upon space.[64] By avoiding or ending close US ties to countries in Russia's "near abroad," blocking any new members from joining NATO, drawing down US forces in Europe, and curbing sanctions on Russia that were previously imposed for its intervention in Ukraine, the United States would "reassure Russia on security issues" and "By minimizing points of friction ... Washington would make it more likely that Moscow would temper its resistance."[65]

Granting a sphere of influence to China would involve a similar bargain, ceding the contested South China Sea that China already occupies, leaving Taiwan's fate to be determined by Taiwan and China despite the lopsided playing field between them, and accepting that the United States cannot prevent settler colonialism or authoritarian oppression in Tibet, Xinjiang, Hong Kong, or even further afield.[66] Mollifying China in this way avoids a confrontation over issues that would make military conflict more likely. Risking war makes little sense when China's security ambitions are contained to its periphery: "defending the Chinese mainland, winning disputes over small border areas and islands, and prevailing in what China sees as its unresolved civil war."[67] Lyle Goldstein, a China expert writing for the Quincy Institute, urged American progressives to support a "policy of military disengagement from the Taiwan issue" on these logical grounds.[68] In both the Russia and China cases, the wager is plausible if their revisionist aims are bounded, making the promise of these compromises the stability of great-power relations.[69] That stability in turn further alleviates the need for the United States to entertain "costly military rivalries and ruinous large-scale wars."[70]

[64] Peter Beinart, "America Needs an Entirely New Foreign Policy for the Trump Age," *The Atlantic* (September 16, 2018), www.theatlantic.com/ideas/archive/2018/09/shield-of-the-republic-a-democratic-foreign-policy-for-the-trump-age/570010/; Graham Allison, "The New Spheres of Influence: Sharing the Globe with Other Great Powers," *Foreign Affairs* Vol. 99, no. 2 (2020), pp. 30–40; David Klion, "How Progressives Can Engage Russia," *The Nation* (May 14, 2018), www.thenation.com/article/archive/how-progressives-should-think-about-russia/.

[65] Wertheim, "The Price of Primacy," p. 29.

[66] Beinart, "America Needs an Entirely New Foreign Policy for the Trump age"; Wertheim, "The Price of Primacy," p. 28.

[67] Wertheim, "The Price of Primacy," p. 28.

[68] Lyle Goldstein, "How Progressives and Restrainers Can Unite on Taiwan and Reduce the Potential for Conflict with China," *Responsible Statecraft* (April 17, 2020), https://responsiblestatecraft.org/2020/04/17/how-progressives-and-restrainers-can-unite-on-taiwan-and-reduce-the-potential-for-conflict-with-china/.

[69] Allison "The New Spheres of Influence"; Peter Beinart, "Bernie Sanders Offers a Foreign Policy for the Common Man," *The Atlantic* (October 15, 2018), www.theatlantic.com/ideas/archive/2018/10/bernie-sanders-and-end-american-century/573001/.

[70] Wertheim, "The Price of Primacy," p. 27.

Finally, anti-hegemonism offers a unique answer to the "non-traditional" problems of terrorism and climate change. Military counterterrorism "perpetuates itself by producing new enemies."[71] If Osama bin Laden justified Al Qaeda's war as a response to US bases in Saudi Arabia, then eliminating those bases in the first place might have foreclosed his jihad before it started.[72] Terrorist attacks on the US homeland are far less likely now that it has a "much improved border security system" since 9/11. And the real solution is to not over-securitize terrorism to begin with – "The one percent doctrine must be permanently discarded, and Americans must learn to live with some level of terrorist risk."[73] This would allow for unilateral demilitarization and base closures that would remove a catalyst for future terrorism.[74]

The climate crisis, meanwhile, is worsened by US dollar supremacy, which "constrains the rest of the world's ability to finance the green transition" because foreign national monetary policies are dependent on fluctuations in the US dollar.[75] The shared threat of climate degradation, moreover, is an opportunity to promote great-power stability while transitioning the world toward renewable energy. Accommodating China's foreign policy ambitions does not only avoid a military confrontation, it also increases the likelihood China cooperates with the United States on climate change – the foremost security concern of most progressives.[76] As the two nations most responsible for greenhouse gas emissions, coordinated policies between China and the United States are the only solution to climate change. Unwinding rivalry with China will reduce the US military's massive carbon footprint, which between 2001 and 2019 the military involved 1.2 billion metric tons of greenhouse gas emissions.[77]

---

[71] Wertheim, "The Price of Primacy," p. 25.

[72] John Ramming Chappell, "A Progressive Domestic Agenda Needs a Foreign Policy Vision to Match," *Progressive Policy Review* (April 15, 2021), https://ppr.hkspublications .org/2021/04/15/progressive-foreign-policy-agenda/.

[73] Daniel Benjamin and Steven Simon, "Beyond Forever War," *Foreign Affairs* (September 10, 2021), www.foreignaffairs.com/articles/afghanistan/2021-09-10/beyond-forever-war.

[74] Wertheim, "The Price of Primacy," p. 26.

[75] Daniel Driscoll, "The Dollar and Climate," *Phenomenal World* (January 14, 2023), www.phenomenalworld.org/analysis/the-dollar-and-climate/.

[76] Tobita Chow and Jake Werner, *U.S.-China: Progressive Internationalist Strategy Under Biden* (New York: Rosa Luxemburg Stiftung, 2021).

[77] "Summary: Pentagon Fuel Use, Climate Change, and the Costs of War," *Costs of War Project* (June 12, 2019), https://watson.brown.edu/costsofwar/files/cow/imce/papers/2019/ Summary_Pentagon%20Fuel%20Use%2C%20Climate%20Change%2C%20and%20 the%20Costs%20of%20War%20%281%29.pdf.

China also has tremendous slack capital that it can steer overseas via state-backed firms, and it is the world's largest manufacturer of renewable energy technologies. Sino-US collaboration makes possible more climate financing and green technology transfers to the Global South than either acting independently.[78] But stability, not climate change, is the higher order payoff. Working with China to address the climate crisis will "help dispel the Cold War environment currently besieging Beijing and Washington and lead to cooperation on other critical issues."[79]

## RISKS

The risks of anti-hegemonism include unintentionally spurring – rather than ameliorating – the militarization of world politics (especially arms-racing), the erosion of democratic peace by signaling that illiberal foreign policy is cost free, and adversary emboldenment. Liberal internationalists often claim that a principal benefit of combining military superiority and alliance commitments is a reduction in arms-racing pressures and a corresponding amelioration of interstate rivalries. If US power protects allies, enforces the rules of the international system, and so outpaces other militaries that even revisionists cannot hope to seriously challenge the United States, then the rationale for arms-racing disappears. What is more, there is little point in other states investing too heavily in military power if it is never sufficient to prevail in a war with the United States. Anti-hegemonism's principal risk, then, is its rejection of a core liberal internationalist wager. States that previously relied on the presumption of US military power, presence, or alliance commitments may feel compelled to resort to internal balancing (that is, military buildups) for their own security. Rivalries previously suppressed, like that between South Korea and Japan, may renew, thereby multiplying new vectors for conflict. Militaries around the world would become more capable and therefore more threatening to others. And a number of states may conclude they need nuclear weapons. Ironically, if states have only been refraining from internal balancing behavior since the end of the Cold War because

[78] Adam Tooze, "Why There Is No Solution to Our Age of Crisis without China," *New Statesman* (July 21, 2021), www.newstatesman.com/long-reads/2021/07/why-there-no-solution-our-age-crisis-without-china.

[79] "U.S.-China Cooperation in Overcoming Climate Change," Committee for a Sane U.S.-China Policy (undated), www.saneuschinapolicy.org/climate-change-cooperation.

of US power, presence, and commitments, then an agenda of restraint and retrenchment could produce a more militarized, weapon-saturated world with numerous rivalry dyads re-emerging.

The second risk of anti-hegemonism – the spread of illiberalism or shrinking the coverage of the democratic peace – follows directly from accommodating rivals' limited ambitions. Spheres of influence are practices of exclusionary control by a foreign power over a local one.[80] Unless the polity being controlled concedes to such an arrangement, the assertion of a sphere of influence is likely to be illiberal and undemocratic, violating the sovereignty of the peoples being treated as an object of control. To grant Russia and China spheres of influence in their respective peripheries is not to directly grant permission for them to deprive weaker states of self-determination, but it is an acknowledgement that great-power conduct within a particular boundary will not be met by US intervention even if it deprives other states of freedom.[81] The risk, then, of accommodating spheres of influence is that their exercise corrupts and undermines democratic governance of areas that constitute great-power peripheries.[82] Without US support, for example, Ukraine's democracy would not have survived against Russia's onslaught for as long as it has. Similarly, without US arms and strategically ambiguous commitments, Taiwan might not be able to maintain political independence in the face of Chinese pressure and political interference.

The third risk in an anti-hegemonist theory of security is a corollary of the second and a classic worry in international politics: adversary emboldenment. The deterrence model of conflict posits how war can result from accommodating an adversary with revisionist intentions, becoming emboldened by acts of appeasement.[83] It is the cautionary tale of British Prime Minister Neville Chamberlain conceding to Hitler's takeover of the Sudetenland at Munich in 1938.[84] For concessions to or compromise with a rival to actually induce restraint in their behavior, the rival must be appeasable, which is to say it must be a status quo state

---

[80] Jackson, "Understanding Spheres of Influence in International Politics."

[81] Allison, "The New Spheres of Influence."

[82] Hal Brands and Charles Edel, "The Disharmony of the Spheres," *Commentary Magazine* (2018), pp. 20–27.

[83] Robert Jervis, *Perception and Misperception in International Politics* (Princeton: Princeton University Press, 1976), pp. 58–113.

[84] Sidney Aster, "Appeasement: Before and After Revisionism," *Diplomacy & Statecraft* Vol. 19, no. 3 (2008), pp. 443–80.

with bounded geopolitical aspirations.[85] The deterrence model and the Munich analogy draw attention to how a combination of simultaneous restraint, retrenchment, and political accommodation of adversaries – not just Russia and China but North Korea and Iran as well – could inadvertently make them more revisionist and more willing to resort to coercion and military force in their foreign policies. The assumption that apparently revisionist states are either in fact status quo states or have only limited revisionist intentions could be wrong. Alternatively, the assumption could be correct about Russia and China now but the act of granting them spheres of influence, combined with retrenchment and restraint, could embolden them to pursue more ambitious revisionist goals for which they may more willingly embrace military actions as the means of achieving them.

[85] Jervis, *Perception and Misperception in International Politics*; Aster, "Appeasement." See also Ralph Dimuccio, "The Study of Appeasement in International Relations: Polemics, Paradigms, and Problems," *Journal of Peace Research* Vol. 35, no. 2 (1998), pp. 245–59.

# 7

# Peacemaking as a Progressive Grand Strategy

There is a third way of doing progressive foreign policy, as peacemaking, whose reasoning can be found in the activist demands of the New Social Movements and the peace intellectuals of the Cold War, as well as in the ideas espoused by some of the leading progressives in Congress. In this way of thinking, peace (internationally and societally) is the priority goal and the crucial means of unlocking other progressive goals like equality. As such, peacemaking as an approach to foreign policy differs from progressive pragmatism in relying less on American power or economic redistribution and more on fostering cooperative engagement among states and at the level of civil societies. It differs from anti-hegemonism in relying more on international institutions, regimes, and transnational activism for a common security, and less on American restraint and great-power bargains.

The logic of peacemaking follows from prioritizing the principle of solidarity. It assumes that military power-balancing is a dead end; that structural violence is the wellspring of conflict; and that adversaries can change. Peacemaking in this way requires coordinating two clusters of action. The first uses cooperative security, multilateral restraint, and mutual threat reduction to reduce risks of war and encourage stability among states. The second wagers that security "across the planet requires more than suppressing violence," and therefore more than military restraint.[1] This involves not the unilateral accommodation of autocracies but rather "waging" peace through transnational civil society-building

---

[1] Marianne Williamson, "Plan for the U.S. Department of Peace," *Marianne 2020* (2019), www.marianne2020.com/issues/us-department-of-peace-plan.

and acts of resistance to ameliorate structural violence.[2] Taken together, these two wagers promise equality and democracy as a result of changing the valence of world politics over time.

## ASSUMPTIONS

Three assumptions translate principles of anti-militarism and solidarity into a foundation for statecraft. One is that internal and external balancing (arms buildups and balance-of-power diplomacy) is risky in the short run and counterproductive in the long run – an extension of the belief that military force is an ineffective means of pursuing political goals. A second, consistent with the concept of national security as human security, is that conditions depriving people of democratic livelihood – whether out of exposure to structural violence or direct oppression – undermine US security. The third assumption is that even if US adversaries are currently revisionist states, they can be converted into defensive, status quo-supporting states in a changed socio-material context.

### Balance-of-Power Games Are Unwinnable

The military is among the worst instruments of policy to secure democratic political ends. Policymakers often rationalize nakedly militarist foreign policy in balance-of-power rhetoric, implying that as long as balancing is the reason for the next missile investment or the next unmanned weapon system, then the decision is sound and therefore legitimate.[3] But balancing, which in practice almost always involves a deliberate effort to accumulate military power, is a path to war rather than a means of peace.[4] Kenneth Boulding, a Cold-War peace intellectual, once observed that "most societies prepared for war seem to get it."[5] This was why the Institute for Policy Studies sought a global "realism divorced from balance-of-power dynamics."[6]

---

[2] For the most comprehensive resource for how civil societies should wage peace, see Gene Sharp, *From Dictatorship to Democracy: A Conceptual Framework for Liberation* (New York: The New Press, 2012); Gene Sharp, *The Politics of Nonviolent Action* (New York: P. Sargent, 1973).

[3] Daniel Nexon, "The Balance of Power in the Balance," *World Politics* Vol. 61, no. 2 (2009), pp. 330–59.

[4] There is a forgotten tradition of equilibrium or "associative balancing," but it is not what policymakers today ever do. See Richard Little, "Deconstructing the Balance of Power: Two Schools of Thought," *Review of International Studies* Vol. 15, no. 2 (1989), pp. 87–100.

[5] Kenneth Boulding, *Stable Peace* (Austin, TX: University of Texas Press, 1978), p. 25.

[6] Mueller, *Democracy's Think Tank*, p. 55.

World War I was the tragic and condemnable apotheosis of balance-of-power diplomacy.[7] G. Lowes Dickinson, horrified by the war, observed in one of the earliest texts of modern international relations that "The fatal defect of the balance of power" has always been that states do comply with the principle of balance but end up in "a perpetual effort to get the better of the balance," which is why "every balance has ended in war."[8]

Today's progressive anti-war activists similarly believe that the policies pursued in the name of the balance of power, including "the empowerment of dictators and human rights abusers ... will not keep us safe."[9] While balancing "can produce temporary stability," it frustrates peace policies with "a gross oversimplification of the complexity of the international system and the decision-making processes within it."[10] Worse, balancing is a "dangerous game" that relies on "fever pitch nationalism" to power it, which in turn creates tripwires of honor, prestige, and indivisible conflicts of interest that activate processes of war.[11] Remarking on the knotty conflict in the South China Sea, progressive activist and former politician Walden Bello explained that "Balance of power as a regulator of conflict is quite unreliable .... Beijing has valid strategic concerns but is going about resolving them the wrong way, like a classic imperial power ... the only viable solution to conflicts in the area lies in multilateral negotiations ... demilitarizing and denuclearizing the area that would demand compliance from third parties like the United States."[12]

This assumption that balancing is a game not worth the candle obviously shares the anti-hegemonist view that militarized violence is counterproductive, but it also goes much further. Peacemakers "... refuse to treat any foreign people as an instrument in the service of state security ends."[13] That commitment to human solidarity precludes strategies like balancing

---

[7] Kazin, *War against War*, p. 140.

[8] G. Lowes Dickinson, *The International Anarchy, 1904–1914* (Honolulu: University Press of the Pacific, 1926, 2003 edition), pp. 5–6.

[9] *Principles of a Progressive Foreign Policy for the United States* (Washington, DC: Win Without War, 2021), https://winwithoutwar.org/policy/principles-of-a-progressive-foreign-policy-for-the-united-states/.

[10] Boulding, *Stable Peace*, pp. 104–5.

[11] Fertik, "Geopolitics for the Left"; Ted Fertik, @TedFertik thread (January 10, 2022), https://twitter.com/tedfertik/status/1480259379823788032.

[12] Walden Bello, "Remarks at Webinar on Asia-Pacific Political Economy: Dynamics and Their Implications," *The Campaign for Peace Disarmament and Common Security* (February 20, 2021), https://cpdcs.org/watch-now-webinar-on-asia-pacific-political-economy-dynamic-and-their-implications/.

[13] Aziz Rana, "Renewing Working-Class Internationalism," *New Labor Forum* (2019), https://newlaborforum.cuny.edu/2019/01/25/working-class-internationalism/.

and formalized spheres of influence because both render people as objects sacrificed for ruling classes. Worse, balancing is a militarized form of what philosopher and activist Olufemi Taiwo called an "antagonistic security" in which "parts of the system ... are secured by way of directing precarity at others."[14] Balancing reflects the logic of state coercion – manipulation of "the threat that leaves something to chance"[15] – which amounts to elites taking risks against greater human existence (gambling with it, essentially) in order to secure the state to which they belong. Peacemakers reject this way of thinking on the grounds that, at best, it traps policymakers in cycles of violence.[16]

## Structural Violence Is Insecurity

Peacemaking also rests on a belief that "the positive aspect of peace – justice – cannot be separated from the negative aspect – elimination of violence."[17] The absence of literal, physical violence is an inadequate measure of security because social groups can be free from war yet afflicted by structural violence – a concept describing conditions of oppression or deprivation as a result of governance, economic, and ecological conditions.[18] Providing for the security of social groups does not only mean shielding them from the physical violence of military invasion, it also means they are not put at heightened risk of death compared to other social groups because of exposure to rights-denying domestic policing or impersonal forces like pandemics and environmental catastrophes. And it means ensuring they have the basic means to make a life that keeps them out of a tyrant's yoke and does not enslave them to subsistence needs.

This sort of violence is quite different from physical violence, yet the two are linked.[19] Not only does each form of violence reify the other;

---

14 Olufemi Taiwo, "Who Gets to Feel Secure?" *Aeon* (October 30, 2020), https://aeon.co/essays/on-liberty-security-and-our-system-of-racial-capitalism.

15 Thomas C. Schelling, *The Strategy of Conflict* (Cambridge, MA: Harvard University Press, 1960), p. 187.

16 On balancing as an impediment to durable security generally, see also Robert Johansen, "Toward an Alternative Security System: Moving beyond the Balance of Power in the Search for World Security," *Alternatives* Vol. 8, no. 3 (1982), pp. 293–349.

17 Quincy Wright, *A Study of War, Vol. 2* (Chicago, IL: University of Chicago Press, 1942), p. 1305.

18 Johan Galtung, "Violence, Peace, and Peace Research," *Journal of Peace Research* Vol. 6, no. 3 (1969), pp. 167–91.

19 Galtung originally hypothesized causal links between structural and physical violence, but others have gone further. See especially Riane Eisler, "Human Rights and

environments free of structural violence are logically ones in which the prospect of war is asymptotically low. Reducing structural violence, then, is a way of reducing risks of conflict and violent extremism.[20] Beyond their causal relationship, this distinction between structural and physical violence also matters because it makes possible the distinction between negative peace (the absence of war) and positive peace (the absence of war and structural violence – i.e., a durable, cooperative peace). And it is building toward a positive peace that is at the heart of much global peacebuilding work.[21]

Consistent with but more ambitious than the human-centered turn in the evolution of security studies research,[22] the logic of peacemaking presupposes that "promoting rights-respecting policies and national security interests are not separate buckets of competing priorities, but fundamentally interlinked."[23] In advocating for Bernie Sanders during the 2016 presidential election, political scientist Charli Carpenter proposed that one of the virtues of a progressive foreign policy was that it would have to acknowledge the "interconnectedness between US interests and human security of those beyond our borders" as part of addressing the "root causes of violent extremism."[24] In defining principles of a progressive foreign policy, Senators Chris Murphy, Brian Schatz, and Martin Heinrich similarly argued that "Human rights and gender equality should not be viewed as secondary to security issues, but appropriately

Violence: Integrating the Private and Public Spheres," in *The Web of Violence: From Interpersonal to Global*, edited by Jennifer Turpin and Lester Kurtz (Urbana, IL: University of Illinois Press, 1997), pp. 161–86; Birgit Brock-Utne, "Linking the Micro and Macro in Peace and Development Studies," in *The Web of Violence*, pp. 149–60.

[20] Caprioli, "Primed for Violence"; Fearon and Laitin, "Ethnicity, Insurgency and Civil War"; Linehan, "Political Instability and Economic Inequality"; Piazza, "Rooted in Poverty?"

[21] Daniel Christie, "Reducing Direct and Structural Violence: The Human Needs Theory," *Peace and Conflict* Vol. 3, no. 4 (1997), pp. 315–32. This is also the heart of the Global Fragility Act that Congress passed in 2020. See "The Global Fragility Act: A New U.S. Approach," *U.S. Institute of Peace* (January 15, 2020), www.usip.org/publications/2020/01/global-fragility-act-new-us-approach.

[22] Barry Buzan and Lena Hansen, *The Evolution of International Security Studies* (Cambridge: Cambridge University Press, 2008), pp. 202–5.

[23] Sarah Leah Witson, "The Human Rights vs. National Security Dilemma Is a Fallacy," *Foreign Policy* (January 10, 2021), https://foreignpolicy.com/2022/01/10/human-rights-national-security-tradeoff-dilemma-defense-lobbyists-corruption-fallacy/?tpcc=recirc_latest062921.

[24] Charli Carpenter, "Why a Progressive Foreign Policy Is Good for US National Security," *Open Democracy* (April 18, 2016), www.opendemocracy.net/en/why-progressive-foreign-policy-is-good-for-national-security-in-us/.

recognized as essential to long-term global stability."[25] 2020 presidential candidate Marianne Williamson built on this point, using her platform to argue that "Large groups of desperate people should be seen as a national security risk."[26] Where there is suffering or oppression, there is no peace. The only viable path to security runs through a foreign policy that centers the protection of human beings – not the state – "from critical and life-threatening danger, regardless of whether the threats are rooted in anthropogenic activities or natural events, whether they lie within or outside states, and whether they are direct or structural."[27]

## Revisionist Actors Can Change

Peacemakers do not share the anti-hegemonist assumption that the world consists of states which are, at root, defensive and security-seeking. To the contrary, many progressives who embrace solidarity as a priority conviction also recognize "a global trend toward authoritarianism and nationalist forms of politics in every continent and in multiple countries, including of course here in the United States."[28] Progressives of this mold have acknowledged that while the current era is "defined by revanchist authoritarianism," rather than confront dictators militarily, "the United States should embody the world order necessary for its survival and think instead in terms of restorative justice."[29]

In a mainstream national security mindset, such belief may seem a puzzling mismatch between problem and response. But recognizing that other actors might have predatory or self-aggrandizing intentions only directs one to responding with instruments of violence if there is genuinely no alternative. The conceit underwriting virtually all peace activism though is that anyone can change given enough time.[30] Revisionist actors

---

[25] Chris Murphy, Brian Schatz, and Martin Heinrich, "Principles for a Progressive Foreign Policy," *Foreign Affairs* (June 8, 2015), www.foreignaffairs.com/articles/2015-06-08/principles-progressive-foreign-policy.

[26] Marianne Williamson, "Plan for a US Department of Peace," *Marianne2020.com* (2019), www.marianne2020.com/issues/us-department-of-peace-plan.

[27] Ramesh Thakur and Edward Newman, eds., "Introduction: Non-Traditional Security in Asia," in *Broadening Asia's Security Discourse and Agenda: Political, Social, and Environmental Perspectives*, edited by Ramesh Thakur and Edward Newman (Tokyo: UN University Press, 2004), p. 4.

[28] Chow and Werner, "The US, China, and the Left."

[29] Patrick Iber, "Patrick Iber: Five Principles," *Fellow Travelers* (October 23, 2018), https://fellowtravelersblog.com/2018/10/23/patrick-iber-five-principles/.

[30] See especially Zinn, *You Can't Be Neutral on a Moving Train*, p. 182.

are capable of changing their character and becoming status-quo actors who unwind their geopolitical rivalries, and that means, "violence is a matter of choice ... there is almost always a less violent alternative, a less violent thought, word, intention, policy, strategy and action ..."[31]

Every regime, moreover, has within it moderates and peace-oriented thinkers; it is only a question of how power within a revisionist regime may work against the moderates' preferences. But even in extreme cases dealing with tyrannical regimes built on cults of personality, how the outside world (and the United States in particular) interacts with the regime can affect which voices in the regime gain credibility or legitimacy.[32] Peace intellectuals believe that "pinpointing cooperative officials" in a rival regime is possible, that cooperation with a rival strengthens the moderates' internal position, and in so doing the foreign policy preferences of the rival can transform.[33]

## WAGERS

Peacemaking is prefigurative. To make the world more just, and therefore safer for democracy, statecraft must make "those ends [cooperative security, mutual threat reduction, and transnational peacebuilding] at the same time our means."[34] A grand strategy of peacemaking therefore seeks in parallel to support reducing structural violence at a grassroots level (via pro-democracy movements and community action) while creating a positive valence in relations among governments by moving toward disarmament and a global cooperative security regime. The former reduces the risk of ethnic and civil wars; the latter reduces the risk of interstate wars.

### Peace from "Above": Toward Disarmament and Cooperative Security

The lodestar of global peacemaking is a project that moves progressively toward a regime of cooperative security and military disarmament.

---

[31] Cynthia Cockburn, *Anti-Militarism: Political and Gender Dynamics of Peace Movements* (London: Palgrave MacMillan, 2012), p. 1.

[32] "Empower the moderates" is an explicit premise of engagement strategies with North Korea. See, for example, Van Jackson, *How to Engage the Enemy: The Case for National Security Diplomacy with North Korea* (Washington, DC: U.S. Institute of Peace, 2020).

[33] Richard Wendell Fogg, "Dealing with Conflict: A Repertoire of Creative, Peaceful Approaches," *Journal of Conflict Resolution* Vol. 29, no. 2 (1985), p. 338.

[34] Cockburn, *Anti-Militarism*, p. 6.

This requires (1) consistently signaling an interest in peace, particularly toward adversaries and (2) materially reducing the ability to destroy and conquer others. The former hinges conceptually on using cooperation to transform how enemies see each other. The latter manipulates the offense-defense balance to favor defensive strategies and postures as the way to disarmament. Neither concept works unless both work, and each relies on unilateral gestures in different ways. Such actions could sustain a system of peace that incentivizes and habitualizes cooperation and puts greater distance between legitimate international behavior and war.[35]

### Signaling Peace, Changing Enemy Images

A common refrain on the activist left is that whereas cooperation is essential to global survival, a new "Cold War with China is a dangerous and self-defeating strategy."[36] Because rivalries tend to legitimize militarism and encourage zero-sum policies, the path to peace requires communicating peaceful intentions in word and deed. This means not only abandoning any pretense of a Cold War-like response to other great powers, but also "affirming the concept of stable peace and setting it as the major goal of national policy."[37] Be the change, stupid. One leftist intellectual pleaded that trying to achieve cooperation with adversaries – specifically China – is "not a naïve or altruistic position ... regimes engaged in security competition have to believe that the other regime earnestly desires peace" in order to step back from rivalry and demilitarize.[38] There is no plausible way to convince a regime like the Communist Party of China (CCP) in China that the United States is interested in peace when it spurns most forms of cooperation and continues to prioritize preparations for war in parallel with China doing the same.[39] The plea is to undertake a process that gradually reconciles enemy images of one another so that mutual threat perceptions

---

[35] Kenneth Boulding described the imperative as strengthening the ability of a peace system to resist against the strain of pressures toward the threshold of violence. Boulding, *Stable Peace*, pp. 32–39.

[36] Sixty five activist organizations endorsed this statement in response to the Strategic Competition Act of 2021. People's Action press release, "Justice is Global Joins 65 Orgs: Cold War with China is a Dangerous and Self-Defeating Strategy" (May 18, 2021), https://peoplesaction.org/2021/05/justice-is-global-joins-65-orgs-cold-war-with-china-is-a-dangerous-and-self-defeating-strategy/.

[37] Boulding, *Stable Peace*, pp. 113–14.

[38] Ted Fertik, @TedFertik thread (January 10, 2022), https://twitter.com/tedfertik/status/1480259379823788032.

[39] Van Jackson, "The Problem with Primacy," *Foreign Affairs* (January 16, 2023), www.foreignaffairs.com/asia/problem-primacy.

soften, risks of war become less acute, and cooperation becomes more politically feasible. The United States must reduce "the scope for the kind of rivalry that bolsters militarism in the US and among the other great powers by expanding the space for constructive international cooperation."[40]

The path to forging peaceable relations out of rivalrous ones is necessarily context contingent, but the common arguments for doing so stress thickening diplomatic engagement, layering multilateral institutional engagement on top of direct diplomacy, and resorting to some amount of unilateral signaling before expecting reciprocal cooperation.[41] Image change comes from positive socialization, a prerequisite for which is engagement. Thickening the density of social ties, especially through institutional sites (like treaties and international organizations), buffers conflict and serves as a counterweight to activities with a militarist character. And unilateral restraint/concessionary unilateralism is the key to unlocking reciprocity or tit-for-tat strategies of cooperation.

The Committee for a Sane Nuclear Policy (SANE), one of America's most important anti-nuclear organizations during the Cold War, had an approach to disarmament that was "not unilateralist," meaning that, while it was willing to undertake unilateral weapons reductions to catalyze cooperative processes, it was not simply prescribing neutering American power as a solution.[42] This also describes the role of unilateral restraint in peacemaking – compromises and accommodations of other international actors are essential, but only to the extent that (1) unilateral gestures can help transform the valence of hostile relations from negative to positive and (2) they do not redirect insecurity toward others in the international system. Establishing patterns of cooperation with otherwise hostile powers, many progressives believe, is the only way to stabilize the ongoing arms race on the Korean Peninsula,[43] or to ensure sufficient

---

[40] Ted Fertik "Geopolitics for the Left," *N-Plus One* (March 11, 2019), https://nplusonemag.com/online-only/online-only/geopolitics-for-the-left/.

[41] Charles Osgood, *An Alternative to War or Surrender* (Urbana, IL: University of Illinois Press, 1962); Boulding, *Stable Peace*, pp. 108–14; Tony Armstrong, *Breaking the Ice: Rapprochement between East and West Germany, the United States and China, and Israel and Egypt* (Washington, DC: U.S. Institute of Peace Press, 1993); Stephen Rock, *Appeasement in International Politics* (Lexington, KY: University of Kentucky Press, 2000); Charles Kupchan, *How Enemies Become Friends: The Sources of Stable Peace* (Princeton, NJ: Princeton University Press, 2010).

[42] Cortright, *Peace*, p. 136.

[43] Jackson, *Risk Realism*; Catherine Killough, "De-Escalation on the Korean Peninsula," *Fellow Travelers* (November 23, 2020), https://fellowtravelersblog.com/2020/11/23/de-escalation-on-the-korean-peninsula/.

collaboration with China to combat climate change, which, while a long-term existential threat, in the short term promises to visit all manner of structural violence, inequities, and even new forms of global colonialism on the world if not managed properly.[44]

By persistently signaling peaceful intentions and boldly embracing "unilateral acts of a tension reducing nature" despite the risks (discussed below),[45] cooperation can build toward a stable peace by increasing the likelihood of "cooperation spirals" – reciprocal trust-building that transforms rivalries into stable, benign relationships.[46] Working with China to address the climate crisis in particular can "help dispel the Cold War environment currently besieging Beijing and Washington and lead to cooperation on other critical issues."[47]

### Non-offensive Defense

One of the arguments easily lodged against the former element of the cooperative security wager is that "signaling peace" is so much cheap talk. Reality is more than rhetoric, and rivals will not disarm or enter some transformational global peace project simply because there are issues like climate change where great-power interests converge. But that is why peace signaling must have a material foundation in mutual threat reduction – the tangible risks involved in moving toward disarmament are what makes commitments to processes of cooperation credible. Disarmament thinking offers any number of proposals that might be mixed and matched for how to do this – multi-track diplomacy with rival regimes, the expansion of nuclear weapons-free zones, mutual nuclear freezes, passing the No First Use Act that would prohibit the United States from using nuclear weapons first, restraining the deployment of nuclear capable weapons systems, diluting the president's nuclear launch authority, eliminating US-based intercontinental ballistic missiles, halting nuclear modernization

---

[44] Fertik, "Geopolitics for the Left"; People's Action press release, "Justice Is Global Joins 65 Orgs: Cold War with China Is a Dangerous and Self-Defeating Strategy"; Bernie Sanders, "Washington's Dangerous New Consensus on China," *Foreign Affairs* (June 17, 2021), www.foreignaffairs.com/articles/china/2021-06-17/washingtons-dangerous-new-consensus-china; Olufemi Taiwo, "The Green New Deal and the Danger of Climate Colonialism," *Slate* (March 1, 2019), https://slate.com/technology/2019/03/green-new-deal-climate-colonialism-energy-land.html?via=recirc_recent.

[45] Mueller, *Democracy's Think Tank*, p. 30.

[46] Lyle Goldstein, *Meeting China Halfway: How to Defuse the Emerging China-US Rivalry* (Washington, DC: Georgetown University Press, 2015).

[47] "U.S.-China Cooperation in Overcoming Climate Change," Committee for a Sane U.S.-China Policy (undated), www.saneuschinapolicy.org/climate-change-cooperation.

investments, allowing international monitors to verify that missiles are inactive (stored or unfueled), and creating a UN-based disarmament agency to name a few.[48] What they tend to share in common is a willingness to undertake unilateral reductions in armaments in a way that shifts the offense-defense balance among major powers toward defense, thereby reducing risks of war and providing a foundation of real stability. Randy Forsberg, best known as the leader of the Nuclear Freeze Movement in the 1980s, brought this approach from Europe, called "nonoffensive defense," which used defense policy to move the world closer to military disarmament.[49] The United States can take actions that make it less risky for others to adopt defensive strategies.

Like the other logics here, peacemaking is incompatible with military primacy (i.e., building a military that unilaterally out-arms the most powerful enemy's *highest* capabilities) as a strategic need or force structure standard. And like anti-hegemonism in particular, peacemaking rejects the proposition that security can come from bilateral defense treaties and a global military presence whose purpose is deterrence and warfighting.[50] But whereas progressive pragmatism is broadly congruent with a forward-balancing defense strategy and anti-hegemonism with an offshore balancing or even garrison defense strategy, peacemaking would repurpose "the role of the military in the direction of soldiers without enemies."[51] The military's roles and missions would need to shift to intergovernmental law enforcement and international peacekeeping – a strategy and structure similar to small-state defense today, including the New Zealand, Canadian, or pre-9/11 "Nordic model."[52] In addition

---

[48] See especially Raskin, *The Politics of National Security*, pp. 115–18; Boulding, *Stable Peace*, pp. 108–22; John Carl Baker, "Restoring Momentum toward Nuclear Zero," *Fellow Travelers* (November 16, 2020), https://fellowtravelersblog.com/2020/11/16/restoring-momentum-toward-nuclear-zero/; Randall Caroline Watson Forsberg, *Toward a Theory of Peace: The Role of Moral Beliefs* (Ithaca, NY: Cornell University Press, 2019).

[49] Randall Forsberg, "Confining the Military to Defense as a Route to Disarmament," *World Policy Journal* Vol. 1, no. 2 (1984), pp. 285–318; Randall Forsberg, "Collective Security: Where Do We Stand Now?" *Mershon International Studies Review* Vol. 38, no. 1 (1994), pp. 121–23; Randall Forsberg, "Creating a Cooperative Security System," *Boston Review* Vol. 17, no. 6 (1992), pp. 7–10.

[50] Kizer, *A U.S. Grand Strategy for a Values-Driven Foreign Policy*; Randall Caroline Watson Forsberg, *Toward a Theory of Peace: The Role of Moral Beliefs* (Ithaca, NY: Cornell University Press, 2019), pp. 36–37.

[51] Boulding, *Stable Peace*, pp. 115–6.

[52] Kathleen Hicks and Joseph Federici, *Getting to Less? Exploring the Press for Less in America's Defense Commitments* (Washington, DC: Center for Strategic & International Studies, 2020), p. 5.

to introducing restraints on the deployment and operationalization of US missiles, nuclear inventory, and nuclear-capable systems on the way to eliminating nuclear weapons entirely, other drastic force structure changes would occur too, including canceling next-generation fighter aircraft development and moving away from "giant, attack-oriented aircraft carriers and battleships" to "smaller but more numerous sea-control vessels" that could be useful for keeping the peace and preserving global commons in a less militarized world without antagonizing the security of others.[53]

Drawing down America's military capabilities, presence, and (existing) commitments in a manner that meets this new benchmark contributes to greater security because it makes the means of policy more closely resemble its desired ends. Prefiguration works here partly through unilateral restraint as a triggering mechanism for ameliorating rivalries, lending credibility to the other peace-signaling actions the government undertakes.[54] Put differently, trading on America's military largesse actually jumpstarts reciprocal restraint by alleviating security dilemmas and arms-racing pressures with rivals: "Because the United States has such an overwhelming edge in arms and technology, American disarmament can be leveraged to gain commitments by others to disarm."[55] Crucially, self-imposed restraint in the form of circumscribed warfighting abilities also ties the hands of the United States to deploy force in the future, making the peacemaker's military transformation a credible signal of benign intent that alleviates the insecurity of competitors.[56] Such costly signals overcome the commitment problem faced by comparatively weaker states, thereby making arms reduction more feasible than it has been since the Cold War.

Shifting the offense-defense balance toward defense raises existentially large questions concerning what to do about existing security architectures built around global forward basing and military alliances. Some peace intellectuals and activists have grappled with these concerns

---

[53] Michael Klare, as quoted in Mueller, *Democracy's Think Tank*, p. 68.

[54] Charles Kupchan, *How Enemies Become Friends: The Sources of Stable Peace* (Princeton: Princeton University Press, 2010).

[55] Lachmann, "How to Build a Socialist Foreign Policy"; Evan Braden Montgomery, "Breaking Out of the Security Dilemma: Realism, Reassurance, and the Problem of Uncertainty," *International Security* Vol. 31, no. 2 (2006), pp. 151–85.

[56] Montgomery, "Breaking Out of the Security Dilemma"; James Fearon, "Signaling Foreign Policy Interests: Tying Hands versus Sinking Costs," *Journal of Conflict Resolution* Vol. 41, no. 1 (1997), pp. 68–90.

in a detailed way, showing how a revolution in common security is plausible.[57] Since peacemakers rule out the balance of power as a security mechanism, arms sales to even democratic allies are mostly unnecessary. North Atlantic Treaty Organization (NATO) and America's bilateral alliances in Asia would not be abandoned but would rather transition to regional collective security arrangements that could eventually be confederated into a global cooperative security regime.[58] In a world of ongoing rivalries and seemingly indivisible conflicts over territory and resources, building a cooperative security peace mechanism at even a regional level may appear fanciful, but that is why the United States in particular must evince a desire for stable peace in word and deed. As the world's only superpower, radical changes the United States makes can transform the context in which other international actors metabolize their own security environments. When you shift how an issue is framed, it becomes possible to shift the kinds of policies that are feasible or desirable. Does it not stand to reason that a superpower changing its patterns of international conduct could change how other regimes perceive or cope with international threats and security? When the United States shifted from rivalry to détente with China in the 1970s, Asian security itself transformed as a result.[59] Even the rivalry between North and South Korea – an entirely separate dyad that up to that point had been in a continuous military struggle punctuated by intermittent violence – entered a period of rapprochement specifically because of the "mood of détente" that Sino-US relations created.[60] And that transformation happened as the consequence of altering just one great-power relationship, without bothering to make peace, and without meaningful military reductions. Peacefulness can cascade just as violence can.

---

[57] See especially, Forsberg, *Toward a Theory of Peace*, pp. 16–36; Andrew Butfoy, *Common Security and Strategic Reform: A Critical Analysis* (London: Palgrave MacMillan, 2016); Sustainable Defense Task Force, *Sustainable Defense: More Security, Less Spending* (Washington, DC: Center for International Policy, 2019); Adam Mount, "Principles for a Progressive Defense Policy," *Texas National Security Review* (December 4, 2018), https://tnsr.org/roundtable/policy-roundtable-the-future-of-progressive-foreign-policy/#essay3.

[58] Mueller, *Democracy's Think Tank*, pp. 55–59.

[59] Jackson, *Pacific Power Paradox*, pp. 29–41.

[60] As one North Korean official explained in 1972, in the shadow of Nixon's opening to China, "In these circumstances, we can't wage war. What should we do? Taking the current situation into account, we thought the best thing to do was launch a peace offensive." As quoted in Van Jackson, *Rival Reputations: Coercion and Credibility in US-North Korea Relations* (Cambridge: Cambridge University Press, 2016), pp. 101–2.

Crucially, since most US allies are not optimized for traditional warfighting anyway, the move to a collective peacekeeping defense posture would involve only minor changes to their militaries; it is the transformation of the US military that is the real "Sinatra test" for the rest of the non-authoritarian world. Rather than measuring US power in terms of the correlation of forces between its military and an adversary's military, then, a cooperative security regime uses a different benchmark entirely, keeping the peace between states by achieving a "ratio of the combined military power of nations supporting [a democratic commitment to nonviolence] to that of nations not supporting – sufficient to deter acts of aggression by the nonsupporters."[61] Peacemaking thus combines collective deterrence (*not* power-balancing under anarchy) with socialization – that is, a deliberate bet that "the establishment of the standard of defensive nonviolence among a few nations might suffice to persuade others of the same view."[62]

### Waging Peace from "Below"

But the peacemaker's other wager is necessarily more antagonistic toward autocratic regimes – transnational partnerships with civil society organizations to support peacebuilding and democracy advocacy across borders. Building toward disarmament can only realize security "if it is sustained and accompanied by other peacemaking efforts."[63] The commitment to solidaristic peacebuilding looks past regimes to the betterment of people within them. It invests "in alternate sources of national power that will empower democratic movements and reinvigorate US influence in the world."[64] Although there are many ways to go about a form of democracy promotion that routes around states in favor of civil societies and communities, there are four major areas of concentrated action: founding a Department of Peace to facilitate peacebuilding, conflict prevention, and restorative justice; transferring portions of Pentagon spending to fund peacebuilding; tailoring sanctions to a "do no harm" principle; and implementing environmental security projects that respond to the climate crisis as a way of improving governance and social stability.

---

[61] Forsberg, *Toward a Theory of Peace*, p. 20.
[62] Ibid.
[63] David Cortright, *Peace: A History of Movements and Ideas* (Cambridge: Cambridge University Press, 2008), p. 108.
[64] Laila Ujayli, *Reimagining US Security Spending for the 21st Century and Beyond* (Washington, DC: Win without War, 2019), https://winwithoutwar.org/wp-content/uploads/2019/09/Reimagining-Security-Spending_Final.pdf.

*A Department of Peace*

The assumption that how you interact with the world must mirror how you wish the world to be translated into an active venture of peacebuilding "designed to prevent the eruption of or return to armed conflict" without the military instrument of statecraft.[65] This wager makes a strategic necessity of non-traditional security initiatives that have long existed on the periphery of strategic analysis but form the core of a peacemaking agenda. Former presidential candidates Marianne Williamson, Dennis Kucinich, Mike Gravel, and others have all backed the creation of a US Department of Peace because it would represent a praxis; a bureaucratic counterweight to the Pentagon that displaces instruments of violence and the militarist mindset that rationalizes them in favor of initiatives that seek to remedy transnational oppression.[66] A peacemaking grand strategy requires coordinating many programs and authorities that need their own institutional champion. There is also ample evidence that peacebuilding in response to events as they happen, or relying organically on the "peacebuilding industry," can easily lead to technocratic projects with good intentions that deliver bad results.[67] A dedicated institutional focal point for peacebuilding is necessary in order to have internal coherence, unity of effort, and ultimately strategic effect.

The proposal for a Department of Peace, which has existed in some form since the early twentieth century and has occasionally been championed by a subset of progressive activists and politicians, would have a widely scoped mandate to "wage peace" by addressing primarily upstream structural causes of violence.[68] Most of the activities that would fall under its purview – dispute mediation, a street-level "peace force" to mute violence in civil societies, election monitoring, economic empowerment of women, knowledge production about nonviolence, multi-track diplomatic engagement, and advocating for non-military solutions to global policy problems – have been part of US policy for decades, but in a thin, scattershot manner. Even during the Trump era, when US foreign

---

[65] Michael Barnett, Hunjoon Kim, Madalene O'Donnell, and Laura Sitea, "Peacebuilding: What Is in a Name?" *Global Governance* Vol. 13, no. 1 (2007), p. 36.

[66] Zack Budryk, "Williamson Unveils Plan to Create Cabinet-Level Department of Peace," *The Hill* (August 20, 2019), https://thehill.com/homenews/campaign/458049-williamson-unveils-plan-to-create-cabinet-level-department-of-peace.

[67] See especially Severine Autesserre, *The Frontlines of Peace: An Insider's Guide to Changing the World* (New York: Oxford University Press, 2021).

[68] "Proposed U.S. Department of Peacebuilding (H.R. 1111)," *Peace Alliance* (2018), https://peacealliance.org/issues-advocacy/department-of-peace/.

policy was a menace to the world, Congress passed the Global Fragility Act, which allocated more than a billion dollars over five years to conflict prevention and peacebuilding initiatives.[69] The juxtaposition of the corruption and hypermilitarism of Trump's statecraft with funds intended to stabilize societies and prevent extremism does not reveal a duality about American power or purpose so much as it exposes the marginal role of the latter peace-related activities in national security thought. Even when peacebuilding activities are funded, they have never had any weight relative to other aspects of US foreign policy, have never been treated as a strategic priority, and have never been concentrated to ameliorate the long-term threats that attract an American military response.

A Department of Peace would give the complex and diffuse work of peacebuilding greater attention-share in US foreign policy. The improved effectiveness of peacebuilding that would result would in turn attenuate "cultures of violence" around the world and strengthen political and economic societal cohesion, which facilitates "peace proliferation."[70] It is through an empowered institutional vehicle like a Department of Peace that US statecraft can advocate – symbolically and materially – for oppressed populations seeking liberation, like the Palestinians, as well as pro-democracy movements like the "Milk Tea Alliance" spanning Taiwan, Hong Kong, Burma, and Thailand.[71]

### Converting to a Peace Economy

A founding priority of the disarmament organization SANE was to "transition to a peacetime economy."[72] US political economy since the 1960s has involved an implicit military Keynesianism – striving for full employment via defense industrial spending rather than domestic investment.[73] That political bargain is potentially threatened by a world at peace, and

[69] "The Global Fragility Act: A New U.S. Approach," *U.S. Institute of Peace* (January 15, 2020), www.usip.org/publications/2020/01/global-fragility-act-new-us-approach.
[70] Alex Nitzberg, "Peace Proliferation? Marianne Williamson Wants to Develop a U.S. Department of Peace," *Townhall* (August 20, 2019), https://townhall.com/tipsheet/alexnitzberg/2019/08/20/peace-proliferation-marianne-williamson-wants-to-develop-a-us-department-of-peace-n2551982.
[71] Wong, "Hong Kong's International Front Line"; Adam Dedman and Autumn Lai, "Digitally Dismantling Asian Authoritarianism: Activist Reflections from the #MilkTeaAlliance," *Contention* Vol. 9, no. 1 (2021), pp. 97–132.
[72] As quoted in Cortright, *Peace*, p. 136.
[73] As Michael Brenes writes, "The politics of a permanent war economy ... also laid the foundation for austerity politics to take shape during and after the 1970s." Brenes, *For Might and Right*, pp. 239–40.

American politics will naturally pull toward military Keynesianism whatever else it does. This is part of the problem that needs fixing. The solution is to not just fund peace but to do so by divesting of defense.

US peace initiatives cannot be part of a "both/and" strategy in tandem with military Keynesianism; the former draws potency from its resources coming at the expense of the latter. Moreover, even when defense funding is reduced but not re-programmed for explicit peace initiatives, it redounds to the benefit of greater security all the same. Military Keynesianism as a political consensus justified *not* investing adequately in domestic renewal after 1964. By eliminating that post-1964 bargain and freeing up federal spending on domestic investment, the United States can finance a healthy democratic society at home, which in turn strengthens America's ability to influence world events through diplomacy: "By working toward a social transformation at home, building up the legitimacy of the American state and the moral legitimacy of its economy, the United States increases its ability to marshal diplomatic pressure on behalf of allies around the world."[74]

This swords-into-ploughshares project is among the most thoroughly developed policy ideas in progressive foreign policy thought. Win Without War, a progressive NGO focused on peace issues, proposed reducing the annual defense budget by $200–350 billion while doubling the spending for the State Department.[75] The Defense Spending Reduction Caucus in the House of Representatives, which has an overlapping membership with the Congressional Progressive Caucus, has proposed shifting 1.3 percent of the defense budget toward a global Covid-19 vaccination program that, in addition to saving lives, "would increase [US] influence with regard to the pandemic fight and other challenges – including the climate crisis, poverty, and regional conflicts."[76] Bernie Sanders and Elizabeth Warren outlined proposals for drawing down the "bloated defense budget" in order to pay for domestic investment.[77] A concrete agenda for transitioning defense spending into peacemaking also appears in a series

[74] Meaney, "What U.S. Foreign Policy Will Look Like under Socialism."

[75] Ujayli, *Reimagining US Security Spending for the 21st Century and Beyond.*

[76] John Nichols, "Cut Military Spending to Deliver Covid-19 Vaccines to the World," *The Nation* (August 20, 2021), www.thenation.com/article/politics/us-military-spending-covid-19-vaccines/.

[77] Remarks by Senator Elizabeth Warren: A Foreign Policy That Works for All Americans (Washington, DC, November 29, 2018), www.warren.senate.gov/newsroom/press-releases/warren-outlines-vision-for-a-foreign-policy-that-works-for-all-americans; Friends of Bernie Sanders, "Issues: How Does Bernie Pay for His Plans?" (undated), https://berniesanders.com/issues/how-does-bernie-pay-his-major-plans/.

of legislative actions proposed by Congresswoman Ilhan Omar. The logic of the seven proposed "pathway to peace" bills in her name "… use some of the money that we decide should be going into militarizing our government, to using it for the prospect of peace around the world."[78] So doing will "not just contain global crises but actually get ahead of them" by remedying the structural violence at their root.[79] As such, the initiatives not only cut defense spending but divert portions of war funding (specifically overseas contingency operations) for conflict mediation and global peacebuilding.[80] They call for international programs that reduce "poverty, inequality, and the lack of opportunity" among disadvantaged global youths by "providing education and employment skills they need for self-sufficiency."[81] They not only withhold security assistance to any government identified as committing human rights violations, but also direct the State Department to work with the offending governments on restorative justice programs that compensate victims and correct undemocratic practices. They confer congressional legitimacy on the International Criminal Court. And they direct the State Department to negotiate a binding international agreement to protect the rights of migrants. This patchwork of direct action and symbolic recognition are financed through military divestment and explicitly grounded in principles of anti-militarism and solidarity.[82]

### Sanctioning Oppressors, Not the Oppressed

Economic sanctions become part of the peacemaking wager only when driven by the imperative for democratic solidarity. Peacemakers generally

[78] "'Our Very Existence is the Resistance': An Hour with AOC, Ayanna Pressley, Rashida Tlaib, and Ilhan Omar," *Democracy Now* (February 10, 2020), www.democracynow .org/2020/2/10/democracy_now_the_squad_sotu#transcript.

[79] Zander Willoughby, "Peacebuilding Coalition Welcomes Peacebuilding Act of 2020," *PR Newswire* (February 12, 2020), www.prnewswire.com/news-releases/peacebuilding-coalition-welcomes-global-peacebuilding-act-of-2020-301003903.html.

[80] Omar's "Pathway to Peace" proposes a $5 billion shift from defense to peacebuilding but others, including #PeopleOverPentagon – which Omar and Justice Democrats support – advocate diverting as much as $200 billion annually from the defense budget. See "The Agenda," #PeopleOverPentagon (undated), https://peopleoverpentagon.org/the-agenda/.

[81] Ilhan Omar, Legislative Statement Introducing "Pathways to Peace" (February 12, 2020), https://omar.house.gov/sites/omar.house.gov/files/wysiwyg_uploaded/Pathway%20to%20Peace%20Summary%2001.11.pdf.

[82] Ben Armbruster, "Q&A: Rep. Ilhan Omar Explains Her New 'Pathway to Peace' and How It's an Antidote to U.S. Militarism," *Quincy Institute for Responsible Statecraft Blog* (February 14, 2020), https://responsiblestatecraft.org/2020/02/14/ilhan-omar-pathway-to-peace-antidote-to-u-s-militarism/.

oppose broad sanctions targeting entire regimes or nations on the grounds that they worsen inequality, widen poverty gaps within countries, and "seriously damage the long-term growth trajectory of the societies they target."[83] For instance, Justice Democrats, led by Representatives Pramila Jayapal and Barbara Lee, sponsored legislation demanding a progressive foreign policy that included "ending the use of broad-based sectoral sanctions."[84] Governing elites often find ways to ensure that individual citizens bear the cost of sanctions rather than the elites themselves. But more than that, "broad financial sanctions create inflationary pressures" that directly harm households.[85] The decision to apply sanctions or not should defer to the judgment, where it exists, of civil society elements on the ground – the people most affected by the decision must be at the center of considerations. This is among the most powerful ways to provide meaningful international solidarity to nonviolent direct action happening locally. Questions about sanctions, in other words, should be subordinate to questions about how to coordinate US economic power with pro-democracy organizing within authoritarian or conflict-ridden regimes.

What this means in practice is that the United States must remove the web of suffocating economic restrictions imposed on North Korea, Iran, Cuba, and more recently Syria – places where the people have long borne the brunt of US sanctions and the strategic effects of sanctions have ranged from negligible to disastrous.[86] Instead, the United States should be using something like the Global Magnitsky Act to target specific individuals involved in illegal weapons proliferation, human rights abuses, and war crimes.[87] This would prevent the worst offenders in the Assad

[83] Mulder, "A Leftist Foreign Policy Should Reject Economic Sanctions."

[84] Office of Congresswoman Pramila Jayapal press release, "Lawmakers Introduce Foreign Policy Resolution" (January 19, 2022), https://jayapal.house.gov/2022/01/19/lawmakers-introduce-foreign-policy-resolution/.

[85] Esfandyar Batmanghelidj, *The Inflation Weapon: How American Sanctions Harm Iranian Households* (Goshen, IN: Sanctions and Security Research Project, 2022), https://sanctionsandsecurity.org/publications/the-inflation-weapon-how-american-sanctions-harm-iranian-households/.

[86] Blaise Malley, "The Enduring Cruelty of Biden's Sanctions Regime," *The New Republic* (November 18, 2021), https://newrepublic.com/article/164450/biden-sanctions-reform-pandemic-diplomacy; Hasan Ismaik, "U.S. Sanctions Are Killing Innocent Syrians," *Foreign Policy* (April 1, 2021), https://foreignpolicy.com/2021/04/01/caesar-sanctions-killing-innocent-syrians/?utm_source=PostUp&utm_medium=email&utm_campaign=31721&utm_term=Editors%20Picks%20OC&?tpcc=31721.

[87] Mulder, "A Leftist Foreign Policy Should Reject Economic Sanctions"; David Klion, "What Should the Left Do about China?" *The Nation* (January 11, 2022), www.thenation.com/article/world/china-left-foreign-policy/.

regime in Syria, the Putin regime in Russia, and the Communist Party of China from offshoring funds and conducting international transactions. On Israel-Palestine, the United States should not impede the Boycott, Sanction, and Divest (BDS) movement against Israel for its occupation and repression of Palestine – a transnational grassroots movement to organize civil society sanctions against Israel – and to the extent that BDS does not harm Israeli civilians, the US government should support it.[88] The United States should also be pursuing "comprehensive economic sanctions" against the military junta in Myanmar – cutting it off from all outside financing and transactions – because civil society there demands it. The Confederation of Trade Unions of Myanmar and the Industry Workers' Federation of Myanmar both issued a global call in 2021 to "cut off the dictatorship's revenue stream ... because of severe violations of workers' human rights, trade unions are no longer able to operate freely in Myanmar .... The military regime must be diplomatic isolated and starved of resources."[89] Myanmar's worker base – which consists of commodity and textile production for export – believes it suffers worse under a junta that receives finance mostly by foreign aid, trade, and investment than if the "national" economy were cut off from the outside world.

### Peace through Environmental Security

The need to respond to the existential threat of climate change also offers a pathway for waging peace from below that did not exist in previous generations. All progressives agree about the importance of reducing environmental harm and mitigating climate change's effects on people, but peacemaking offers a unique way to think about and use the issue to facilitate peace, emblematic of a strategy that augurs for its means to resemble its ends.

Peacemakers believe that "if we cut the Pentagon budget, we could have an actual Green New Deal on the scale we need to stop climate change."[90] That funding could "expand on current models of

---

[88] This was why, for example, Bernie Sanders has been vocally critical of Israeli settlement policies, approved withholding security assistance to Israel, yet opposed BDS in 2017. "Bernie on Palestine and BDS," *AJ+* (May 4, 2017), www.facebook.com/watch/?v=953404734801034.

[89] IndustriALL Global Union, Call to Support the Campaign for Comprehensive Economic Sanctions against the Military Junta in Myanmar (August 31, 2021), www.industriall-union.org/sites/default/files/uploads/documents/2021/MYANMAR/call_for_campaign_on_myanmar.pdf.

[90] Ashley Smith in "China and the U.S. Left: A Dialogue Between Critical China Scholars and *Spectre*," *Spectre* (July 17, 2021), https://spectrejournal.com/china-and-the-u-s-left/.

peacebuilding trust funds," which already allocate portions of their budget to climate-related initiatives.[91] Addressing climate change by making societies resilient to its effects and introducing methods of more efficient natural resource management occurs through community-based projects that peacebuilding organizations have used to reduce structural violence and mend communal disputes and tensions.[92] The opposite is also true – the majority of the UN's peace operations are vulnerable to climate-related disruptions, meaning peace is literally harder to pursue when the damage of climate change is greater.[93] Climate justice and community peace are coterminous.

## RISKS

The peacemakers' wagers accept the interrelated risks that arise from the mistrust and relative-gains thinking they reject – defection by states with whom the United States enters into arms control and mutual threat reduction agreements, vulnerability to coercion by states that retain or increase military advantages relative to the United States, and authoritarian interference in democracies as a reaction to transnational civic engagement. They also potentially harbor a major strategic blind spot to the extent that they prioritize resolving structural violence over distributions of wealth and power.

### Vulnerability to Military Predation

Realist and strategic bargaining literatures foreground the difficulty of trusting other international actors, particularly competitors. For realists, states under international anarchy can never trust the intentions of others; prioritizing relative gains means avoiding relative vulnerability.[94] This is why security dilemmas can be difficult to ameliorate even though cooperation is a logical pathway out of them. If one party's defection from an arms control agreement would result in military advantages

---

[91] Kate Kizer, "American Fans of Putin," *Inkstick Media* (March 3, 2022), https://inkstickmedia.com/american-fans-of-putin/.

[92] Florian Krampe, Farah Hegazi, and Stacy VanDeveer, "Sustainable Peace through Better Resource Governance: Three Potential Mechanisms for Environmental Peacebuilding," *World Development* Vol. 144 (2021), www.sciencedirect.com/science/article/pii/S0305750X21001200?via%3Dihub.

[93] Florian Krampe, "Why United Nations Peace Operations Cannot Ignore Climate Change," *SIPRI* (February 22, 2021), www.sipri.org/commentary/topical-backgrounder/2021/why-united-nations-peace-operations-cannot-ignore-climate-change.

[94] Montgomery, "Breaking Out of the Security Dilemma."

relative to a competitor, or if adhering to an unfulfilled agreement generates military disadvantages, then negotiations between relative-gains thinkers either will not happen or will fail upon implementation. Contra expectations that the means of policy should resemble its ends, pursuing arms control and threat-reduction agreements irrespective of external conditions, or unilaterally reducing US military capabilities and commitments, risks deception and betrayal by the counterparty – especially if the offense-defense balance favors offensive military strategies.[95] The strategic bargaining literature treats this cooperation-vulnerability dilemma as an information problem. Actors have incentives to misrepresent their risk tolerance and preferences, making it difficult to know whether the words and deeds of others are accurate representations of intent.[96] Anyone seeking advantage will "pocket" US restraint or reductions in its power by ultimately failing to emulate it. The risk, then, is that the United States makes itself less capable of projecting force while the world fails to imitate, thus militarily weakening the United States to others' benefit.

### Autocracy's Revenge

The transnational aspect of peacemaking also risks incurring the backlash of state oppression against civil societies and reciprocal authoritarian interference in democracies. When Bernie Sanders rebuked Vladimir Putin on the presidential campaign trail, he stated baldly that, "our goal is to not only strengthen American democracy, but to work in solidarity with supporters of democracy around the globe, including in Russia."[97] Sanders, and the Progressive International he helped found, have determined that transnational activism is part of what is necessary to realize peace and democracy. Yet, history suggests that the world's dictators may react to attempts to seek out solidarity with democracy movements abroad by pursuing a mirror-image strategy of promoting authoritarianism and societal ruptures within democracies abroad.

Whereas in the late- and post–Cold War era, transnational activist networks operated around the world on behalf of liberal causes, by the turn

---

[95] Robert Jervis, "Cooperation under the Security Dilemma," *World Politics* Vol. 30, no. 2 (1978), pp. 186–90.

[96] James D. Fearon, "Rationalist Explanations for War," *International Organization* Vol. 49, no. 3 (1995), pp. 379–414; Andrew Kydd, "Game Theory and the Spiral Model," *World Politics* Vol. 49, no. 3 (1997), pp. 371–400.

[97] Bernie Sanders as quoted in Alex Ward, "Read: Bernie Sanders's Big Foreign Policy Speech," *Vox* (September 21, 2017), www.vox.com/world/2017/9/21/16345600/bernie-sanders-full-text-transcript-foreign-policy-speech-westminster.

of the century autocratic states were routinely using a variety of tactics to restrict, subvert, and shut them down. Consequently, dictators started succeeding in insulating their rule from pressures for democratic reform and respect for human rights.[98] Worse, in Russia, Vladimir Putin came to see "Western" NGOs as engaging in a form of political interference that threatened his kleptocracy and challenged Russia's dominion over its near abroad, which some see as essential context for making sense of Putin's hostility to the United States.[99] Putin not only subsequently facilitated the rise and connectivity of far right parties across Europe, he also reinvigorated Soviet-era practices of divide-and-rule information warfare targeting democratic polities, including the United States in the 2016 and 2020 presidential elections.[100]

Russia's playbook for entrenching authoritarianism and crushing liberalism has also spread to Africa, Asia, Europe, and Latin America.[101] The Trump-era ascendance of authoritarian populism globally had many causes, but transnational illiberal networks – fostered foremost by Russia as a reaction to pro-democracy transnational activism – were undoubtedly among them. Consequently, in places like Brazil, where Progressive International has issued statements and organized protest action against authoritarian demagogue Jair Bolsonaro, the latter's supporters have portrayed the Progressive International itself as a subversive group aligned with Bolsonaro's political opponents.[102] The risk is clear enough – the more effective pro-democratic transnational activism appears to be, the more it will antagonize the interests of tyrants, who surely will not sit idly by as their existence is threatened.

### *"Peacewashing" Oppression*

A final risk of peacemaking is that political economy proves a devastating blind spot. Even if peacemaking appears to reduce interstate war and improve the balance of democracy in the world, it may leave untouched patterns of economic domination within societies and between the Global

---

[98] Cooley and Nexon, *Exit from Hegemony*, pp. 141–44.

[99] See, for example, Charles Ziegler, "A Crisis of Diverging Perspectives: U.S.-Russian Relations and the Security Dilemma," *Texas National Security Review* Vol. 4, no. 1 (2020/21), pp. 11–33.

[100] Thomas Rid, *Active Measures: A Secret History of Disinformation and Political Warfare* (New York: Farrar, Straus, Giroux, 2020), pp. 377–422.

[101] Cooley and Nexon, *Exit from Hegemony*, pp. 144–48.

[102] Q24N, "Marches in Favor of Bolsonaro Shake the Progressive International," *Q Costa Rica* (September 8, 2021), https://qcostarica.com/marches-in-favor-of-bolsonaro-shake-the-progressive-international/.

North and South. It is possible, in other words, that the peacemaker's logic does not go far enough upstream in diagnosing the causes of insecurity. At the risk of stating it too simply, the logic of peacemaking has no answer to problems of class or class-based racial conflict. For instance, if neocolonialism or racial capitalism is the core problem in world order – a contested view but one that has ample historical ammunition[103] – then the peacemaker's wager at best offers a way of treating the racial part of global insecurity without resolving the ills associated with the capitalist part. This would be untenable because structures of racial hierarchy are co-constitutive of the structure of global capitalism, meaning racial and economic justice are indivisible.[104]

And so while it may be true that there is no national security without human security, it may likewise be that there is no human security without economic security. Indeed, exploitation, a mechanism that produces structural violence, is also a mechanism of durable economic inequality.[105] Peacemaking's "democracy from below" wager subsumes the question of power redistribution; if everyone gets to be part of civic life and have a say in governance, then problems of material deprivation should sort themselves out. But there is no necessary relationship between political democracy (elections, civic participation) and economic democracy. Procedural and deliberative democracy, in fact, can become the source of legitimacy for sustaining depraved levels of inequality, as the American experience has shown.

A materialist account of solidarity should presuppose redistributing power relationships. The structure of the global economy, which all but guarantees capital mobility, prevents the economic sovereignty necessary to ameliorate extreme economic inequalities within any given country.[106] While structural violence is an underlying cause of insecurity, it often arises from inequitable access to resources. And if the valence of

---

[103] For an excellent summary of racial capitalist literature and the controversy it evokes even within the left, see Olufemi Taiwo and Liam Kofi Bright, "A Response to Michael Walzer," *Dissent* (August 7, 2020), www.dissentmagazine.org/online_articles/a-response-to-michael-walzer. For Walzer's original critique of racial capitalism, see Michael Walzer, "A Note on Racial Capitalism," *Dissent* (July 29, 2020), www.dissentmagazine.org/online_articles/a-note-on-racial-capitalism.

[104] Adom Getachew, *Worldmaking after Empire: The Rise and Fall of Self-Determination* (Princeton: Princeton University Press, 2019), pp. 14–36.

[105] Johan Galtung, "Cultural Violence," *Journal of Peace Research* Vol. 27, no. 3 (1990), pp. 291–305; Tilly, *Durable Inequality*.

[106] Tim Barker, "The End of Development," *Dissent* (Spring 2021), www.dissentmagazine.org/article/the-end-of-development.

world politics changes to be more apparently peaceful and cooperative but the global economic order does not fundamentally change, then attempts at inclusion, societal cohesion, and the narrowing of gender and tribal differences will amount to so much goodwill dodging the need to redress the core problematic – imbalances of power among classes or races, kleptocracy, and/or worker precarity. The consequence of sidestepping economic security in this way may be that ethnonationalism, demagogic authoritarian politics, and violent extremism persist despite best efforts.

# 8

# Varieties of Progressive Political Economy

Political economy plays an outsized role in progressive thinking. The anti-militarist character of progressive foreign policy necessarily assigns greater relative weight to public policy (including economic policy) as a strategy resource than do traditional national security perspectives. The progressive pragmatist theory of security in particular finds the sources and remedies for global insecurity primarily in the domain of political economy. And even though the anti-hegemonist and peacemaking strategies de-center the economy in their reasoning about security, they do not deny a role for economic statecraft. Just as "foreign policy may have many goals beyond security,"[1] and just as liberal internationalism has historically served political purposes beyond international order-building or calculations about national security,[2] so too do progressives see foreign policy as an extension of politics generally. That means using American

---

[1] Barry Posen, *Restraint: A New Foundation for U.S. Grand Strategy* (Ithaca: Cornell University Press, 2014), p. 2.

[2] Regardless of its strategic rationales, liberal internationalism has also been a way of maintaining political bipartisanship around a military-centric political economy at home. See especially Brenes, *For Might and Right*. NSC-68, the Cold War blueprint of liberal internationalism, was motivated not primarily by military concerns but sustaining/preventing a collapse of the capitalist economic order in Western Europe especially. See Curt Caldwell, *NSC-68 and the Political Economy of the Cold War* (New York: Cambridge University Press, 2011). For certain sects of American Christianity, liberal internationalism has been part of a crusade for souls. See Jeremy Menchik, "Woodrow Wilson and the Spirit of Liberal Internationalism," *Politics, Religion and Ideology* Vol. 22, no. 2 (2021), pp. 231–53. And for neoconservatives, liberal internationalism has been a universalizing project of democracy promotion. See Justin Vaisse, *Neoconservatism: The Biography of a Movement* (Cambridge, MA: Harvard University Press, 2010), pp. 136–40.

conduct abroad to serve interests other than that which might be minimally required to realize the sustained absence of conflict.

Any progressive foreign policy worthy of its name would concern itself with economic policy regardless whether it nests within a logic of security.

As Chapter 3 explained, opposition to neoliberalism – because of the inequities and environmental destruction that result from its veneration of capital at workers' expense – is an anchoring preference that contemporary progressives tend to share. Advocates of the neoliberal economic order that has prevailed since the 1970s brand it as "grounded in the belief that market forces had to be liberated from government regulatory controls."[3] As an ideology though, neoliberalism represents the primacy of capital over labor, and subordinates public policy accordingly.[4] Neoliberalism's proponents pitched deregulation, austerity, and unencumbered foreign investment as a set of prescriptions that might increase short-run inequality but that would generate absolute gains – all could be better off as a result of capital mobility, barrier-free trade, and global production networks.

But neoliberalism's shortfalls have created a breach in the discourse about economic policy that progressive ideas have entered. For the last decade or so, there has been an intellectual ferment fusing progressives' ongoing resistance critiques against neoliberalism with positive demands that range from modest reform policies to radical transformations of the international system toward a post-capitalist imaginary. This chapter takes stock of the most coherent of these various proposals for a more progressive global political economy, most of which have only emerged since the 2008 financial crisis.

The chapter essentially makes two arguments. First, left-progressive policy proposals can be organized based on how they align with competing "models" for global order: neo-Keynesianism; justice for the Global South; a Global Green New Deal (GGND); and degrowth. Each has distinct priorities driving its approach, prescribes distinct ways of overcoming neoliberalism, and is logically compatible with only a finite range of policies. Second, while all four approaches pursue the same broad goals – reducing inequality within the Global North, raising standards of living

---

[3] Gary Gerstle, *The Rise and Fall of the Neoliberal Order: America and the World in the Free Market Era* (New York: Oxford University Press, 2022), 2.

[4] Quinn Slobodian, *The Globalists: The End of Empire and the Birth of Neoliberalism* (Cambridge: Harvard University Press, 2018).

and buffering structural violence in the Global South, and responding to the climate crisis – these goals potentially exhibit the tensions of a trilemma. While there are some policies that would advance all three, most government action would not advance them equally, implicitly privileging one above the others. Optimizing policy for responding to the climate crisis and reducing inequality within the North limits how you reduce economic precarity in the South. Optimizing policy for responding to the climate crisis and improving life chances in the South constrains the ability to reduce inequality within the North. And optimizing policy for reducing inequality within the North and precarity in the South requires compromising how you respond to the climate crisis. Knowing where and why the policy imaginary that reaches to the left of neoliberalism implicates competing models helps ensure awareness of what progressive goals are being subordinated in order to realize others.

## COMPETING APPROACHES TO A PROGRESSIVE ECONOMIC ORDER

Table 8.1 contrasts the alternative approaches to post-neoliberal economic order-building and how they implicitly rank-order progressive goals differently. Neo-Keynesianism asserts the power of the state on behalf of skilled jobs and infrastructure. Justice for the Global South insists that addressing inequality starts with correcting historical power imbalances between the Global North and South, which translates into resources that help the developing world achieve both ecologically and economically sustainable governance. The GGND tells us that massive financial investments in renewable energy production and measures to mitigate the effects of climate change on the world's poor offer an economically just pathway for getting the world to net-zero carbon emissions. And the degrowth movement offers prescriptions that would do the most to directly arrest the climate crisis, albeit by halting some forms of economic productivity and focusing instead on economic redistribution.

Progressives may agree that neoliberal policies worsen environmental degradation, kleptocracy, and oligarchy, but their idea ecosystem consists of multiple alternatives emphasizing different virtues and strategic judgments.

Surveying the various models of progressive political economy discussed in this chapter is a way to (1) foreground the ways in which they are not fully fungible, (2) identify the kinds of specific policy actions that might be areas of convergence, (3) and clarify the compatibility of

TABLE 8.1 *Varieties and priorities of progressive political economy*

| | Neo-Keynesianism | Justice for the South | Global Green New Deal | Degrowth |
|---|---|---|---|---|
| Approach to political economy | Fiscal activism to stimulate full employment and redistribute capital within borders | Redressing wealth and power imbalances between Global North and South | Middle-class jobs and infrastructure investment to achieve a "just energy transition" | Ecosocialism – radically reduce carbon emissions by ending labor exploitation linked to economic growth |
| Priority goals | (1) Northern inequality (2) Climate crisis (3) Southern precarity | (1) Southern precarity (2) Climate crisis (3) Northern inequality | (1) Climate crisis (2) Northern inequality (3) Southern precarity | (1) Climate crisis (2) Southern precarity (3) Northern inequality |
| Tension | Northern equality limits Southern development, modestly responds to climate crisis | Southern development ignores intra-North inequality, modestly responds to climate crisis | Middle class and green infrastructure forsakes Southern precarity, still requires massive environmental exploitation | Arresting climate crisis forsakes intra-North inequality, reduces the means by which to improve Southern precarity |
| Risks | Empowers nationalists, exploits nationalism, worsens imperialism and militarism | Cuts off from Northern capital or perpetuates elite capture (dependence on North) | Empowers technocracy over workers, can't meet its own climate goals | Politically unrealistic, can't resolve precarity without growth |

different economic approaches with the progressive grand strategies of the earlier chapters. Table 8.2 summarizes dozens of concrete policy choices in the progressive discourse about political economy and cross-references their compatibility with different progressive approaches to the international economic order.

## Neo-Keynesianism

Keynesian economics became the basis for the Democratic Party's fiscal and monetary policies during the New Deal era.[5] It encourages counter-cyclical government stimulus spending and interest-rate setting on the belief that it increases aggregate demand and has a positive effect on economic output.[6] During periods of economic depression, government intervention may be the only source of demand growth.

Although Keynesianism fell out of favor in the 1970s as neoliberalism became dogma in both the Democratic and Republican Parties, it has seen a revival since the global financial crisis of 2008, the lesson of which was that "if you have an activist central bank, you can do whatever the fuck you like in terms of fiscal policy. There's really no shit you can't pull. You can double your bet, you can run up debt like you did in World War II."[7] This is the essence of what might be called neo-Keynesianism – sometimes called "productivism" or "supply-side progressivism"[8] – a fiscally activist approach to political economy that channels government resources toward domestic worker power, national public infrastructure investment, and full employment.[9] These are all classically

[5] Stephanie Mudge, *Leftism Reinvented*, pp. 191–209.

[6] The classic text is John Maynard Keynes, *The General Theory of Employment, Interest and Money* (New York: Harcourt-Brace and Co., 1936).

[7] Adam Tooze, as quoted in Seth Ackerman, "All That Was Solid: An Interview with Adam Tooze," *Jacobin Magazine* (November 29, 2018), https://jacobinmag.com/2018/11/all-that-was-solid.

[8] Dani Rodrik, "The New Productivism Paradigm?" *Project Syndicate* (July 5, 2022), www.project-syndicate.org/commentary/new-productivism-economic-policy-paradigm-by-dani-rodrik-2022-07; Amy Capczynski, "What's Beyond 'Beyond Neoliberalism?'" *Law and Political Economy Project* (January 9, 2023), https://lpeproject.org/blog/whats-beyond-beyond-neoliberalism/.

[9] Edoardo Saravelle and Ben Judah, "Trans-Atlantic Ties Should Put Finance, Not Security, First," Foreign Policy (July 30, 2020), https://foreignpolicy.com/2020/07/30/transatlantic-us-nato-germany-finance-security-biden/; Jennifer Harris, "Making Trade Address Inequality," *Democracy Journal*, no. 48 (Spring 2018), https://democracyjournal.org/magazine/48/making-trade-address-inequality/; Nik DeCosta-Klipa, "Read the Transcript of Elizabeth Warren's Big Foreign Policy Speech," *Boston.com* (November 29, 2018), www.boston.com/news/politics/2018/11/29/elizabeth-warren-foreign-policy-speech-american-university/.

progressive priorities whose realization inherently requires breaking away from neoliberal austerity and privatization in favor of more ambitious government spending, taxation, and regulation. The positive logic is to "move ... against the natural tendency of the private capitalist economy today ... to force a state policy of investment that would never be supported in any other way."[10]

At the international level, a neo-Keynesian orientation could privilege policies that center the American worker and leverages US power. For instance, a global minimum wage and a global minimum tax would make US labor more competitive internationally while raising global living standards. So would "employee funds," which is a sovereign wealth fund owned by corporate wage earners (usually via unions) and is capitalized by a portion of corporate profits.[11] It is a social-democratic structure that could generate the capital needed for international projects and a green energy transition at home and abroad. In a similar vein, a Tobin tax is a form of national capital control that would impose a nominal, proportional tax on global currency transactions to suppress the kinds of currency speculation that triggered the Asian Financial Crisis in 1997/98.[12] American labor, the most direct beneficiaries in neo-Keynesian schemes, have also been champions of increasing market-access quotas for international economies that show progress on labor power or allowing unions to form, which reduces the labor-based competition between domestic and foreign workers. The United States granted increased import quotas in textiles to Cambodia in 1997 on the condition that Cambodia permitted its garment workers to unionize.[13] So the developing nation gets larger export volume and the nation's workers get basic bargaining rights. This shows that the needs of US labor unions are not necessarily at odds with those of labor unions abroad, as does the movement to seek "floor wages" in certain sectors of the global economy like textile production.

---

[10] Suzi Weissman interview with Robert Brenner, "Behind the Economic Turbulence," *Against the Current* (February 10, 2019), https://againstthecurrent.org/atc200/economic-turbulence/.

[11] Dylan Matthews, "Bernie Sanders's Most Socialist Idea Yet, Explained," *Vox* (May 29, 2019), www.vox.com/2019/5/29/18643032/bernie-sanders-communist-manifesto-employee-ownership-jobs.

[12] Mahbub ul Haq, Inge Kaul, and Isabelle Grunberg, eds., *The Tobin Tax: Coping with Financial Volatility* (New York: Oxford University Press, 1996).

[13] Erik Loomis, "A Left Vision for Trade," *Dissent* (Winter 2017), www.dissentmagazine.org/article/left-vision-trade-tpp-isds-international-law.

Neo-Keynesianism grants far greater economic sovereignty to national governments than neoliberalism, which makes possible policies like the "right to ban" foreign imports even under conditions of zero tariff barriers for reasons of national well-being (for instance, genetically modified food restrictions).[14] Yet this approach to political economy also limits economic sovereignty. Progressives have argued that Investor State Dispute Settlement Courts (ISDS) – a global legal mechanism that allows companies to sue national governments outside national courts – either be shut down or expanded to allow individuals and civil society groups to bring cases against corporations or governments.[15] The neo-Keynesian model has also stressed corporate supply-chain accountability, making multinational corporations liable for labor, human rights, and environmental standards implicated by any of their contractors or partners anywhere in their supply chain.

Contra the neoliberal ethos, supply-chain accountability would require much greater regulation of large corporations than has previously been the case, but it would also make companies much warier of offshoring and outsourcing based purely on the cheapest labor inputs. As an adjunct to this revolutionary form of corporate responsibility, progressives have proposed social dumping tariffs as a pro-labor, pro-justice way of making it easier for corporations to operate clean supply chains. Just as the United States can impose anti-dumping tariffs on imported goods whose price and supply undercut domestic markets, the United States could impose tariffs on imports whose price and supply undercut domestic markets when relying on exploitation of wage-starved and precaritized workers.[16]

As an essentially nation-first perspective on economics, American neo-Keynesianism provides a distinct answer to the climate crisis. The most direct, mainstream response is legislation like the Green New Deal – large public investments in renewable energy, sustainable national infrastructure, and a green-jobs program. Another is by drawing on national economic power to impose "green" sanctions in the form of tariff penalties or restrictions for products manufactured at the expense

---

[14] Martin Sanbu, *The Economics of Belonging: A Radical Plan to Win Back the Left Behind and Achieve Prosperity for All* (Princeton: Princeton University Press, 2020).

[15] Loomis, "A Left Vision for Trade."

[16] Gregory Shaffer, "Reconceiving Trade Agreements for Social Inclusion," in *The Shifting Landscape of Global Trade Governance: World Trade Forum*, edited by Manfred Elsig, Michael Hahn, Gabriele Spilker (Cambridge: Cambridge University Press, 2019), pp. 157–81.

of environmental damage or with excessive carbon emissions. A passive method of green sanctions would be the EU's carbon border adjustment tax. A more activist method would involve targeting sanctions against corporations or international actors who are causing environmental damage.[17] Neo-Keynesianism could also address climate change through monetary policy. The practice of "quantitative easing," a national tool, gives the Federal Reserve the ability to infuse capital into the economy through commercial banks. This practice could be extended to public banks, capitalizing them for the purpose of making investments in sustainable energy transitions.[18]

### Justice for the Global South

"De-colonize international political economy" is a vastly different rallying cry – with vastly different implications for economic order – than the neo-Keynesian "Build Back Better" mantra. As many colonial territories converted to nation-states after World War II, the extractive economic order that had been part and parcel of European and American empire did not transform to the same degree that the political order did. Conceptualizing the very existence of a Global North and South was a prerequisite to making sense of patterns of economic dependency through which the enrichment of the North or "core" in perverse ways had required deprivation and impoverishment of the South or "periphery."[19] The new forms of economic exploitation sustained through international financial institutions (IFIs) and global power imbalances favoring the North over the South came to be understood as neo-colonialism or neo-imperialism.[20]

Taking the progressive imperative for economic equality seriously means taking seriously the dramatic development inequalities dividing the Organization for Economic Co-Operation and Development (OECD)

---

[17] John Feffer, "The Case for a Coercive Green New Deal," *The Nation* (July 30, 2019), www.thenation.com/article/archive/china-coercive-green-new-deal/.

[18] Varoufakis, "A Progressive Monetary Policy is the Only Alternative."

[19] Fernando Henrique Cardoso and Enzo Faletto, *Dependency and Development in Latin America* (Berkeley: University of California Press, 1979); Walter Rodney, *How Europe Underdeveloped Africa* (New York: Verso, 2018); James Caporaso, "Dependency Theory: Continuities and Discontinuities in Development Studies," *International Organization* Vol. 34, no. 4 (1980), pp. 605–28.

[20] Kwame Nkrumah, *Neo-Colonialism: The Last Stage of Imperialism* (New York: International Publishers, 1965); Leo Panitch and Sam Gindin, *The Making of Global Capitalism: The Political Economy of American Empire* (New York: Verso, 2011).

nations and what used to be referred to as the Third World. Many progressive policy initiatives aim to center the Global South, rebalancing its wealth and power with that of the Global North and unwinding the processes of resource extraction and structural violence perpetuated there. But there is more than one imagined path to justice for the Global South.

## NIEO

The New International Economic Order (NIEO) emerged as a set of Third World demands during the Cold War and passed as a UN General Assembly resolution in 1974. So many different proposals were part of the NIEO concept that the acronym became something of a floating signifier, but the common denominator in those demands was a material redress of colonial pillaging of the Global South.

This included price stability for commodities that Global South economies relied on for export, ending Western subsidies in those commodities so as not to undermine Southern development, increased market access for Southern exports, development aid that did not include "structural adjustment" conditions and that instead respected the economic sovereignty of the South, debt restructuring or forgiveness, and support for building infant industries in the South through non-reciprocal protectionism.[21] And although the NIEO was overtaken by neoliberalism before it ever gained traction, it became the center of global policy debates again in 2012, when the appointment of the new World Bank president came from the United States (again) rather than one of the candidates from the Global South.[22]

## South–South Interdependence

The NIEO remains the keystone for Global South-first strategies of reforming the economic order, though the vision has evolved. In one version that draws on Third Worldism, black internationalism, and anti-imperialism, the Global South needs to build interdependence within itself, forging strong South-South bonds that decrease reliance on the North.[23] The

[21] On the NIEO, see especially, Getachew, *Worldmaking After Empire*, pp. 142–75; Nils Gilman "The New International Economic Order: A Reintroduction," *Humanity* (Spring 2015), pp. 1–15.

[22] Vinod Aggarwal and Steve Weber, "The New New International Economic Order," *Harvard Business Review* (April 18, 2012), https://hbr.org/2012/04/the-new-new-international-econ.

[23] Rohini Hensman, *Workers, Unions, and Global Capitalism: Lessons from India* (New York: Columbia University Press, 2011), p. 334. See also Getachew, "The New Black Internationalism."

South must "shift from the external [North] to the internal [South] market so as to ensure that the poor majority of our population participates in the growth process both as consumers and as producers."[24]

The policy agenda for South-South interdependence overlaps with the NIEO, but the principal effect it seeks to achieve involves breaking patterns of export dependency and eliminating the compromises of fiscal sovereignty that come with dealing with IFIs and Western nations on an individual basis. That means the NIEO approach of seeking greater market access in (and offshoring capital accumulation in) the United States and Europe is contrary to South-South aims. Rather than Southern economies exporting capital to finance American military adventures, "Expanding domestic markets, reorienting trade, and shifting away from the US dollar as a reserve currency [toward dollar multilateralism] would remove this source of support for imperialism."[25]

### Progressive Globalization

An alternative path to better conditions in the South is "progressive globalization," which argues for "the management of globalisation by multilateral institutions under principles of social justice."[26] It seeks to embed capitalism within an international social democratic order, demanding many of the reforms sought as part of the NIEO – for Global South trade barriers to fall only after a period of sufficient sectoral development, to end OECD agricultural subsidies, to fix pricing systems in commodities that the South exports, and for intellectual property exemptions that would allow the South to address its public health needs.[27]

In addition to these, progressive globalization's two major planks involve strategically directing capital from the Global North to investment in the South, and ending the neoliberal practice of liberalizing public services, national infrastructure, and utilities. By avoiding deregulation and austerity and capitalizing projects in developing economies, progressive globalization will power global growth via increased consumer and production demand in the South (where demand has been held much lower than its potential by a neoliberal order that starves it of

---

[24] Amit Bhaduri as quoted in Barker, "The End of Development."
[25] Hensman, *Workers, Unions, and Global Capitalism*, p. 334.
[26] Michael Jacobs, Adam Lent, and Kevin Watkins, *Progressive Globalisation: Towards an International Social Democracy* (London: Fabian Society, 2003), p. 5.
[27] Jacobs, Lent, and Watkins, *Progressive Globalisation*, pp. 72–3; Thomas Meyer and Lewis Hinchman, *The Theory of Social Democracy* (Cambridge: Polity Press, 2007), pp. 166–87.

equity investment).[28] Some of the neo-Keynesian schemes like the Tobin tax and "employee funds" would generate the capital necessary for the Global North to play this altered role toward the South. But intellectual property covenants, which formed a large part of US complaints in its Trump-era trade war with China, should be seen as a rigged game against not just China but the Global South generally.[29]

### Reparations and Restorative Justice

A reparations-based approach to the Global South is a hybrid of progressive globalization, the NIEO, and South-South interdependence. Its policy prescriptions are not that different from progressive globalization, but its reasoning has to do with a forward-looking restorative justice. Those with the most resources – that is, the "people and institutions that have benefited the most from these historical processes" of imperialism, slavery, and later neo-colonialism – should bear the disproportionate cost of building a just international economic order.[30]

Put to that purpose, American statecraft should be expanding climate financing and technology transfers to aid developing economies with their transitions to environmentally sustainable modes of development. It should be granting zero-tariff market access to exports from the Global South. And it should favorably reallocate to the Global South the International Monetary Fund's (IMF) "Special Drawing Rights (SDRs)" quotas – dollarized coupons allocated on a country basis that national financial institutions can exchange for real money to pay for public goods, emergencies, or currency reserves. Just as voting rights in IFIs are allocated overwhelmingly in favor of the United States and Europe, so too are SDRs, which the IMF grants disproportionately to the world's richest countries, even though they rarely make use of them (and which the United States never uses).[31]

---

[28] Eric Levitz, "Only the Left Can Save Globalization Now," *New York Magazine* (February 9, 2021), https://nymag.com/intelligencer/2021/02/only-the-left-can-save-globalization-now.html.

[29] Jake Werner, "China is Cheating at a Rigged Game," *Foreign Policy* (August 8, 2018), https://foreignpolicy.com/2018/08/08/china-is-cheating-at-a-rigged-game/.

[30] Olufemi Taiwo as quoted in William Jones, "How to Repair the Planet," *Dissent* (February 4, 2022), www.dissentmagazine.org/online_articles/how-to-repair-the-planet?utm_source=Dissent+Newsletter&utm_campaign=daa3eeadco-EMAIL_CAMPAIGN_The_First_Democratic_Debates_COPY_0&utm_medium=email&utm_term=0_a1e9be8ode-daa3eeadco-102061977.

[31] Michael Franczak and Olufemi Taiwo, "Here's How to Repay Developing Nations for Colonialism – and Fight the Climate Crisis," *The Guardian* (January 22, 2022), www.theguardian.com/commentisfree/2022/jan/14/heres-how-to-repay-developing-nations-for-colonialism-and-fight-the-climate-crisis; Eric Martin, "Warren, Sanders Urge IMF to

This is a waste of resources that could benefit developing economies, and it results directly from an unfair imbalance of power in the international economic order. Immediately correcting this problem entails either eliminating the IMF's quota system for SDRs in favor of some South-favoring ruleset for allocation, or else re-directing the SDRs that the United States and OECD nations receive toward climate investment funds and multilateral development banks. Longer term, the IMF should not be allocating voting share within the institution on the basis of a country's share of the global economy because that literally means the richer you are, the more power you are given. Undoing legacies of colonialism like this are not just penance; they are *how* to realize better conditions in the world.

One of the most powerful proposals to transform both North-South relations and the living conditions of the Global South also happens to be among the most antagonistic to neoliberal capitalism – debt justice. Progressives concerned with the developing world – including the Justice Democrats in Congress – have urged for the United States to concentrate its influence, bureaucratic attention, and resources toward alleviating debt burdens in the Global South.[32] Sovereign debt involves the public debts accrued by a foreign government, which can come from either private borrowing in financial markets or from IFIs and public finance (lending by other governments). "Odious" debt is sovereign debt accrued by autocrats or kleptocrats whose people carry the debt burden even after the regime has changed. For embattled economies in the South, debt is a mechanism of direct harm to social welfare and national development. When servicing interest payments on debt to creditors who largely reside in the Global North becomes literally unpayable or requires imposes fiscal austerity on a government's people, the debt ought to be renegotiated.

Debt also has geopolitical consequences and the justice that debt relief provides is the optimal way to manage their risks and costs. Cambodia, for example, as of 2022 owed more than $500 million to the US government for loans in the 1970s made to a different (and highly

Create $2.1 Trillion More in Reserve Assets for Covid Help," *Bloomberg* (February 1, 2022), www.bloomberg.com/news/articles/2022-01-31/warren-sanders-urge-creating-2-1-trillion-more-in-imf-reserves.

[32] Alexandria Ocasio-Cortez, for instance, introduced a bill in the House of Representatives that would require the United States to use its power to furnish debt relief to developing nations with unsustainable levels of debt. See H.R. 6549, 117th Congress, 2nd Session (February 1, 2022), www.congress.gov/117/bills/hr6549/BILLS-117hr6549ih.pdf.

corrupt) regime.[33] The Cambodian people never saw most of that money. The current government in Cambodia, which considers the loans "a dirty debt," has asked for the United States to either drop the interest rates on the debt to 1 percent, or else to reclassify 70 percent of the debt as "development aid" to fund education and landmine clearance activity in Cambodia.[34] Cambodia belongs to a basket of countries, including Sri Lanka and the Philippines, that US officials worry about because of their reliance on Chinese aid and investment. These countries, to varying degrees, also find their economic development stunted by old debt and needing China's patronage – which comes free from "structural adjustment" conditionalities – to obtain new financing. American national security types worry about China's "debt-trap diplomacy" and other forms of strategic dependency on China, but show little concern for remedying the conditions that make countries ripe for reliance on China. Debt relief is the key, and there are numerous ways to furnish it.[35]

In cases where the debt is owed to the US government or an IFI, canceling debt outright should be a US priority, especially if the debt can be legally classified as odious debt.[36] In cases where the debt is a private creditor or consortium of creditors, the United States should be using its influence to negotiate debt restructuring and partial forgiveness, either by slashing interest rates on the loans, extending the life of repayment, or securing a repayment moratorium. If that sounds impossible, the US government did precisely that for Iraq after its invasion of the country in 2003.[37] The United States could, depending on the circumstances, also either offer "grant-in-aid" funds as a vehicle to take over paying sovereign debts for another country or, barring any of the above, could secure or offer "concessional terms" on exports from the indebted country as an offset for debt repayment. The point is that there are many, many

[33] David Hutt, "America's Debt Trap Diplomacy in Cambodia," *Asia Times* (July 1, 2021), https://asiatimes.com/2021/07/americas-debt-diplomacy-in-cambodia/.

[34] Luke Hunt, "Cambodia Offers US Three Options to Resolve War Era Debt," *UCA News* (June 2, 2021), www.ucanews.com/news/cambodia-offers-us-three-options-to-resolve-war-era-debt/92710#.

[35] On the case for debt justice in various forms, see Progressive International, "A Blueprint for Debt Justice," *Progressive International* (December 4, 2021), https://progressive.international/blueprint/606164ba-c29f-4f32-b464-50bc9b7f1a26-a-blueprint-for-debt-justice/en.

[36] Chayes, *Thieves of State*, pp. 198–9.

[37] Simon Hinrichsen, "Tracing Iraqi Sovereign Debt Through Defaults and Restructuring," *LSE Economic History Working Papers*, No. 304 (December 2019), www.lse.ac.uk/Economic-History/Assets/Documents/WorkingPapers/Economic-History/2019/WP304.pdf.

creative solutions that are possible in the realm of debt relief, but they require recognizing that debt is in many cases an unresolved legacy of historical injustice, an albatross around the neck of developing economies, *and* a source of long-term geopolitical risk. All of that makes prioritizing debt relief as a problem set worthy of strategy and statecraft.

### Global Green New Deal

In neo-Keynesian and Global South approaches to progressive political economy, the threat of climate change is instrumental rather than essential – an area of policy activism and a means of realizing other goals, but not the focal point. For the GGND and its derivative proposals though, saving humanity from environmental destruction is the goal orchestrating political-economic action; generating middle-class jobs and infrastructure happens to be instrumental to the vision for how to save the planet.[38]

Sometimes also referred to as plans for a "just energy transition," the GGND concentrates policy change and resources on reducing man-made harm to the environment and environmental harm to humanity, seeking "a fair transition to a carbon free economy." To reach this goal, advocates have called for four broad priorities: the world's governments must achieve large reductions in greenhouse gas emissions by 2030 (somewhere between 45 percent reductions and net zero, depending on the proposal); renewable energy resources must be dramatically expanded; workers in the fossil fuel industry must not experience economic insecurity; and the economic order must be both environmentally sustainable and raise "mass living standards."[39] Although addressing climate change is its ultimate raison d'etre, the GGND's proponents also see it as a way

---

[38] See especially, United Nations Environment Programme, *Global Green New Deal Policy Brief* (New York: United Nations, 2009).

[39] Kevin Gallagher and Richard Kozul-Wright, *A New Multilateralism for Shared Prosperity: Geneva Principles for a Global Green New Deal* (Boston: Boston University Global Development Policy Center, 2019); Kate Aronoff, "A New Global Group of 21 Lawmakers Will Pressure Countries on Climate Change," *New Republic* (July 20, 2021), https://newrepublic.com/article/162999/ilhan-omar-global-green-new-deal?utm_source=newsletter&utm_medium=email&utm_campaign=tnr_daily. For the 45 percent reductions by 2030 proposal, see Noam Chomsky and Robert Pollin, with C.J. Polychroniou, *Climate Crisis and the Global Green New Deal: The Political Economy of Saving the Planet* (London: Verso, 2020), p. ix. For the net zero demand, see "Why the World Needs a Global Green New Deal," *War on Want* (November 6, 2021), https://waronwant.org/news-analysis/why-world-needs-global-green-new-deal.

of "driving the transformation of capitalism away from its current inter-regnum between neoliberalism and neofascism."[40]

The Global South features prominently in the GGND for two reasons. One is because "it is poor countries and poor people who stand to bear the greatest cost of global warming"; they lack technological adaptations for daily life (sea walls, air conditioners), and they live in places where climate change is already having the greatest impact.[41] The other is because there is no solution to climate change without arresting carbon emissions from those parts of the world. OECD countries are responsible for most historical carbon emissions, but the developing world collectively accounts for 63 percent of emissions today, and close to 90 percent of emissions growth projected out to 2040.[42] At best, a green energy transition limited to the Global North marginally slows but does not stop the effects of climate change.

Accordingly, the GGND calls for massive outlays of climate financing – low- and no-interest loans or grants-in-aid to developing economies. The Inflation Reduction Act of 2022 serves as a down payment on this funding ($369 billion over ten years), but, by design, virtually all of it goes to US-based companies (not the Global South).[43] The GGND requires some $2 trillion per year for *global* projects, of which the United States should be providing at least $680 billion annually [the amount proportional to the US share of Gross Domestic Product (GDP) among OECD countries, 34 percent].[44] Some of this could come from a carbon border adjustment tax and a domestic carbon cap that imposes taxes on carbon-producing firms beyond a specified ceiling. Some could come from monetary policy, directing quantitative easing toward capitalizing climate sustainability programs at public investment banks. Some funding could also come from industrial policy. For instance, the United States can use (and encourage foreign governments to also introduce) "feed-in tariffs" to direct public utilities to buy renewable energy from private renewable

---

[40] Chomsky and Pollin, *Climate Crisis and the Global Green New Deal*, p. 75. The Global Alliance for a Green New Deal also sees the GGND as a way to transcend neoliberalism. See Aronoff, "A New Global Group of 21 Lawmakers Will Pressure Countries on Climate Change."

[41] Chomsky and Pollin, *Climate Crisis and the Global Green New Deal*, p. 93.

[42] Jacob Fawcett, *The Global Green New Deal* (New York: People's Policy Project, 2019).

[43] Justin Worland, "Why The World Is Protesting America's Climate Plan," *Time* (January 15, 2023), https://time.com/6247230/inflation-reduction-act-global-response-climate-trade-protectionsim/.

[44] This calculation comes from Fawcett, *The Global Green New Deal*. However, multiple NGOs offer similar estimates, as do Chomsky and Pollin.

energy producers, reducing the risk and increasingly the profitability of investing in renewable energy production.[45] But most of the funding for the GGND would necessarily come from the United States issuing climate-related bonds that would direct money raised to a fund managed by multilateral institutions (for instance, the United Nations manages a "Green Climate Fund"). The bond could be a one-time issuance of $10. 8 trillion of treasury bonds on the open market, which would ensure domestic politics did not disrupt annual US financial contributions, or the United States could pass a law making its contribution of $680 billion/year a "mandatory spending" item in the federal budget.[46]

The purpose of all this financing is to help the South transition to green economies that substitute renewables like solar and wind power for fossil fuels, that build greater resilience to climate-induced natural disasters (droughts, fires, flooding, and tsunamis), that provide public insurance programs, that support transitional income for workers leaving the fossil fuel industry, and that pay for the transfer of more energy-efficient technologies so that national production activity has a lower carbon footprint.[47] Supporting measures that further the GGND's larger aims include green sanctions, intellectual property waivers that would support organic agricultural production and lower-carbon manufacturing practices, renegotiating debt burdens in exchange for carbon emission reductions, and reallocating voting share in the World Bank and IMF. But the kernel of the GGND project is unlocking world-historic levels of funding to move the global economy to renewable energy while improving global standards of living.

### Degrowth

The conceit of the degrowth movement is that humanity can live happily and healthily on earth with "radically smaller resource throughput" than currently used to sustain it.[48] It sees capitalist production

---

[45] Joern Huenteler, "International Support for Feed-In Tariffs in Developing Countries – A Review and Analysis of Proposed Mechanisms," *Renewable and Sustainable Energy Reviews* Vol. 39 (2014), pp. 857–73.

[46] Fawcett, *The Global Green New Deal.*

[47] Chomsky and Pollin, *Climate Crisis and the Global Green New Deal*, pp. 98–99; United Nations Environment Programme, *Global Green New Deal Policy Brief*, pp. 3–5; Gallagher and Kozul-Wright, *A New Multilateralism for Shared Prosperity.*

[48] Giorgos Kallis, Vasilis Kostakis, Steffen Lange, Barbara Muraca, Susan Paulson, and Matthias Schmelzer, "Research on Degrowth," *Annual Review of Environment and Resources* Vol. 43 (2018), p. 291.

and consumption as both unnecessary and the ultimate source of global carbon emissions wreaking havoc on the environment.[49] Consequently, degrowth as an approach to international economic order urges breaking away from "development" and growth as measures of global and national success in favor of an ecologically sustainable economic life.

There is more than one way to do degrowth, but three goals are common to most proposals: reducing human impact on the environment; increasing economic redistribution/equality; and forging a new cooperative way of life that relates human beings to each other and to the environment.[50] These goals converge with the GGND in many specific policy areas. Utilizing green sanctions, technology transfers to the South, climate finance, intellectual property waivers, the renegotiation of debt burdens, democratizing voting share in the IMF and World Bank – all of these measures would advance a GGND and degrowth agenda because they address global inequality and reduce humanity's carbon footprint. Some degrowth proponents have even argued for a "Green New Deal without Growth" that would incorporate degrowth policies into the GGND agenda.[51]

But there are two points of differentiation between degrowth and the GGND that make them clash and affect how one narrates the policy changes sought. One is that degrowth advocates see the GGND and other mainstream pro-environmental policies as inadequate to the urgent task of preventing increases in global temperatures beyond 1.5 degrees Celsius. Keeping the temperature from changing that much requires, in the most modest version, halving global emissions by 2030. As ambitious as the GGND is, it will not reach that target,[52] which the Intergovernmental Panel on Climate Change (IPCC) believes is the critical tipping point for the planet.[53] Moreover, degrowth critics of the GGND believe that

---

[49] See especially Giacomo D'Alisa, Federico Demaria, and Giorgos Kallis, eds., *Degrowth: A Vocabulary for a New Era* (Abingdon: Routledge, 2014).

[50] Ines Cosme, Rui Santos, and Daniel O'Neill, "Assessing the Degrowth Discourse: A Review and Analysis of Academic Degrowth Policy Proposals," *Journal of Cleaner Production* Vol. 149, no. 15 (2017), pp. 321–34.

[51] Riccardo Mastini, Giorgos Kallis, and Jason Hickel, "A Green New Deal Without Growth?" *Ecological Economics* Vol. 179 (2021), https://doi.org/10.1016/j.ecolecon.2020.106832.

[52] Max Krahé, "The Whole Field," *Phenomenal World* (April 30, 2022), www.phenomenalworld.org/analysis/climate-planning/.

[53] Intergovernmental Panel on Climate Change, *Climate Change 2021: The Physical Science Basis* (New York: United Nations Environmental Programme, 2021).

renewable energy cannot be generated at a scale sufficient to sustain economic growth, and further that simply substituting renewable energy for fossil fuels reduces carbon emissions at the expense of even greater heavy metal and mineral extractions that will lead to ecological breakdown.[54]

Degrowth, by contrast, presumes that "the slower the rate of economic growth, the easier it is to achieve emissions reductions."[55] The world can reach IPCC-designated climate targets if OECD countries bring an end to processes of overaccumulation and prioritize policies of redistribution within the North (rather than growth) while facilitating "green" forms of development in the South.[56]

The other difference with the GGND is that advocates of degrowth understand the growth obsession of modern governments as constitutive of the historical processes of colonial exploitation and extraction; theirs is a green anti-colonial critique of capitalism.[57] That makes shifting to a more cooperative, inclusive political economy – which presupposes greater justice for the Global South – *the* way of ending governments' GDP-focused mindset and thereby reducing productivity in environmentally harming sectors. If the world allows economic growth to continue being treated as a political necessity, governments will not be able to halt productivity in ecologically damaging sectors of the economy.[58]

## GRAND STRATEGIC COMPATIBILITIES
### AND SIGNS OF A TRILEMMA

These different proposals for a more progressive economic order broadly respond to the entwined problems of economic inequality and the climate crisis. As such, they all share an aim of discarding the neoliberal version of capitalism and its corresponding policy prescriptions. And as Table 8.2 indicates, they even share a number of the same policies. But each tells a slightly different story about how to reduce inequality, for whom, and whether it ought to take precedence over the climate crisis in instances where progress toward the two goals does not advance simultaneously.

---

[54] Mastini, Kallis, and Hickel, "A Green New Deal Without Growth?"
[55] Ibid.
[56] Hickel, "What Does Degrowth Mean?"
[57] Kallis, Kostakis, Lange, Muraca, Paulson, and Schmelzer, "Research on Degrowth"; Jason Hickel, *Less is More: How Degrowth Will Save the World* (London: Penguin Random House, 2021).
[58] Jason Hickel, "What Does Degrowth Mean? A Few Points of Clarification," *Globalization* Vol. 18, no. 7 (2021), pp. 1105–111.

TABLE 8.2 *Policy compatibility and models of progressive political economy*

| Policy | Neo-Keynesianism | Justice for the South | Global Green New Deal | Degrowth |
|---|---|---|---|---|
| Global minimum tax | Yes | Yes | Yes | Yes |
| Global minimum wage | Yes | Yes | Yes | Yes |
| End or open ISDS courts | Yes | Yes | Yes | Yes |
| Supply chain accountability | Yes | Yes | Yes | Yes |
| Labor rep. in trade deals | Yes | Yes | Yes | Yes |
| End structural adjustment | Yes | Yes | Yes | Yes |
| End multistakeholder governance | Yes | Yes | Yes | Yes |
| Feed-in tariffs | Yes | Yes | Yes | Yes |
| Climate finance | Maybe | Yes | Yes | Yes |
| Green sanctions | Yes | Maybe | Yes | Yes |
| Tech transfer | Maybe | Yes | Yes | Yes |
| Sectoral floor wages | Yes | Yes | Maybe | Maybe |
| Raised quotas for foreign unions | Yes | Yes | Maybe | Maybe |
| IMF SDRs | Maybe | Yes | Yes | Maybe |
| Capital diversion to South | Maybe | Yes | Maybe | Maybe |
| Social dumping tariffs | Yes | Yes | Maybe | Yes |
| Carbon border adj tax | Yes | Maybe | Yes | Yes |
| QE w/public investment banks | Yes | Maybe | Yes | Maybe |
| Sanctions on oligarchs | Yes | Maybe | Maybe | Yes |
| Tobin tax | Yes | Yes | Maybe | Maybe |
| Employee/wage earner funds | Yes | Maybe | Maybe | Maybe |
| Retire "odious" debt | No | Yes | Yes | Yes |
| Restructure debt | No | Yes | Yes | Yes |
| IP waivers | No | Yes | Yes | Maybe |
| Commodity price stability | No | Yes | Maybe | Maybe |
| End OECD agric. Subsidy | No | Yes | Maybe | Maybe |
| Zero tariff trade for South | No | Yes | Maybe | Yes |
| End US veto in IMF/ World Bank | No | Yes | Yes | Yes |
| Stop offshoring tax incentives | Yes | No | Maybe | Yes |
| Dollar multilateralism | No | Yes | Maybe | Maybe |

Neo-Keynesianism asserts the power of the state on behalf of green jobs and infrastructure. Justice for the Global South insists that addressing inequality starts with correcting historical and ongoing power imbalances between the Global North and South, which translates into resources that help the developing world achieve both ecologically and economically sustainable governance. The GGND tells us that massive financial investments in renewable energy production and measures to mitigate the effects of climate change on the world's poor offer an economically just pathway for getting the world to net-zero carbon emissions. And the degrowth movement offers prescriptions that would do the most to arrest the climate crisis, albeit by halting some forms of economic productivity and focusing instead on economic redistribution.

But how do these progressive economic projects square with progressive theories of security?

### Progressive Pragmatism and Economic Order

The grand strategy of progressive pragmatism is uniquely grounded in political economy, but its assumptions and wagers are more amenable to some progressive approaches than others. It diagnoses economic inequality as the core problem driving insecurity. Its wagers seek to remedy that inequality at a global level. Climate change figures into its theory of security as a point of leverage against petro-dictators and as a condition that, if unremedied, exacerbates pre-existing durable inequalities in society and the world. But progressive pragmatism is agnostic about *how* to reduce inequality in a world of finite resources and time.

Neo-Keynesianism, the GGND, and certain configurations of justice for the Global South (specifically progressive globalization and restorative justice variants) are most congruent with progressive pragmatism. Because it assumes that the exercise of American power is a means of realizing security, economic policies that constrain US power may be at cross purposes with progressive pragmatism. Degrowth would directly undercut the influence the United States derives from the growth-oriented capitalist order, as would most of the policies of the NIEO. The South-South interdependence approach, meanwhile, would cut off the United States from financial flows that would remain in the Global South, which would also dilute America's economic power there.

Yet the Fabian character of progressive globalization would see the United States putting its wealth and influence to work investing in the Global South and helping developing-world economies deliver better conditions for its workers. The United States would also have a prominent role in a political economy grounded in restorative justice, which would see the United States lobbying in favor of diluting Global-North voting shares at the IMF and World Bank, and using its statecraft to negotiate debt relief for the Global South.

But neo-Keynesianism fits best with progressive pragmatism. State power is central to both, and both tend to direct that power toward problems facing the Global North. Waleed Shahid, a founder of the Justice Democrats, once comically remarked that the Biden administration's agenda was "Great power rivalry with China while also decarbonizing the economy, led by macho dudes in electric vehicles."[59] The quip conveys how the neo-Keynesian and progressive pragmatist agendas can converge on a nationalism whose internationalist implications are colored by the dark perils of geopolitical rivalry. The anti-kleptocratic initiatives in progressive pragmatism, for instance, concentrate state power on corruption and tax evasion globally, which basically renders greater equality by preventing theft. Even when dirty money comes from the Global South, it is encased in the Global North, where the white-collar intermediaries that launder it in various ways also reside. And the risk of far-right authoritarian configurations within Global North democracies – a threat progressive pragmatists optimize against – justifies the neo-Keynesian prioritization of reducing inequalities within the United States and the Global North.

### Anti-hegemonism and Economic Power

The grand strategy of anti-hegemonism is grounded in restraint – bridling American power not just militarily but economically too. In this view, the only guiding criterion in adopting progressive political economy is whether it constrains the coercive capacity of the United States. Some versions of justice for the Global South are optimal alternatives to US economic hegemony, as are the economic strategy of degrowth and the NIEO. Parts of the GGND and progressive globalization fit with anti-hegemonism too, but most of the neo-Keynesian agenda is in conflict with the logic of anti-hegemonism.

The South-South interdependence model of political economy would serve the larger anti-hegemonist project best because it would end

---

[59] "Build Back Green New Deal?" *Bloc Party Podcast* (February 23, 2021), www.listennotes .com/podcasts/bloc-party/build-back-green-new-deal-K_5wjL-gQRe/.

reliance on the Global North – and especially on the United States. The degrowth movement would also uplift the Global South while constraining American influence. Not only would degrowth decenter America in the global economy, it would also reduce the high levels of production, consumption, and trade on which US economic power depends.

The other forms of justice for the Global South – through the NIEO, progressive globalization, or restorative justice – would ultimately have the effect of rolling back American domination of the global economy but in ways that employ rather than restrain its power. For example, re-allocating voting shares at the IMF, campaigning for restructuring unsustainable debt, or steering capital toward underserved developing economies are changes that depend on US government activism. Such approaches consist of means that clash with the anti-hegemonist logic but promise to further its restraint-oriented ends.

The GGND, similarly, can be compatible with anti-hegemonism, though it does not necessarily aid the project of reducing US power. The GGND involves major global efforts from the United States to exercise something like international leadership, a role that has historically made anti-hegemonists chafe because it has always been the rhetorical apparatus helping legitimate the illegitimate exercise of American coercion against others. But unlike the justice-for-the-South approaches, nothing in the content of a GGND would dilute American power.

Still, only neo-Keynesianism is wholly incompatible with anti-hegemonism. The anti-hegemonic left has raised major concerns about the "imperialist Keynesianism" that manifests in projects like Biden's "Build Back Better" ethos. They claim that investment in national renewal via government spending and policy activism offers no theory for building a better world, but instead merely offers ways to compensate for how neoliberalism has "undercut US capitalism's ability to compete within – and by extension dominate – the world system."[60] They note how all the political framing around neo-Keynesian political economy has to do with competing with China, not the creation of a just society or world. For such critics, the way in which all America-building projects in Washington are yoked to an anti-China pathology is not just rhetorical

---

[60] Ashley Smith, "Imperialist Keynesianism," *Tempest* (May 18, 2021), www.tempestmag .org/2021/05/imperialist-keynesianism/?fbclid=IwAR0CxydV2qol1MOSR7G3dwJpVm yBTtX9MT9Gyhe178CN29SndtX3rEFdoiU.

packaging out of political expedience, it betrays the very nature of neo-Keynesianism, which heightens clashing imperialist competition between the United States and China. Because neo-Keynesianism fuels Sino-US rivalry, it inhibits the ability of the United States and China to address the needs of the Global South or to collectively address the climate crisis – collective great-power action is not possible in Cold War-like conditions.[61] And changing the rhetoric around neo-Keynesian policies to simply not reference China does not change the policies' ultimate raison d'etre (a US-centered capitalist system), which for anti-hegemonists is itself dubious.

And if industrial policy really just cashes out as economic nationalism in response to a low-growth world where the size of the economic pie is no longer expanding, then the world is being setup to suffer cycles of antagonistic prosperity – the most modern economies securing productivity and financial capital for themselves in a manner that condemns everyone else to stunted growth and eternal dependency. A nationalist approach to anything eventually runs up against logical tension with others' nationalisms; it is hard to be at once inclusive and boundary-drawing. For instance, one of the policy proposals for more progressive trade that directly targets benefits to the middle class in the Global North has been to use free-trade negotiations to prevent other economies from offering tax incentives and subsidies to relocate Northern corporations overseas. To the same extent that this "saves" Northern jobs, it also fore-closes on those jobs growing in the country where they would have been relocated. For China and many nations in the Global South, legal and financial incentives are policy tools to entice investment from the Global North on their (the South's) terms.

Such an example is congruent with a larger tendency of neo-Keynesian ideas to implicitly privilege the Global North above the Global South. A global regime of carbon border adjustment taxes would disproportionately benefit OECD countries economically. Supply-chain accountability benefits everyone, but is going to be far easier to implement for resource-endowed American and European corporations than Southern ones. Quantitative easing and central-bank coordination of monetary policies is mostly a US and European affair. And the "right to ban" imports for wooly, idiosyncratic

---

[61] See especially Tobita Chow and Jake Werner, "The US, China, and the Left," *Socialist Forum* (Fall 2021), https://socialistforum.dsausa.org/issues/fall-2021/the-us-china-and-the-left/.

reasons obviously works against export-dependent economies, which includes much of the Global South.

## Peacemaking and Economic Justice

Although economic questions largely fall outside peacemaking's theory of security, economic statecraft can complement its project of "peace from below" as long as it is targeted at reducing structural violence. Because each model of progressive political economy promises to curb economic precarity in some way, peacemaking accommodates all of them in principle; there is no intrinsic antagonism between a grand strategy of peacemaking and progressive visions of economic order. While the GGND and forms of justice for the Global South would play the greatest role in advancing the logic of peace, neo-Keynesianism and degrowth could facilitate reductions in structural violence as well.

Justice for the Global South offers the least circuitous route to making a more peaceful world. Progressive globalization, South-South interdependence, and a project of restorative justice with real materialist foundations all involve a large shift of resources toward improving the living and working conditions of the Global South. The NIEO would also reduce structural violence in the Global South via "socialism among states," but if it leaves individual states to organize themselves internally however they wish, it risks the same problems of the Asian "miracle" economies – reducing structural violence for some at the expense of precaritizing the mass and accommodating extreme elite graft.

The GGND and degrowth movements – as with peacemaking – do not reduce structural violence by way of reducing wealth and income inequality. Instead, both directly address the "slow violence" of climate degradation – a threat unique to the Global South that other approaches to political economy implicitly de-prioritize.[62] Peacemaking's use of environmental resilience and sustainability projects as sites of community cohesion and tension reduction suggests a synergy between making peace and managing the climate crisis.

While neo-Keynesianism would do the least to ameliorate structural violence in the South, it does not necessarily impede peacemaking. By

---

[62] Rob Nixon, *Slow Violence and the Environmentalism of the Poor* (Cambridge: Harvard University Press, 2013).

prioritizing the Global North, neo-Keynesianism might reify patterns of economic development that help some in the South while leaving most precarious. And its answer to the slow violence of climate change is indirect, amounting to incremental shifts in renewable energy production. But some of the neo-Keynesian proposals that improve conditions for workers in the United States do not come at the expense of labor in the South but rather improve their lot. Ideas like social dumping tariffs, a global minimum wage, and a global minimum tax could improve working conditions in the Global South despite centering American workers.

# 9

## Political Terrain and Social Democratic Statecraft

This book has laid out three internally coherent but starkly competing visions for progressive grand strategy – worldmaking anchored in progressive principles. Each has its own reasoning about what it takes to realize greater security. Each makes different assumptions about world politics, stresses different aspects of the history of the progressive movement, sets different priorities, configures the repertoire of statecraft in different ways, and accepts different kinds of strategic risks in the process of making a better world.

But they can all make a claim to being grounded in the progressive commitment to economic equality, solidarity, and anti-authoritarianism. They all represent critical revisions of liberal internationalism. And they all understand that the conditions of security – peace, democracy, and equality – are indivisible in the final analysis, even if their pursuit must sometimes be sequential. Consequently, all three approaches to progressive grand strategy offer rationales for dialing down the role of the military and dialing up the role of public policy beyond the national security state.

On one level, the point of all this was to expand the imagination of those who study and practice grand strategy and security studies. By revealing alternative vistas for how America relates to the world, it exposes otherwise muted assumptions, costs, and risks in simply persisting with the wagers of a highly militarized liberal internationalism that services a neoliberal economic order (and increasingly a rapacious geoeconomic order). It also provides a basis for evaluating the analytical claims implied in progressive foreign policy demands. And it makes a case for policymakers to consider or reconsider options for engaging with the world that have mostly fallen outside of Washington foreign policy debates.

On another level though, this book is intellectual ammunition for the left. It organizes (in an analytically transparent way) the policy repertoires available for making a progressive statecraft. By thinking differently about the first principles and ultimate ends of strategy, it vastly expands the toolkit of ways and means that policymakers might draw upon to pursue a more democratic and egalitarian security.

But two questions remain.

First, what might a synthesis of progressive grand strategies look like? That is, to what extent can you fashion a consensus progressive foreign policy agenda? Just as the divergences within the left are worth understanding, so too are the convergences. We can look across these three schools of thought and triangulate policies that would be faithful to progressive commitments without coming at the expense of one or more progressive theories of security.

Second, what are the prospects for a more progressive statecraft actually happening, and how? Progressive policy ideas do not exist in a vacuum, and it is worth contemplating the potential openings and constraints of the contemporary political terrain.

## SYNTHESIS: TOWARD A COMMON PROGRESSIVE POSTURE

A foreign policy agenda constructed from a mix of progressive pragmatism, anti-hegemonism, and peacemaking is bound to have less internal coherence than the individual grand strategies themselves, but not only is that to be expected when bringing ideas into practice, but also it is not necessarily a bad thing. These grand strategies, like any others, are freighted with risks. Deviations from the ideal type can potentially be a way of managing them.

Identifying consensus policies across these different modes of reasoning is a basis for savvy progressive politicians to navigate the universe of leftist foreign policy opinion. It provides a possible focal point for widening the coalition working for a progressive foreign policy. And it clarifies the "low-hanging fruit" choices that can be advanced without antagonizing or dividing the left. Below I explain six areas of progressive consensus and the kinds of policies that would advance them.

## Nuclear Restraint Policies

The demand for nuclear disarmament has been part of left politics for as long as nuclear weapons have existed.[1] All three progressive grand strategies seek to restrain America's nuclear arsenal and accept the most basic insight about the nuclear revolution – that nuclear weapons made unrestricted warfare unwinnable and therefore too costly to undertake.[2]

But they are either agnostic about or disagree with other implications embedded in debates over nuclear weapons – specifically, whether nuclear weapons lessen the severity of security dilemmas and therefore make cooperation easier, and the corollary of whether nuclear weapons favor defensive strategies and are therefore stabilizing. Peacemakers are resolved to pursue gradual disarmament. Anti-hegemonists want restraint – to tie up America's ability to use and deploy its nuclear arsenal – and would accept gradual disarmament. And progressive pragmatists might seek only to retain a secure second-strike capability, leaving ample room for nuclear reductions and restraints of various kinds short of disarmament.[3] Accordingly, a progressive consensus not only supports subjecting US nuclear weapons to arms control treaty negotiations, it also supports proactively bridling America's nuclear posture.

This preference for nuclear restraint needs to be understood in relation to a nuclear-saturated status quo. Beyond Trump and into the Biden era, liberal internationalists continued to argue for preservation of the nuclear triad (bombers, submarines, and intercontinental ballistic missiles (ICBMs)). As of this writing, they still champion a nuclear modernization project that costs up to $1.7 trillion over 30 years and invests in new versions of all three legs of the nuclear triad, more interceptors for the GMD system, and 145 B-21 stealth bombers (more than six times the number of its B2 bombers). They refuse to acknowledge a condition of mutual vulnerability with China, despite that being the actual character of Sino-US nuclear stability. And they oppose declaring a no-first-use (NFU) nuclear policy that would forswear employing US nuclear weapons except in retaliation for an adversary launching nuclear weapons first.

---

[1] Lawrence Wittner, *The Struggle against the Bomb, Volume I: One World or None: A History of the World Nuclear Disarmament Movement* (Palo Alto: Stanford University Press, 1993), pp. 56–59, 171–210.

[2] Robert Jervis, *The Meaning of the Nuclear Revolution: Statecraft and the Prospect of Armageddon* (Ithaca: Cornell University Press, 1990).

[3] If changed conditions made disarmament more feasible than it is today, the logic of progressive pragmatism too would support a disarmament policy. The need to sustain balances of power involving nuclear states is the only reason for demurring at the call for disarmament today.

Anyone who believes in the virtue of American power enough to stake out these positions on nuclear policy will be reluctant to restrain it. This is why the Biden administration's announcement of an $813 billion defense budget in 2023 (which Congress boosted to more than $858 billion) was justified on the grounds that it "restores American leadership and confronts global threats."[4] For liberal internationalists, American primacy (or what remains of it) is still seen as an essential public good.

A progressive consensus opposes virtually all of this. Bernie Sanders, Elizabeth Warren, and Julian Castro all endorsed an NFU declaratory policy during the 2020 presidential election. The Congressional Progressive Caucus supports NFU too, and has lobbied with progressive legislators in other countries to adopt NFU.[5] Liberal internationalists resist NFU on the grounds that allies would find US nuclear commitments on their behalf less credible and that adversaries would not believe an NFU commitment anyway.[6] But allies would surely find much more comfort in a world with greater strategic stability than in a world of more credible threats of mutual nuclear death. And adversaries are much more likely to find an NFU commitment credible (thereby making it more stabilizing) if it is pursued not in isolation but in concert with other restraint-oriented nuclear policies. Credibility depends on context, and if US policy reshaped the context of an NFU declaration, it would be evaluated differently. As such, the United States should also:

- *Hold itself to the old terms of the Intermediate-Range Nuclear Forces (INF) treaty*, even if Russia and China do not.
- *Seek restoration of the anti-ballistic missile treaty* it abandoned in 2002.
- *Reduce instability risks in space* by codifying and expanding the Biden administration's 2022 unilateral moratorium on anti-satellite testing (ASAT).

---

[4] Press Release, "Fact Sheet: President's FY23 Budget Restores American Leadership and Confronts Global Threats," *White House* (March 28, 2022), www.whitehouse.gov/omb/briefing-room/2022/03/28/fact-sheet-presidents-fy23-budget-restores-american-leadership-and-confronts-global-threats/.

[5] Press Release, "Progressive Lawmakers in US, Japan Call on Biden to Reduce Risk of Nuclear War," *Union of Concerned Scientists* (April 1, 2022), www.ucsusa.org/about/news/progressive-legislators-call-no-first-use.

[6] For a summary of this debate, and the progressive rejoinder put forward here, see Van Jackson, "Time for US Nuclear Strategy to Embrace No First Use," *East Asia Forum* (July 4, 2021), www.eastasiaforum.org/2021/07/04/time-for-us-nuclear-strategy-to-embrace-no-first-use/.

- *Ratify the Comprehensive Nuclear Test-Ban Treaty* that the UN General Assembly passed in 1996, and if necessary unilaterally comply with it via an executive order.
- *Establish a policy to not develop "tactical" low-yield nuclear weapons*, as a starting point for encouraging others (especially North Korea, Pakistan, and Russia) to abandon their development.
- *Assert congressional war powers to take away the president's authority to launch nuclear weapons except when Congress has authorized war.* Congressional Democrats introduced legislation in 2016 and 2021 to introduce restraints on presidential nuclear launch authority.[7]
- *Work with allies and adversaries alike to introduce US-compliant "Nuclear-Weapons-Free Zones" (NWFZ)* – geographic areas where nuclear weapons are prohibited – in the South China Sea, parts of Northeast Asia, and Oceania.[8] Several NWFZ have been established by treaty and observed by the UN Office for Disarmament Affairs, but the United States does not abide by them because they cover large portions of the globe that the US Navy and Air Force transit with nuclear-capable delivery systems.[9] Applying the NWFZ concept to areas of potential territorial contest provides a focal point for international cooperation and helps reduce catastrophic geopolitical risks in those areas.

### Arms Control and Mutual Threat Reduction

Progressives roundly reject a strategy of primacy because it entails military superiority and arms-racing dynamics.[10] As the world's leading military power, the United States is in an optimal position to take political risks in the name of diplomacy rather than just taking militarily competitive risks in the name of demonstrating resolve or achieving military

---

[7] Press Release, "Senator Markey and Rep. Lieu Announce Reintroduction of Bill to Limit U.S. President's Ability to Start a Nuclear War," *Office of Senator Ed Markey* (January 19, 2021), www.markey.senate.gov/news/press-releases/01/19/2021/senator-markey-and-rep-lieu-announce-reintroduction-of-bill-to-limit-us-presidents-ability-to-start-a-nuclear-war.

[8] Elizabeth Mendenhall, "Nuclear Weapon Free Zones and Contemporary Arms Control," *Strategic Studies Quarterly* Vol. 14, no. 4 (2020), pp. 122–51.

[9] "Overview of Nuclear-Weapon-Free Zones," UN Office for Disarmament Affairs, www.un.org/nwfz/content/overview-nuclear-weapon-free-zones.

[10] Van Jackson, "Relational Peace Versus Pacific Primacy: Configuring US Strategy for Asia's Regional Order," *Asian Politics & Policy* Vol. 15, no. 1 (2023), pp. 141–52.

overmatch or signaling negative reciprocity. Campaigns of arms control and mutual threat reduction are a tangible way to curb the global military modernization and missile proliferation trends that, heretofore, US policies have helped propel.

Sane people everywhere – not just progressives – would support negotiations with China, Iran, North Korea, and Russia aimed at halting or reversing the growth of their nuclear and missile capabilities. But even conservative primacists sometimes pose as if they support arms control, in theory. Endorsing arms control is easy, even if, like primacists, you have no real interest in it; what is hard is taking the risks necessary to make arms control materially meaningful and not just performative or a bad-faith box-checking exercise on the road to arms-racing.

The novelty of a progressive statecraft is in the investments that it is willing to make to build more stable, restrained relations and to reduce the material danger states pose to one another. The purported moral hazard risk of literally buying an adversary regime out of its nuclear or missile production – specifically North Korea and Iran – is no risk at all compared to the risks of senselessly goading them to maximize their military capabilities. Therefore, the United States must explore the extent to which it can offer sanctions relief or financial remuneration in exchange for fewer weapons and less lethality; that is a great deal compared to the alternatives.

If arms reductions can only be bought in like-terms, through mutual capability reductions (which is likely the case with China and Russia), even better. As of this writing, the most acute non-nuclear areas of danger include China's massive naval ship-building expansion, missile proliferation in Asia, and US investments in intermediate-range ground-launched cruise missiles previously banned under the INF Treaty (which the United States withdrew from in 2019). Progressives support the United States putting its own forces and defense research and development on the table as potential compromises in order to address these dangers. Specifically, the United States should be willing to:

- *Forego INF-range missiles*, which its Asian allies have openly opposed hosting in their territory and the existence of which increases the risks of crisis instability because adversaries cannot tell if they carry nuclear payloads or not.
- *Curb the support it extends to allies developing long-range ballistic and hypersonic (atmospherically maneuverable) missiles* if it would rein in China's naval modernization and missile proliferation.

- *Eliminate the Missile Defense Agency* entirely, and be willing to negotiate limits and curtailments of certain missile defense investments – specifically the ground-based midcourse defense (GMD) system that Russia and China have viewed as destabilizing because it undermines mutual vulnerability (a state of mutual deterrence that the United States has not accepted with China).[11]
- *Eliminate or drastically reduce the "ground-based strategic deterrent"* – that is, the number of nuclear ICBMs it operates.[12]
- *Seek a freeze or moratorium in advanced conventional weapons testing, production, and deployment* – heretofore freeze initiatives have only ever applied to nuclear arms.

Unilateral reductions in US force structure – which can be driven by adopting a different defense strategy rather than by imposing haphazard cuts – aid this bid for threat reduction. The most traditional-looking defense posture among the progressive grand strategies – progressive pragmatism – sets the ceiling for the capacity and capability of the US military at that which would be necessary to sustain a forward-balancing defense strategy (i.e., sharing the burden of force structure investment in such a way that the United States cannot realistically engage in a war with China except in coalition with other democracies). Anti-hegemonists and peacemakers might oppose the forward military presence and capabilities necessary to sustain a democratic power-balancing strategy, but they would support the unilateral defense cuts that such a strategic shift would entail. Thus, the forward-balancing conversation – that is, what a US military that has thoroughly multilateralized its force structure must look like – sets the ceiling (not the floor) for a consensus progressive stance on the defense budget.

By being willing to not only submit the United States to reciprocal arms control negotiations but also to combine that with new declarations and some unilateral reductions that inhibit America's ability to do

---

[11] Press Release, "65 National Security Leaders Urge President Biden to Put Missile Defense on the Table," *Council for a Livable World* (June 3, 2021), https://livableworld.org/63-national-security-leaders-urge-president-biden-to-put-missile-defense-on-the-table/.

[12] Emma Claire-Foley, *The Real Cost of ICBMs: U.S. Economic Development Beyond Defense Spending* (Washington, DC: Global Zero, 2022), www.globalzero.org/wp-content/uploads/2022/06/The_Real_Cost_of_ICBMs.pdf; Sarah Lazare, "Biden Is Using the Ukraine Crisis to Justify Dangerous Investments in Nuclear Weapons," *In These Times* (March 28, 2022), https://inthesetimes.com/article/biden-budget-pentagon-nuclear-weapons-icbm-russia-ukraine; Fred Kaplan, "The Missile Trap," *Slate* (March 10, 2021), https://slate.com/news-and-politics/2021/03/icbm-gbsd-missile-lobby.html.

military interventions unilaterally, adversaries may be willing to take US arms control efforts more seriously than in recent years where the United States has appeared primarily focused on ensuring it retains nuclear and conventional superiority no matter the costs or risks.

### From National Defense to Global Public Goods

The peacemaker's grand strategic gambit hinges partly on not just reducing the defense budget but funding public goods provision with the money saved. This swords-into-ploughshares position is compatible with alternative progressive theories of security and is among the most widely shared foreign policy sentiments on the left. Diverting defense spending toward virtually any purpose that reduces inequality or structural violence would advance progressive visions for the world and how America relates to it. Included among the most popular proposals that progressives have championed are:

- *Getting the world vaccinated.* In 2021, the Defense Spending Reduction Caucus introduced legislation to take 1.3 percent of the defense budget and re-program it for global vaccine donations. They estimated that amount would provide vaccines for 30 percent of the world, ensuring that the most vulnerable and destitute are provided for, but also reducing the risk of new Covid-19 variants mutating in unvaccinated populations.[13]
- *Financing climate adaptation and emissions reductions.* Closing most of the US military bases projected to be overwhelmed by flooding and climate catastrophe over the next 30 years would help bankroll climate adaptation.[14] At home, this includes restoring pre-Trump era funding levels to Federal Emergency Management Agency (FEMA)'s Flood Hazard Mapping and Risk Analysis Program, increasing funding for the Department of Energy's Weather Assistance Program, and paying for some of the care provisions built into the proposed Green New Deal.[15] Abroad, this includes

---

[13] Nichols, "Cut Military Spending to Deliver Covid-19 Vaccines to the World."

[14] Mandy Smithberger, "The United States Needs to Cut Military Spending and Shift Money to Two Pressing Threats: Pandemics and Climate Change," *Bulletin of the Atomic Scientists* (September 7, 2021), https://thebulletin.org/premium/2021-09/the-united-states-needs-to-cut-military-spending-and-shift-money-to-two-pressing-threats-pandemics-and-climate-change/.

[15] Ujayli, *Reimagining U.S. Security Spending for the 21st Century and Beyond,* p. 15.

the Global Green New Deal initiatives discussed in Chapter 8. Congressional Democrats have also introduced amendments to the defense budget that would allocate $7.6 billion (less than 1 percent of the defense budget) toward climate accounts at the Department of State, US Agency for International Development, and the US International Development Finance Corporation.[16]

- *Reducing global poverty and investing in peacebuilding.* Progressive Non-governmental organizations (NGO)s have identified over $200 billion in defense savings that could be reprogrammed to fund "community foundations" in the Global South – local clearing-houses that take responsibility for how the money will be deployed to alleviate structural violence and promote peace.[17] Congress-woman Ilhan Omar introduced a salvo of legislation called "Path-ways to Peace" that proposed transferring $5 billion of the defense budget to global peacebuilding initiatives.[18] Alternatively, dozens of Nobel laureates launched a "Peace Dividend campaign" in 2021, demanding that 2 percent of military spending by all governments be directed to UN funds that would not only address public health and climate change, but also global poverty and inequality.[19]

In 2022, the United States secured only $1 billion for climate financ-ing abroad – less than a tenth of what the Biden administration initially promised and only 2 percent of what the Overseas Development Institute estimated would be America's necessary share toward making a green energy transition real. But in the first half of 2022 alone, the United States spent $13.6 billion on military aid to Ukraine (an amount that quadrupled shortly thereafter).[20] This exemplifies an egregious mismatch between US resources and global security needs.

---

[16] See, for example, Press Release, "Senator Markey Files NDAA Amendment to Redi-rect Defense Dept. Funds to Address Climate Crisis" (November 18, 2021), www .markey.senate.gov/news/press-releases/senator-markey-files-ndaa-amendment-to-redirect-defense-dept-funds-to-address-climate-crisis.

[17] Ujayli, *Reimagining U.S. Security Spending for the 21st Century and Beyond*, p. 17. See also "The Agenda," #PeopleOverPentagon (undated), https://peopleoverpentagon.org/ the-agenda/.

[18] Omar, Legislative Statement Introducing "Pathways to Peace."

[19] Dan Sabbagh, "'Colossal Waste': Nobel Laureates Call for 2% Cut to Military Spending Worldwide," *The Guardian* (December 14, 2021), www.theguardian.com/world/2021/ dec/14/nobel-laureates-cut-military-spending-worldwide-un-peace-dividend.

[20] "'Betrayal': US Approves Just $1 Bn Climate Finance for Developing Countries in 2022," *Climate Home News* (March 11, 2022), www.climatechangenews.com/2022/03/11/ betrayal-us-approves-just-1bn-climate-finance-for-developing-countries-in-2022/.

To point this out is not to argue against support for Ukraine. There is room to debate the security logic of providing military assistance to Ukraine, but only in a world where the United States is also tending to graver and more widely impactful threats, like the climate crisis. To back Ukraine militarily while failing on most other fronts of international security gives the lie to liberal rhetorical idealism. Spending on global public goods by drawing down defense spending helps rebalance the obvious overmilitarization of US statecraft. For this reason, there is a great deal of fungibility in what public goods the United States invests in and how, but all progressives desire using the savings acquired through defense spending reductions to invest in greater peace, democracy, and equality.

### De-securitizing Terrorism

The left (as distinct from the Democratic Party) has been opposed to the Global War on Terror (GWOT) from the outset. That the GWOT has come at a high price in blood and treasure – while inflaming rather than arresting global terrorism – suggests countering violent extremism with the extreme violence of the national security state has been a costly and avoidable error. *If* terrorism is the grave threat that justified it becoming the focal point of national security for the better part of two decades, then America's militarized response was precisely the wrong approach. The persistence of vital threats requires root-cause remedies, not 20-plus years of emergency measures and whack-a-mole violence. And if the United States has misjudged the significance of terrorism – inflating the threat it poses – then it never warranted the moral and democratic compromises that have been made in fighting it, nor the lost civilian lives (over 350,000) it has caused.[21] From every left vantage point, the answer to terrorism thus lay at least partly in de-militarization of US counterterrorism efforts, which includes:

- *Repealing the Authorization to Use Military Force (AUMF).* The legal authority to prosecute the GWOT – the AUMF – was written after 9/11 in haste, and with language so broad that it has allowed for literally global military counterterrorism operations. During the 2020 presidential election, Sanders, Warren, and Castro advocated

---

[21] "Human Costs of Post-9/11 U.S. Wars: Direct War Deaths in Major War Zones," Costs of War Project (September 2021), https://watson.brown.edu/costsofwar/figures/2021/WarDeathToll.

for a repeal of AUMF, which would force counterterrorism operations to occur with a narrower remit, within pre-9/11 presidential
authorities.

- *Ending military weapons transfers to police.* The large-scale weapons manufacturing needed to equip US forces in the GWOT – especially Iraq and Afghanistan – produced a glut of unneeded advanced
conventional small arms and armor-plated vehicles. Some of these
weapons and equipment made for warfighting go to foreign police
services, but most of it get transferred into local communities across
America through a basket of federal programs.[22] It has been the
material dimension of the militarization of American policing that
has created an atmosphere of fear and antagonism between the
police and civil society.[23]

- *Drawing down the US military presence in the Middle East.* Every
progressive approach to foreign policy supports reducing America's military footprint in the Middle East – anti-hegemonists and
peacemakers advocate eliminating it entirely. To the extent that
US forces in the region exist to prosecute the GWOT or protect
oil monarchies, their existence does not serve peace, equality, or
democracy.

- *Joining the International Criminal Court (ICC).* It is unrealistic to
expect good policy judgment about matters of war and peace when
US officials are unaccountable for their actions. The US legal system
has shown itself incapable of this self-accountability; the national
security state routinely rewards and promotes officials who stand
credibly accused of war crimes, torture, and human rights violations.[24] The best alternative, therefore, is for the United States to
join the ICC so that it can investigate and prosecute US officials
responsible for violating international law.

---

[22] The program to receive the most public scrutiny is the Defense Logistics Agency's 1033
Excess Property Program, but other programs to transfer military materiel to civilian
policing organizations include the Homeland Security Grant Program, the DoJ's Justice
Assistance Grants and Equitable Sharing programs, Treasury's Forfeiture Funds Equitable Sharing program, and the General Services Administration's Federal Surplus Personal Property Donation program.

[23] Schrader, *Badges without Borders*; Brian Barrett, "The Pentagon's Hand-Me-Downs
Helped Militarize Police: Here's How," *Wired* (June 2, 2020), www.wired.com/story/
pentagon-hand-me-downs-militarize-police-1033-program/.

[24] None of the senior officials involved in the CIA's extraordinary rendition program of
systematized torture have been held to account and one, Gina Haspel, later became
the director of the CIA. Nobody was criminally tried – or even purged from polite

## Ghosting Dictators

Progressives broadly agree that the United States should not aid and comfort despotic regimes – a position held consistently since at least the dawn of the Cold War. This aligns with the rhetoric of American liberal internationalism, but flies in the face of its practice. US foreign policy has repeatedly mobilized military and intelligence resources on behalf of dictatorship over the generations.[25] Sometimes it was in the name of Manichean anti-communism. Sometimes it was to secure oil, to manipulate a regional balance of power, or to defeat terrorism. More recently, it has been to contain Chinese "influence."

There is always a reason to justify aiding the world's oppressors, but rarely is it even plausible to claim that doing so serves the cause of peace, democracy, or equality. The "Leahy amendments" to US foreign security assistance budgets – which prohibit forms of military aid to human rights violators – would seem to agree with this view, in principle. The problem is that the vetting process for known and suspected human rights violations is weak and inconsistent, and there is very little precedent for prosecuting violations of the laws on the backend.[26] Specific policies to correct for this moral and strategic deficiency in American statecraft include:

- *Limiting alliance commitments to democracies only.* Progressives disagree about whether to retain a system of formal security alliances, but agree that it should not extend to autocratic regimes. This means the United States must end its North Atlantic Treaty Organization (NATO)-based commitment to Hungarian and Turkish defense, and remove US nuclear weapons and basing in Turkey.

---

society – for the US invasion of Iraq in 2003. Nobody has gone to prison or been fired for the civilian casualties resulting from counterterrorism operations. Henry Kissinger remained until his death a darling of Washington – endowing chairs at think tanks and universities in his name – despite standing credibly accused of war crimes in the 1970s. Impunity is the political culture of national security. On Kissinger especially, see Christopher Hitchens, *The Trial of Henry Kissinger* (New York: Verso, 2001).

[25] Steven Cook, "Loving Dictators Is as American as Apple Pie," *Foreign Policy* (April 26, 2019), https://foreignpolicy.com/2019/04/26/loving-dictators-is-as-american-as-apple-pie/. Some view the practical embrace of dictators within a commitment to liberal internationalism as essential. See, for example, Stephen Krasner, *How to Make Love to a Despot: An Alternative Foreign Policy for the Twenty-First Century* (New York: Liveright, 2019).

[26] Winifred Tate, "Human Rights Law and Military Aid Delivery: A Case Study of the Leahy Law," *Political and Legal Anthropology Review* Vol. 34, no. 2 (2011), pp. 337–54; Ujayli, *Reimagining U.S. Security Spending for the 21st Century and Beyond*, pp. 18–19.

If other European governments flip regime type, their future as an American client ought to also be at risk. In Asia, the future of the US alliances with the Philippines and Thailand should also be contingent on how far they drift away from good governance and toward violent, kleptocratic authoritarianism. The United States should be able to co-exist peacefully with non-democracies, but it should not protect them at the price of perpetuating militarism and strengthening the hand of regimes that disenfranchise their people.

- *Denying support to autocracies at war.* The United States has materially and symbolically backed Saudi Arabia's war in Yemen since 2015, which makes the US government complicit in causing large numbers of internally displaced persons, a food crisis plaguing the entire country, and well over 200,000 casualties.[27] Even if Saudi Arabia continued prosecuting this bloodletting on its own, it should have to do so without US arms, intelligence, or moral and political legitimation. This represents a more universal principle on which progressives agree – the US national security state should not be taking the side of autocracy in wars of choice, even if there is some tactical realpolitik advantage for the United States in an autocrat's victory.

- *Forbidding weapons transfers to despotic regimes and unstable societies.* There should be a policy to prohibit Foreign Military Financing/Foreign Military Sales programs for military juntas, kleptocratic regimes, any authoritarian regime actively at war, any regime governing a society in rebellion or civil conflict, or any regime known to be engaged in torture, extrajudicial killings, or ongoing human rights violations. This would mean that, for example, Saudi Arabia loses US military patronage entirely, and Foreign Military Sales (FMS) transactions with India would be suspended as long as it continues to persecute its Muslim population and control Kashmir. It would also mean that the United States cannot provide military aid to the Philippines while it has a fascistic leader. It should have suspended military aid to the Philippines when its former president, Rodrigo Duterte, was directing mass extrajudicial killings and suppressing freedom of speech. Given that the Philippines has many features of democracy and the Armed Forces of the Philippines has not been part of Duterte's suppression of free speech, mass street

---

[27] "UN Humanitarian Office Puts Yemen War Dead at 233,000, Mostly from 'Indirect Causes'," *UN News* (December 1, 2020), https://news.un.org/en/story/2020/12/1078972.

murders, or extrajudicial drug war, the fate of the US–Philippines alliance is a separate and thorny question. But military aid should be suspended when the governing regime is cosplaying fascism.

- *Ending QME for Israel.* The policy of ensuring Israel's "qualitative military edge" (QME) over the rest of the Middle East is dangerously nonsensical while the United States also sells arms to and maintains bases in nations throughout the region. America has found itself actively stoking ceaseless arms competition in the Middle East, arming both Israel and all of its antagonists other than Iran (and for decades it armed Iran too). The fate of US policy toward Israel overall is a lightning rod for controversy within the left, but the imperative to end the QME policy is far less controversial.[28] There should be no standing requirement to ensure Israel's military superiority over its neighbors.

## Reform International Financial Institutions

As Chapter 8 showed, progressives seek to reduce inequality but vary substantially in how best to go about it. Even commonsense anti-corruption measures at home and abroad are a point of contention.[29] But progressives widely support reform of international financial institutions (IFIs), either because they have locked in unjust power imbalances or because they have been the key agents of neoliberal globalization (or both). Consensus policy proposals aimed at the social democratic reformation of IFIs include:

- *Ending "structural adjustment" programs.* The World Bank and IMF have a decades-long tradition of conditioning its aid and loans to governments in need on the implementation of neoliberal economic policies – a package of fiscal austerity, deregulation, and privatization euphemistically known collectively as "structural adjustment" programs. The results have been disastrous, worsening structural violence and inequality while enriching kleptocrats and large multinational corporations. In recent years, the IMF has come to recognize that this had negative consequences, and does

---

[28] For a critical view of intra-left debates about Israel, see Marc Lamont Hill and Mitchell Plitnick, *Except for Palestine: The Limits of Progressive Politics* (New York: The New Press, 2020).
[29] Benjamin Fogel, "The Problem with 'Anti-Corruption'," *Jacobin* (February 12, 2021), https://jacobinmag.com/2021/02/anti-corruption-biden-samantha-power-jake-sullivan.

not impose them with the same zeal as during their heyday from the 1970s through the 1990s ... but it still imposes them all the same. As recently as 2022, the IMF made structural adjustment contingencies a requirement of restructuring a 2018 loan to Argentina.[30] Loans and support from IFIs should not perpetuate the fiction that economic life is somehow severable from political self-determination, nor should it inhibit investments in social welfare.

- *No more "surcharges."* The IMF has a longstanding practice of charging low-income and distressed government recipients of loans with surcharges in addition to structural adjustment conditions and normal interest payments, "accounting for 45% of all expected non-principal debt service owed by the five largest borrowers."[31] These charges must be eliminated, or else shifted to the richest countries with the largest voting shares – otherwise the institution's existence is subsidized by perpetuating inequality in a very direct sense.

- *Buffering the Global South against financial volatility.* Or more precisely, allow and encourage the South to protect itself via national capital controls and a Tobin tax.[32] The IMF spent much of the late- and post-Cold War era pushing deregulation of cross-border currency movements. This exposed the South to extreme financial volatility due primarily to currency speculation by hedge funds, leading to substantial financial instability in "emerging markets" that spilled over into developed economies.[33] In some places, like Indonesia, that financial instability fed a process of political instability, societal violence, and eventually regime change. In a 2012 review, the IMF acknowledged that currency regulation could be useful in a crisis. But this does not go far enough; economic authorities need to be able to prevent crises, not just respond to them.[34]

---

[30] Joseph Stiglitz and Mark Weisbrot, "Argentina and the IMF Turn away from Austerity," *Foreign Policy* (February 1, 2022), https://foreignpolicy.com/2022/02/01/argentina-imf-austerity-debt-economics-inflation/.

[31] Francisco Amsler and Michael Galant, *The Growing Burden of IMF Surcharges: An Updated Estimate* (Washington, DC: Center for Economic and Policy Research 2023), https://cepr.net/report/the-growing-burden-of-imf-surcharges-an-updated-estimate/.

[32] Mahbub ul Haq, Inge Kaul, and Isabelle Grunberg, eds., *The Tobin Tax: Coping with Financial Volatility* (New York: Oxford University Press, 1996).

[33] Joseph Stiglitz and Kevin Gallagher, "The IMF's Unfinished Business," *Project Syndicate* (March 7, 2022), www.project-syndicate.org/commentary/imf-review-must-embrace-capital-controls-by-joseph-e-stiglitz-and-kevin-p-gallagher-2022-03?barrier=accesspaylog.

[34] Luma Ramos, Lara Merling, and Kevin Gallagher, "Evaluating the Implementation of the IMF's Institutional View on Capital Flows," *GEGI Working Paper* No. 54 (March 2022), www.bu.edu/gdp/files/2022/03/GEGI_WP_054_FIN.pdf.

Moreover, the IMF has not demonstrated an ability to evenly apply this modest crisis-based deviation from its historical position against capital controls.[35]

- *Invigorating the International Labor Organization (ILO).* The global labor movement has shriveled and fractured in the era of neoliberal globalization, and it has been to the detriment of equality and democracy. As a consensus starting point for revitalizing the UN's ILO, which in theory is the organizational champion for worker power across borders, the United States should prioritize a global minimum wage campaign and make the ILO its responsible agent. A global minimum wage, as Chapter 8 explained, would benefit workers in the United States and abroad. The ILO has expressed interest in playing this role, and can be an ally should the United States channel its political capital toward making it a reality.[36]

- *Setting up new rules for voting allocations at the IMF.* Voting power at the IMF goes disproportionately to the Global North, and especially to the United States, which can exercise a veto. Instead of weighting voting share according to financial contribution, a more democratic alternative would simply grant each IMF member one vote, or at least to ensure that non-OECD countries receive at least half of total voting power.[37]

- *Reallocating "special drawing rights" (SDRs) at the IMF.* The poorest nations have the greatest need for SDRs because they can be used to pay for emergency supplies, vaccines, and other public goods. For this reason, in 2022, progressives in the House and Senate coalesced around a proposal to authorize $1.5 trillion in SDRs as an emergency measure.[38] A more lasting alternative would involve changing the rules for how the IMF allocates SDRs. Instead of pegging SDRs to the amount of a state's financial contribution to the IMF – which gives the richest nations the greatest access to SDRs, which they do

---

[35] Lara Merling, "After the Argentina Debacle, the IMF Endorses Weakening Capital Controls in Ecuador," *Open Democracy* (December 18, 2019), www.opendemocracy.net/en/oureconomy/after-argentina-debacle-imf-endorses-weakening-capital-controls-ecuador/.

[36] Hickel, *The Divide*, pp. 252–3.

[37] Ibid., p. 247.

[38] Press Release, "Warren Leads Colleagues in Calling on Senate Majority Leader Schumer to Support Additional Assistance to Low-Income and Developing Countries," (January 31, 2022), www.warren.senate.gov/oversight/letters/warren-leads-colleagues-in-calling-on-senate-majority-leader-schumer-to-support-additional-assistance-to-low-income-and-developing-countries.

not need – allocations should be based on an alternative standard such as need, poverty level, or social instability risk.[39]

## STRATEGIC PATHWAYS FOR PROGRESSIVE POLITICS

The prospects for seeing the United States relate to the world in a more peaceful, egalitarian, and democratic way depend on the constraints of the political landscape. If America's new right is fascist (or bears that family resemblance) and ends up capturing the institutions and authorities of the federal government, then all bets are off. Progressive world-making in an illiberal, undemocratic, and hyper-militarized society riven by internal conflict would be like aiming to grow a vineyard on a sand dune – your goals and resources are hopelessly mismatched. Some people believe this is already the case or will soon be. And I will not deny that there are signs of America's political situation being too far gone.

But that would be a threshold that requires revisiting everything. In that case, the principles guiding strategy (equality, democracy, and peace) become only strategy's visionary ends while the agents, objects, and instruments of strategy get re-sorted entirely – organized violence may need to be a tool, and the state may no longer be a representative agent of democratic will but rather a more acute threat to it. Most Americans, and in particular leftists, are not ready to disrupt their daily lives with the ways and means required of truly anti-fascist ends. For now, career- and life-risking campaigns of sustained civil disobedience, general strikes, sabotage, insurgency, or rebellion are almost entirely absent from their political imagination. Today, unlike in Franklin D. Roosevelt's (FDR's) day, there is not even a popular consciousness that sees redressing economic precarity as a means of inoculating the nation against reactionary forces, and "It's tough to slay neo-fascism when you can't even raise the minimum wage."[40]

I would like to think that Americans are not ready for such an existential battle because the circumstances do not demand it. Yet. And as long as the United States retains trappings of liberal democracy, there is a basis for steering policymakers and the Congress toward a more progressive statecraft through something resembling normal politics.

Still, ours is an era in flux. There are ways in which the Biden era represented an amalgam of liberal primacist continuity, a break from neoliberalism, an interregnum before American oligarchic neo-fascism, and the

---

[39] Franczak and Taiwo, "Here's How to Repay Developing Nations for Colonialism – and Fight the Climate Crisis."

[40] Timothy Shenk, "Born into the Dark," *Dissent* (Winter 2022), www.dissentmagazine .org/article/born-into-the-dark.

reincarnation of an FDR-style New Deal liberal progressivism. That all of these are plausible near futures at the same time is discomfiting, yet it also means it is not too late for a progressive statecraft to make a difference.

But how?

Constituencies within the left are currently following multiple paths to power, and each has unique implications for the prospects of a more progressive statecraft: (1) forming an anti-liberal, red-brown alliance with cross-sections of the anti-establishment right; (2) rallying around Democratic Socialists of America (DSA) as an alternative to the Democratic Party; (3) organizing a global left; and (4) working for change within the Democratic Party, through some combination of insider politics and outsider movement-based pressure. None of these are particularly promising for progressive futures but they are not equally dismal paths, and what emerges on the left could end up being a mashup of them.

## Red-Brown Alliance-Making

For those who believe progress toward political equality has come at the expense of economic equality,[41] aligning with reactionaries against left-liberals and moderates is a way of bringing about radical change in material betterment for workers. This topsy-turvy political logic, which forces progressives to bargain against themselves, might be alluring to people feeling frustrated and powerless. Lenin argued for something along these lines as the only way to seize power.[42] For foreign policy, it promises not only a mass political alignment in favor of military restraint and selective anti-war politics, but also the ruthless prioritization of neoliberalism as a threat.

Of course, the problem with red-brown alliances, as Scott Lemieux quipped, is that they are just brown.[43] They gesture at military restraint while forcing you down the path of extreme militarism. Parts of the "Make

---

[41] As Chapter 3 discussed, the New Left did not stress economic equality so much as the discrete political equality and anti-war issues that later became the New Social Movements. A fashionable criticism of the New Left today is that this prioritization meant that demands for equality came at the expense of critiques of capitalism and therefore an abandonment of economic equality.

[42] V.I. Lenin, *"Left Wing" Communism: An Infantile Disorder* (Detroit, MI: The Marxian Educational Society, 1921), pp. 42–51.

[43] Scott Lemieux, "Red-Brown Alliances Are Just Brown," *Lawyers, Guns, & Money* (March 23, 2022), www.lawyersgunsmoneyblog.com/2022/03/red-brown-alliances-are-just-brown.

America Great Again" right ("MAGA right") like Tucker Carlson and Senator Josh Hawley, for example, were opposed to war against Russia in Ukraine and sometimes postured as "anti-interventionist" in that context. But their arguments gave the game away, reasoning variously that China was the real threat, that fighting in Russia would distract from the real fight against China, and that ultimately Russia was the vanguard of the global far right; Putin sat atop a regime that was manifestly white, Christian, and "traditional," making him symbolically attractive rather than an adversary.[44]

Neither the "New right" nor the MAGA right, assuming we can disentangle them, is anti-war; they redirect nationalist animosity toward the grander anti-China (and occasionally anti-Semitic, anti-leftist, anti-black, anti-Asian, and anti-LGBTQ) struggle. These versions of the right have no interest in slashing the defense budget, narrowing the scope for nuclear weapons use, de-militarizing police at home, or ending programs of national security surveillance at home and abroad. Militarism and democracy are incompatible, and the aim of this kind of right-wing project "is not to end US militarism but to seize control of it."[45]

More generally, economic and political equality should not be severable, and just because a mode of economic-power relations is not "neoliberal" does not mean it is good or fair. Far right populists and neofascist sympathizers who reach out to the left do so in the name of a purported common enemy – liberalism.[46] Steve Bannon did this with the progressive *American Prospect* magazine in 2017, reaching out to its editor, naming China as a shared opponent in an interview, and subtly conflating the China threat with "globalist" liberals themselves.[47] Similarly, the amorphous but radically anti-liberal, anti-egalitarian new right is nothing less than "a project to overthrow the thrust of progress, at least such

---

[44] Tobita Chow and Ben Lorber, "Tucker Carlson's Flip Flops Mask a Deep Militarism," *The Nation* (March 28, 2022), www.thenation.com/article/politics/carlson-russia-nationalism-far-right/.

[45] Chow and Lorber, "Tucker Carlson's Flip Flops Mask a Deep Militarism." For a political philosophy of how militarism prevents rational problem-solving, see Mark Beeson, *Environmental Anarchy: Security in the 21st Century* (Bristol: Bristol University Press, 2021).

[46] Compact Magazine is an avowedly anti-liberal publication whose board is primarily right-wing intellectuals, but who has captured a handful of fringe left-wing provocateurs like Slavoj Zizek.

[47] Robert Kuttner, "Steve Bannon, Unrepentant," *American Prospect* (August 16, 2017), https://prospect.org/power/steve-bannon-unrepentant/.

as liberals understand the word."[48] The new right is a Peter Thiel-funded re-brand of the alt-right, leading one leftist blogger to ask, "aren't these guys just fascists? I mean come on, right?"[49] And yet they attract some of the fringes of the left all the same.[50]

The advances made on behalf of social justice over the decades are a threat to reactionary politics, and the right entertains a red-brown alliance only to thwart them. As Karl Kautsky argued, "Where democracy does not exist, the most urgent task before Labor and Social Democracy is to establish political freedom. It is quite erroneous to say that the workers must emancipate themselves economically, and that only then will 'true' democracy be possible."[51] The left, then, must ask whether abandoning or risking hard-won gains in political equality creates a terrain more favorable to demanding economic equality for all rather than for just whites, Christians, or men. It does not. A worthwhile left-right coalition should not entail sacrificing political equality. The fact that ethnonationalists find social justice threatening should be taken as a sign that it is a firm foothold for greater progress and unfavorable terrain for them. Indeed, the new "pink tide" of democratically elected leftist governments in Latin America has built its electoral success on strategies that leveraged inclusion and representational issues as the basis for coalitional solidarity and an agenda of economic security; political democracy as the on-ramp to economic democracy.[52]

Ultimately, the idea that you could secure working-class livelihoods by way of discriminatory, rights-denying political alliances is a chimera.

---

[48] James Pogue, "Inside the New Right, Where Peter Thiel Is Placing His Biggest Bets," *Vanity Fair* (May 2022), www.vanityfair.com/news/2022/04/inside-the-new-right-where-peter-thiel-is-placing-his-biggest-bets.

[49] Max Read, "Four Questions about the New Right," *Read Max Newsletter* (April 22, 2022), https://maxread.substack.com/p/four-questions-about-the-new-right?token=eyJ1c2Vy X2lkIjoxMDgwOTc3LCJwb3N0X2lkIjoxMjYxNjgwMiwiXyI6IldvclhNIiwiaWFoIjox NjUwNTcwMTc3LCJleHAiOjE2NTTA1NzM3NzcsIml1zcyI6InB1YiozOTI4NzMiLCJ zdWIiOiJwb3N0LXJlYWNoaW9uIn0.uWboVHRS-8uMlw3ZNeCiiNas1BBH5Hq0g1 tQ5Wxpvqs&s=r.

[50] Pogue, "Inside the New Right, Where Peter Thiel Is Placing His Biggest Bets."

[51] Karl Kautsky, "Chapter 8. Socialism and Democracy," in *Social Democracy versus Communism* (Rand School Press, 1946), www.marxists.org/archive/kautsky/1930s/demvscom/ch08.htm.

[52] Veronica Gago, "What Latin American Feminists Can Teach American Women about the Abortion Fight," *The Guardian* (May 10, 2022), www.theguardian.com/commentisfree/2022/may/10/abortion-roe-v-wade-latin-america; "The Government of Hope Has Arrived," *Progressive International* (June 20, 2022), https://progressive.international/wire/2022-06-20-the-government-of-hope-has-arrived-/en.

Playing with ethnonationalists, conspiracy theorists, and reactionary post-liberal traditionalists who pine for a past that never really existed as they imagine it risks ending in fascism of some sort. Policies that perpetuate a white supremacist or neofascist order, for instance, by definition can only elevate a slice of the working class, and they do so by way of depriving others of the same rights and privileges. A shared red-brown desire to move away from neoliberalism is not especially meaningful if there is total disagreement about what to move toward.

### A Socialist Bloc

Democratic socialism has existed in the United States for more than a century, but always on the fringes.[53] Not only has America's two-party system stacked the deck against socialism institutionally, American political culture has nurtured an anti-socialist attitude since well before the first "red scare" in 1919. Despite this, DSA, a successor organization to both the older Socialist Party of America (SPA) and the New Left's Students for a Democratic Society (SDS),[54] has seen massive growth since 2016.[55] Polls also indicate that overall attitudes toward socialism are softening, and that younger generations of voters – who grew up in the shadow of the war on terror, Iraq, the great recession, and a global pandemic – view socialism far more favorably than older generations.[56]

Although DSA is arguably more radical than progressive, it is not entirely shut out of competition for power in the US electoral system. DSA was a vocal bloc of support endorsing Bernie Sanders for president in 2016 and 2020. It runs candidates at the state and local level throughout the country. It counts as progressive members some of the Justice Democrats in Congress, including Alexandria Ocasio-Cortez, Rashida Tlaib, Jamaal Bowman, and Cori Bush. And DSA – not the Democratic Party or even organized labor – was the only political constituency of

---

[53] Dorrien, *American Democratic Socialism*.

[54] Joseph Schwartz, "A History of Democratic Socialists of America, 1971–2017," *Democratic Socialists of America* (July 2017), www.dsausa.org/about-us/history/.

[55] As of 2021, DSA touted a little over 94,000 members. Democratic Socialists of America, *Financial Report: National Convention of 2021* (undated), https://docs.google.com/document/d/19cy7DOQH7582rJxqgY2ABqFWtWuJ3JP8AVIvGEYiGy8/edit.

[56] Igor Derysh, "New Poll Finds 70% of Millennials Say They're 'Likely' to Vote for Socialist," *Salon.com* (October 29, 2019), www.salon.com/2019/10/29/new-poll-finds-70-of-millennials-say-theyre-likely-to-vote-for-a-socialist/.

note actively campaigning in support of Amazon warehouse employees in New York when they secured a remarkable success in voting to unionize in 2022.[57]

On foreign policy, the organization's members formulate its positions, which are inflected with class consciousness. Accordingly, DSA's statements about foreign policy have stressed a mix of anti-hegemonist and peacemaking themes, making it a reliable advocate for military restraint and cutting defense to invest in public goods. Opposition to American hegemony has been by far DSA's most stable foreign policy preference, and socialism of any sort presupposes the end of neoliberal policy prescriptions.

But there are large challenges with DSA as a path for realizing a progressive foreign policy. Just as liberalism is capacious enough to produce wide-ranging variations in foreign policy, so too is socialism. You still find substantial disagreement among American democratic socialists about the character of the Chinese Communist Party,[58] the gravity and imminence of the fascist threat,[59] how best to support Palestine,[60] and the proper response to Russia's invasion of Ukraine.[61] And when democratic socialists thought they might be on the cusp of power in the 2020 presidential election, at least one mused in a major mainstream publication about the possibility of a socialist foreign policy supporting wars

---

[57] Indeed, an old communist pamphlet about organizing in the steel industry was the playbook on which Amazon workers relied for organizing the union vote. See Luiz Feliz Leon, "Amazon Workers on Staten Island Clinch a Historic Victory," *Labor Notes* (April 1, 2022), www.labornotes.org/2022/04/amazon-workers-staten-island-clinch-historic-victory.

[58] Contrast, for example, Tobita Chow and Jake Werner, "The US, China, and the Left," *Socialist Forum* (Fall 2021), https://socialistforum.dsausa.org/issues/fall-2021/the-us-china-and-the-left/; Travis S., "Building a Mass Movement with No Apologism."

[59] Udi Greenberg, "What Was the Fascism Debate?" *Dissent* (Summer 2021), www.dissentmagazine.org/article/what-was-the-fascism-debate.

[60] See Lamont Hill and Plitnick, *Except for Palestine*; Andy Sernatinger, "On (Not) Expelling Jamaal Bowman," *Tempest* (December 10, 2021), www.tempestmag.org/2021/12/on-not-expelling-jamaal-bowman/; "DSA Leadership Dissolves BDS Working Group: DSA in Crisis," *Socialist Alternative* (March 20, 2022), www.socialistalternative.org/2022/03/20/dsa-leadership-dissolves-bds-working-group/.

[61] Contrast, for example, Eric Levitz, "The Left Has Half-Baked Answers on Ukraine," *New York Magazine* (March 20, 2022), www.tempestmag.org/2021/12/on-not-expelling-jamaal-bowman/; John Ganz, "Assessing DSA's Ukraine Statement," *Unpopular Front Substack* (February 10, 2022), https://johnganz.substack.com/p/assessing-dsas-ukraine-statement?s=r; Ben Burgis, "No, Left-Wing Opponents of War Aren't Isolationists," *Jacobin* (April 14, 2022), https://jacobinmag.com/2022/04/antiwar-internationalists-isolationists-eugene-debs-russia-ukraine; John Ganz, "Ben Burgis's Bad History," *Unpopular Front Substack* (April 16, 2022), https://johnganz.substack.com/p/ben-burgiss-bad-history?s=r.

against "climate chauvinists."[62] The point being that socialism has not yet been developed into a theory of foreign policy, and what it means in practice to foreground in your analysis class, capitalism, or imperialism is often indeterminate at the level of state decision-making and therefore very contested.

Building power through DSA, or socialist organizing generally, is also just a circuitously hard slog to transforming foreign policy. Despite its growth the past decade, DSA is still very small. At less than 100,000 members as of 2021, it is literally a rounding error compared to the size of the Democratic Party (more than 48 million as of 2021). There is no foreseeable DSA member entering the presidency anytime soon; to date, Sanders was unique among twenty-first-century presidential candidates. DSA, moreover, is not technically a political party, which means it lacks institutional advantages that the Democratic and Republican Parties enjoy. And critical voices within DSA are torn about whether to be agitators, an independent voting bloc, or popular-frontists.[63]

Some want a socialism that confronts and opposes Democrats (an outsider strategy); others see as essential partnering with Democrats or subsuming DSA as a de facto caucus aligned with the Democratic Party.[64] After Sanders lost the presidential primary in 2020 to Joe Biden, DSA declined to endorse the latter, exposing an open disagreement about political strategy that lingers.[65] And some, charting a "left populism," see DSA rather derisively as "an organization of young, precarious members [sic] college-educated people who are aspirational PMC [professional managerial class] ... could be working class oriented but is not."[66]

These power realities and internal fissures matter because they augur against expecting DSA to be the channel through which US foreign policy

---

[62] Meaney, "What U.S. Foreign Policy Will Look Like under Socialism."

[63] In essence, socialists today face the same strategic tension Adam Przeworksi mapped out decades ago: whether to seek power through elections, the working class directly, or overturning capitalism entirely. Adam Przeworski, *Capitalism and Social Democracy* (Cambridge: Cambridge University Press, 1986).

[64] Nick French and Neal Meyer, "Socialists Need a Clear, Confrontational Strategy to Win," *Socialist Call* (April 13, 2022), https://socialistcall.com/2022/04/13/socialists-strategy-legislature-new-york-dsa/.

[65] Former Leaders of the Students for a Democratic Society, "An Open Letter to the New New Left from the Old New Left," *The Nation* (April 16, 2020), www.thenation.com/article/activism/letter-new-left-biden/; Daniel Finn, "An Open Letter from SDS Veterans Haranguing Young Socialists to Back Biden Was a Bad idea," *Jacobin* (April 17, 2020), https://jacobinmag.com/2020/04/sds-new-left-joe-biden-letter.

[66] Catherine Liu, "/231/ New Class Analysis," *Bungacast Podcast* (November 9, 2021), www.podbean.com/media/share/pb-dtgw8-1150f7.

might be transformed. DSA has no influence over the Executive Branch of government, which stewards American power in the world, and it has no post-Cold War track record of placing socialists in civil servant or political appointee roles.[67] Its ability to impact foreign policy comes from influencing the opinions of individual members in the Congressional Progressive Caucus, and pushing the boundaries of public opinion on discrete issues in the same way that any advocacy organization does. That means the socialist path to a more progressive American statecraft hinges on Overton window work (shifting the boundaries of acceptable opinion about specific policies) or getting many more DSA members elected to Congress.

## A Global Left

The formation of a "global left" could also shape a more progressive foreign policy. The left's outlook is inherently internationalist. Marxists saw/see global class solidarity as a basis for revolutionary change.[68] The early formations of the American progressive movement exchanged ideas and resources transnationally, not only with Europe but also progressives in British settler colonies across the Pacific.[69] The Black Panthers played global balance-of-power politics against the US national security state, although doing so quickly became a liability.[70] Influencers within the pre-Cold War civil rights movement looked to the ongoing independence movement in colonized India as a model for organizing at home.[71] And American civil rights during the Cold War were part of a global civil rights struggle – an understanding that made it possible to secure the former by advancing the latter and vice versa.

---

[67] Prior to the McCarthy-era Second Red Scare, it was quite common for socialists to enjoy careers in public service. See Storrs, *The Second Red Scare and the Unmaking of the New Deal Left.*

[68] It is easy to overstate how literally to take the quote that "The working men have no country." For a nuanced reading of Marx on internationalism, see Daniel Finn, "Two Centuries of the National Question," *Jacobin* (February 15, 2023), https://jacobin.com/2023/02/two-centuries-of-the-national-question.

[69] Marilyn Lake, *Progressive New World: How Settler Colonialism and Transpacific Exchange Shaped American Reform* (Cambridge, MA: Harvard University Press, 2019); Daniel Rodgers, *Atlantic Crossings: Social Politics in a Progressive Age* (Cambridge, MA: Harvard University Press, 2000).

[70] Sean Malloy, *Out of Oakland: Black Panther Party Internationalism during the Cold War* (Ithaca: Cornell University Press, 2017).

[71] William Jones, *The March on Washington: Jobs, Freedom, and the Forgotten History of Civil Rights* (New York: W.W. Norton & Co., 2014), pp. 54, 58, 63–4.

The Student Nonviolent Coordinating Committee (SNCC), that bastion of organizing in the American South, had a global perspective on racial capitalism that situated their struggle as part of a global network of liberationists.[72] And the SNCC was deeply internationalist – opposing apartheid in South Africa, coming out early against the Vietnam War, and increasingly criticizing Cold War foreign policy, especially in the Caribbean and Africa.[73]

In keeping with the internationalist tradition, Progressive International and the Transnational Institute – two of today's more prominent organizations among a much larger milieu – aim to build a transnational infrastructure and consciousness for a progressive global order. Progressives are increasingly forging transnational ties that selectively route around and ally with the state in the name of bringing greater pressure to bear on the state – national politics need not be "the dominant arena for resolving contradictions of capital and representing the interests of the working class."[74] The condition of possibility for a global left is a shared problematic – neoliberal globalization, American hegemony, the global far right, and the climate crisis are all sources of insecurity in their own ways, and all are global in nature. The response, logically, must also be global.

A global left with some ability to concentrate political activism, messaging, and money could massively reshape the incentive structure of national politics in the United States and elsewhere. Progressive International in particular has achieved some success in supporting progressive movements in Latin America, as well as convening the Havana Congress on the New International Economic Order in 2023 – an ambitious effort to align the G-77 and the Global South with forces in the Global North seeking a progressive economic order.[75] Progressives in the US House of Representatives, remarkably, have established thin connections to some social democratic politicians in parts of Asia, Europe, and Latin America. And in Brazil, progressive Lula da Silva's re-election as president (and defeat of neofascist Jair

---

[72] Dan Berger, "SNCC's Unruly Internationalism," *Boston Review* (November 16, 2021), https://bostonreview.net/articles/snccs-unruly-internationalism/.

[73] Ibid.

[74] Nihal El Aasar, "The Only Way We Win: The Progressive International," *Verso Books Blog* (May 14, 2020), www.versobooks.com/blogs/news/4711-the-only-way-we-win-the-progressive-international.

[75] Kenny Stancil, "Havana Declaration Outlines Vision for Building Just World Economy," *Common Dreams* (January 30, 2023), www.commondreams.org/news/havana-declaration-just-world-economy.

Bolsonaro) has given the global left project an institutionalized political anchoring, for now.[76]

Yet the left has always struggled to sustain transnational solidarity in a world dominated by nation-states and intergovernmental organizations. European socialists overwhelmingly subordinated themselves into nationalist projects once World War I broke out.[77] The Black Panthers found themselves trafficking in illegal arms and setting up alliances with despots and violent revolutionary regimes abroad.[78]

Today, Brazil's President Lula is a vanguard of global progressivism, straddling the core and periphery of the world system, yet, it is not clear what this means for transnational forces or progressives in the United States, where political institutions are mostly *not* occupied by progressive policymakers. And while the global insecurity challenges faced today may require a global response, the threats they pose are not evenly distributed, making the urgency of prioritization dependent on your position in the world system and local circumstances: "progressives need a quantum leap in transnational networking .... What is needed is strategic coordination .... The challenge ... how to combine the horizontality of organizing that respects local differences with the verticality of politics that the scale of the global problems demands."[79] This is no small dilemma, and it is worsened by the left's limited financial resources. Reactionary political movements have a continuing advantage because their interests tend to align with capital interests – the richest sources of funding are generally antagonistic to truly progressive ends.

What a global left needs is some kind of blueprint that has broad buy-in as a focal point and is at once global and local. That is, it must narrate unity of effort and common direction while accommodating both a "diversity of tactics" and functional differentiation based on a world-systems perspective – the optimal national policies in a global progressive order will depend on where a nation sits in the world system. It is not just about *how* to organize horizontally and hierarchically, but also *who* should organize for *what* given the different political, geographic, and

---

[76] Alex Burns, "Lula's Plan: A Global Battle against Trumpism," *Politico* (April 13, 2023), www.politico.com/news/magazine/2023/04/13/lula-global-battle-against-trumpism-00091794.

[77] See especially Kazin, *War against War*; Finn, "Two Centuries of the National Question."

[78] Joshua Bloom and Waldo Martin, Jr., *Black against Empire: The History and Politics of the Black Panther Party* (Berkeley: University of California Press, 2016), pp. 1–4, 309–38.

[79] Feffer, *Right across the World*, pp. 138–9.

developmental constraints and advantages that individual states face.[80] States remain the dominant actors in world politics.

## The Democratic Machine

The Democratic Party is an eclectic, big-tent political coalition, and as such has always thought of itself as the tribune of democracy (hence the name). Yet what it has stood for has changed dramatically with the times. For basically all of its history, it has been inescapably liberal, with all the good and bad that can be smuggled into that characterization.[81] During Reconstruction, it was for the white working man and against corporate monopolies. But it was also staunchly pro-settler colonialist and deeply racist. In the 1930s, it became the party of labor, and since then has been the primary electoral home for self-identified progressives, even though prior to the Civil Rights Act of 1964 and the Voting Rights Act of 1965 it was also a party filled with white supremacists. From the end of the Cold War through Trump's election, the Democratic Party has incorporated many of the political values of the old New Left – racial and gender equality, environmentalism, a cosmopolitan ethos. Yet it has also alienated labor, repudiated the New Left's anti-war politics, and championed corporate interests and Wall Street.[82]

What the Democratic Party stands for today is an unsettled matter. The 2020 presidential primary saw the party's platform move left, especially on domestic and economic policy.[83] Keynesianism became en vogue again. FDR had replaced Wilson as the totem of Democratic politics. Although Joe Biden was among the most conservative of the many candidates running for the Democratic nomination, he too embraced a more Rooseveltian political posture.

As such, many leftists who pinned all their hopes on a Bernie Sanders presidency tried to make the most of Joe Biden, for a time. After the Trump

---

[80] Immanuel Wallerstein saw the problem of prioritization as a key obstacle to a Global Left, and he did not seem to think it was so simple as just claiming a "chain of equivalence." Immanuel Wallerstein, *The Global Left: Yesterday, Today, Tomorrow* (Abingdon: Routledge, 2022), pp. 26–8.

[81] Michael Kazin defines the throughline of the Democratic Party as "moral capitalism," balancing greater equality for workers and the poor with rights to private accumulation. Kazin, *What It Took to Win*, pp. xi–xiii.

[82] See especially Geismer, *Left Behind*.

[83] Matt Yglesias and Milan Singh, "Democrats Have Changed a Lot Since 2012," *Slow Boring Newsletter* (May 11, 2022), www.slowboring.com/p/shifting-left?r=1g1myl&utm_medium=ios&s=r.

years, the Biden administration and the Congressional Progressive Caucus "came in hoping to crush the pandemic, clear a path beyond the wreckage of neoliberalism, and take major steps toward saving the planet from climate change. Instead, they gave a leftish tilt to a string of ad hoc responses."[84]

Early measured hope soon gave way to a major tension – whatever shift to the left the Democratic Party's grassroots might have made during the Trump years, the party leadership was still dominated by centrists and opportunists. A Democratic majority in Congress was only possible if it included conservative-leaning politicians like Senator Joe Manchin who, opposing much of the party's leftward shift, stood in the doorway blocking President Biden's most ambitious legislative proposals for infrastructure investment and a green energy transition. When the Inflation Reduction Act did finally become law in 2022, it unleashed massive investments in a green energy transition and the rebuilding of domestic industrial capacity, but it did so on a much smaller scale than the Green New Deal proposal from which it took its inspiration; it did so almost entirely via corporate and personal tax credits; it did so without the progressive care and worker-power provisions that were why the left was part of the legislative coalition in the first place; and it did so by legitimizing and heightening Cold War-like geopolitical rivalry with China. Accordingly, the Biden-era Democratic Party remains something of a Rorschach test.

The Biden presidency itself, as distinct from the Democratic Party, moved left on domestic and economic policy compared to its predecessors, but it is easy to overstate how far left – especially given that Biden's economic policy activism primarily serves (and has been driven by) the interests of the national security state. To his credit, he introduced a moratorium on student loan payments and $10,000 of debt forgiveness, extended a moratorium on landlords evicting renters, made direct cash transfers to every American as part of pandemic relief, and prioritized free nationwide vaccine distributions. Biden himself even spoke out favorably on behalf of organized labor while his administration remained mute and continued working on behalf of capital rather than labor.

At the same time, Biden openly antagonized those within the party calling for reforms to community policing around the country.[85] Despite

---

[84] Timothy Shenk, "Born into the Dark," *Dissent* (Winter 2022), www.dissentmagazine.org/article/born-into-the-dark.

[85] Peter Nickeas, "'The Answer Is Not to Defund': Here's What's in President Biden's Increased Budget for Policing," *CNN* (March 31, 2022), https://edition.cnn.com/2022/03/31/us/biden-police-budget-increase/index.html.

his rhetorical support for unions, he prevented rail workers from striking for paid time off, siding with the bosses. His industrial policies were "worker-friendly" in absolute terms, but did nothing to enhance worker power in relative terms. Biden could not raise the minimum wage, despite campaigning to do so. Inequality, which was already extreme, worsened during his presidency. Biden did not remotely rise to the challenge of climate change. He said in February 2020 that there would be "no more drilling on federal lands. Period, period, period."[86] Yet the Biden administration even outpaced Trump in issuing permits for oil and gas drilling on federal lands during the first half of his presidency.[87] And only a year after taking office, Biden began touting "deficit reduction" (in parallel with sky-high defense spending) as a virtuous necessity that would actually make national security stronger.[88]

It is unclear how much of Biden's yo-yo-ing between Keynesianism and neoliberalism was thrust upon him by the pandemic, by the contradictions of "supply-side progressivism,"[89] or by centrist Democrats holding his efforts to "Build Back Better" hostage. While there is definitely evidence of a shifting policy landscape, you could look at the sum of US political economy and confirm any bias you wish.

The same, however, could not be said of foreign policy – a domain where the Biden administration showed the fewest signs of change from his predecessors, hewing to a staunchly liberal primacist outlook. Its rhetoric touted all the things we have come to expect of American exceptionalism – claims to leadership, an insistence on domination through favorable imbalances of power, autocracies versus democracies, and the logical inconsistency of denying others spheres of influence while protecting (and refusing to acknowledge) your own spheres. In these ways, Biden foreign policy bore a strong resemblance to Obama's, but in a less favorable context that made it even more distant from progressive priorities.

---

[86] As quoted in Coral Davenport, "Biden Plans to Open More Public Land to Drilling," *New York Times* (April 15, 2022), www.nytimes.com/2022/04/15/climate/biden-drilling-oil-leases.html?smid=tw-share.

[87] Ibid.

[88] Jeff Stein, "Biden Budget Pivots to Deficit Concerns While Boosting Military, Domestic Programs," *Washington Post* (March 28, 2022), www.washingtonpost.com/us-policy/2022/03/28/biden-budget-white-house/.

[89] Paul Baran and Paul Sweezy surfaced the contradiction at the heart of what some now call "supply-side progressivism" long ago – Keynesian-style policies require socialist politics. See Benjamin Feldman, "A Capital for the Age of Growth: Paul Baran, Paul Sweezy, and the Critique of Keynesian Civilization," *Critical Historical Studies* Vol. 6, no. 2 (2019), pp. 195–221.

Unlike Obama, Biden no longer resisted and instead leaned into "strategic competition" with China.[90] Biden spent more on defense than not only Obama but Trump too, closing in on a trillion-dollar defense budget. And Biden gave up promoting trade deals in favor of an approach to international political economy that lacked any real coherence beyond simply trying to sustain what remains of American global primacy in a historical conjuncture where that is self-defeating and unrealistic.[91]

Borrowing from the foreign policy platforms of the most progressive presidential candidates in 2020, the Biden White House elevated the role of corruption and kleptocracy to being a priority national security issue, going so far as issuing the first-ever strategy to combat it. It launched a campaign for a global minimum tax, which progressives had long touted. And it unlocked some badly needed funding for climate financing in places like India. But whatever good that represented must be weighed against the Biden administration's fixation on what can only be described as national-security Keynesianism – leaving in place and expanding on the largely arbitrary Trump-era tariffs against China, building out a more deliberate industrial policy, reshoring supply chains, restricting foreign access to US technologies, and leveraging the allure of US tax credits to prohibit foreign firms from investing in Chinese technology firms. These are not morally innocent moves but rather a techno-containment strategy that is actively trying to rewrite the rules of the so-called rules-based international order.[92]

The history of the Democratic Party shows that "... pressures exerted within social movements by their left wings can enlarge liberals' ambitions and urge them on to reforms that might not otherwise occur."[93] The best of what the party stands for owes something to the pressure it receives from radical and mass sentiment. If we extend that observation to foreign policy, the diversity of the party itself means that, while its policies can be malleable, the trudging nature of intra-party coalition politics also makes it an unlikely champion of radical reform. The question is how to view progress that proceeds in this manner. Most foreseeable versions of the Democratic Party would enact a shift toward progressive statecraft only slowly, piecemeal, and from a baseline of an obscenely large national security state and globally present military.

---

[90] On Obama's resistance to Sino-US rivalry despite laying the groundwork for it, see Jackson, *Pacific Power Paradox*, pp. 131–63.

[91] Jackson, "Relational Peace versus Pacific Primacy."

[92] Jackson, "The Problem with Primacy."

[93] Brick and Phelps, *Radicals in America*, p. 13. See also Kazin, *What It Took to Win*.

Critics would point out that the way the Democratic Party evolves on policy evokes what Antonio Gramsci called "passive revolution" – a ruling-class response to the need for social change that preserves the basic social hierarchy or distributions of political power.[94] It thus stands to reason that the more urgently you view the need for a progressive shift in foreign policy, the more dissatisfied you will be with banking on the deeply flawed vessel that is the Democratic Party.

And yet, it is possible that a rapid transformation of foreign policy into something more progressive comes from within the Democratic machine anyway. Owing to the work of the Justice Democrats, Congress and the party now contain within them a social democratic bloc.[95] It is conceivable that the Justice Democrats' strategy of primarying centrist Democrats in solidly progressive districts will continue paying off, growing the size of that bloc and changing the composition of the party itself.[96] That could shift the politics of the party in favor of workers, social justice, and the environment.

Alternatively, or perhaps concurrently, the revitalization of American labor could become a new power-political constituency for Democrats. The upsurge of worker organizing since the pandemic, and the success of unionization drives at Starbucks and Amazon, as well as in less high-profile sectors, antagonizes the corporate base of the Clintonite neoliberal-friendly Democratic leadership over the past generation. It cannot be taken as a given that labor will align with Democrats, but there is an organic convergence between labor priorities and progressive ones.

It is also possible that a charismatic left-populist could win the presidency as a Democrat. Eugene Debs was a socialist who got close to a million votes for the presidency in 1920 *while imprisoned*.[97] Upton Sinclair was a socialist who nearly became California governor in 1934 as a Democrat. Bernie Sanders was leading all contenders for the Democratic

---

[94] On Gramsci's concept of passive revolution, see Adam David Morten, "Waiting for Gramsci: State Formation, Passive Revolution, and the International," *Millennium* Vol. 35, no. 3 (2007), pp. 597–621.

[95] Kazin, *What It Took to Win*, p. 312.

[96] Andrew Marantz, "Are We Entering a New Political Era?" *New Yorker* (May 31, 2021), www.newyorker.com/magazine/2021/05/31/are-we-entering-a-new-political-era.

[97] Debs was a victim of Woodrow Wilson's crackdown on civil liberties and his imprisonment owed to his opposition to US involvement in World War I. Terence McArdle, "The Socialist Who Ran for President from Prison – and Won Nearly a Million Votes," *Washington Post* (September 22, 2019), www.washingtonpost.com/dc-md-va/2019/09/22/socialist-who-ran-president-prison-won-nearly-million-votes/.

Party presidential nomination in 2020 for most of that campaign season, and deserves much of the credit for removing mainstream stigma around democratic socialism in America. And to the extent that the voting public chooses its presidents based on criteria other than foreign policy anyway – which is certainly the conventional wisdom – even a centrist Democratic president has tremendous latitude to pursue a radically more progressive vision for America's place in the world without it damaging their electoral prospects.

Progressive worldmaking needs a political home to be viable, and Michael Kazin was not wrong to observe, however reluctantly, that "the Democrats remain the only electoral institution in twenty-first-century America able to help solve the serious problems facing the United States and, to a degree, the rest of humanity as well."[98] The growth of the Justice Democrats, the emergence of a transformational figure, or the revitalization of an American labor movement once again aligned with the Democrats would open enough space to introduce a more self-consciously progressive approach to the world. But each of those eventualities would be a stark political shift from the Democratic Party as we have known it since the 1970s.

## A SECURITY BEYOND TRAGEDY

Progressives tend to see the tragic view of world politics – consisting of little more than power hoarding, war optimization, and great-power status competitions – as tragically self-entrapping. Widening our conception of security, thinking differently about risk, and elevating statecraft to emphasize public policy – not just national security policy in the conventional sense – promises to narrow the space for tragedy, and possibly change the way the game of global politics is played. Progressive principles are no panacea, and pregnant with dilemmas in practice. But they also provide a basis for beginning to address the root problems plaguing international politics, by guarding against imperialism and ruling-class theology (for example, neoliberalism), but also against Herrenvolk social democracy. All such possibilities not only betray the goals of economic democracy and equality in a multiethnic society, but they also create space for perpetual war by reinforcing boundaries dividing who gets to be secure and who is vulnerable to being sacrificed.

---

[98] Kazin, *What It Took to Win*, p. xvi.

During the Cold War, left-leaning scholars tried to broaden the security agenda as a way to dilute the importance of the military. What I have attempted here, by contrast, is to reconfigure how we think about the "security agenda" altogether, showing how public policy – not just defense policy – is a space for making a world that is *not* more securitized, but rather more peaceful, democratic, and egalitarian.

Leftists remind us that the state is a mechanism that extracts the blood and treasure of workers, converts it into power, and then deploys it to perpetuate a political status quo that favors a society's elites ... unless the people that states govern direct it to do otherwise. Progressive worldmaking recognizes this reality, and suggests ways of wielding the state on behalf of a durable, not chimerical, security – one that foregrounds security for the many, not the few. As distinct repertoires of statecraft, progressive grand strategies reveal many things, good and bad depending on your perspective. But what they make indisputable is that anyone who claims "There Is No Alternative" to liberal primacy is wrong.

# Index

China (cont.)
  and climate crisis, 137
  and Cold War mindset, 113, 125, 135
  and Communist Party, 147
  and democracy, 55, 104
  and economic interdependence, 102
  foreign policy of, 124
  and global economic order, 101
  and the Global South, 175
  and great-power competition, 33, 173
  and human rights abuses, 5, 93
  and the INF treaty, 181
  and Joe Biden, 20, 207
  and labor, 85
  military, 116
  and military aggression, 83
  and multilateral coalitions, 91
  and mutual vulnerability, 180
  and nuclear policy, 113, 115, 183
  and oppression, 1
  and patronage, 165
  and rivalry with the US, 205
  and spheres of influence, 94, 122, 123, 126
  and tariffs, 207
  and trade, 163
  as US adversary, 117, 120, 127
  and US dollar supremacy, 106
  and US policy, 92, 105, 118, 140, 174, 184
  and US progressives, 6, 75, 110, 183, 196
  and Uighurs, 36
Chinese Communist Party, 86, 135
Chomsky, Noam, 77, 120
civil rights, 45, 50, 53, 54, 56, 70, 71, 76, 201
climate change, 1, 6, 20, 22, 34, 77, 84, 100, 107, 124, 137, 147, 155, 160, 166, 167, 172, 177, 186, 205, 206
climate crisis, 10, 100, 124, 137, 141, 144, 155, 156, 159, 170, 172, 175, 176, 187, 202
Clinton, Bill, 42, 43, 57, 58
Clinton, Hillary, 58
Cold War
  and arms reduction, 139
  and civil rights movement, 201
  critiques of foreign policy, 20
  and disarmament, 136
  end of, 57, 73, 125, 204
  and financial crises, 32

  and foreign intervention, 35
  and imperialism, 73
  and Institute for Policy Studies, 112
  liberals, 33, 39, 53
  and military primacy, 33
  and New Left, 18
  onset of, 16, 25, 34, 54, 72, 122, 189
  and peace intellectuals, 128
  and security agenda, 210
  and the Third World, 69, 161
Cold War liberalism, 52, 53, 55, 57
colonization, 33, 42, 75, 86
communism, 41, 51–54, 71
Communist Party, 71, 85, 147, 199
Communist Party of China, 85
Comprehensive Nuclear Test-Ban Treaty, 182
Congress, 47, 119, 128, 143, 164, 181, 182, 194, 198, 201, 202, 205, 208
Congressional Progressive Caucus, 44, 58, 144, 181, 201, 205
cooperative security, 4, 9, 14, 128, 134, 137, 140, 141
corruption, 9, 29, 44, 45, 65, 66, 79, 83–85, 92, 94, 96, 98, 100, 105–8, 143, 173, 191, 207
credibility, 24, 25, 78, 134, 139

defense
  and alliances, 104
  and communism, 71
  and NATO, 189
  and non-interventionism, 109, 115
  and peacekeeping, 141
  research and development, 183
  of Taiwan, 118
defense commitments, 88
defense industry, 119
defense intellectuals, 19, 112
defense spending, 1, 32, 33, 90, 115, 143, 144, 181, 185–87, 196, 199, 206, 207
democracy
  advocacy of, 141
  and alliances, 94
  balance of, 150
  and capitalism, 26, 42, 70, 95
  in Eastern Europe, 55
  and economic equality, 82, 95
  and freedom, 197
  and human rights, 17
  and imperialism, 109
  and inequality, 84

9 781009 009881